Savings Bond Alert
November 2005

Tom Adams

Alert Media
New York

Savings Bond Alert

November 2005 Issue

Alert Media – New York

email: savings-bond-alert@alert-media.com

web: http://www.alert-media.com/

Information in this book is subject to change without notice. Updated information, links mentioned in the text, and reduced-price annual book upgrades are available on our web site at:

http://www.Savings-Bond-Advisor.com/

ISBN: 0-9760645-1-0

ISSN: 1552-1249

WARRANTY AND LIMITATION OF LIABILITY – We guarantee that the information in this book is useful and correct. If you are unsatisfied with the quality of the information, return the book to us within 30 days of your purchase with documentation showing when and how much you paid. We will refund your full purchase price. OUR LIABILITY FOR ERRORS AND OMISSIONS IS LIMITED TO THE PRICE YOU PAID FOR THIS BOOK. In no case shall we be liable for any incidental or consequential damages, nor for ANY damages in excess of the price paid for the book by the reader.

The Vanguard Group, Inc. offers the Vanguard 500 Index fund. Standard & Poor's®, S&P®, S&P 500®, Standard & Poor's 500® and 500® are trademarks of The McGraw-Hill Companies, Inc.

Printed and bound in the United States of America.

Dedicated to
Amelia Weishaar

Acknowledgements: We are indebted to the Treasury's Bureau of Public Debt – particularly its Public Affairs and Customer Service personnel, who have patiently answered our many questions. Daniel J.. Pederson's books about Savings Bonds have been invaluable in helping us understand some of the quirks of Savings Bonds. Ken Evoy's system of starting small businesses led us to Savings Bonds to begin with. There are many others we have learned from and been encouraged by through the years. Heartfelt thanks to all.

Table of Contents

Introduction

Is this book for you?

Part 1 – Creating Your Investment

An introduction to Savings Bonds

Today's choices – Series I and Series EE

Electronic at TreasuryDirect or paper at your bank?

Naming the new baby: registration

Why Savings Bonds?

Part II – Managing your investment

Savings Bond A, B, Cs

Current interest rates paid by all Savings Bonds

How much are my Savings Bonds worth?

Keeping track of your Savings Bond inventory

Lost and stolen Savings Bonds

Changing the registration

Managing the deferred-tax time bomb

Is this book for you?

Lose the commissions and fees

Do you want to know a secret?

Getting the most from this book

Getting the most from our web site

Lose the commissions and fees

Most financial professionals don't recommend Savings Bonds. If you find one who does, listen carefully, because you're finally hearing more than just a commission talking.

Compared to the "smart and sophisticated" investments that financial professionals earn commissions on, Savings Bonds are an excellent, low cost, do-it-yourself investment.

But at least seven out of ten Savings Bond investors lose money because their investment doesn't work the way they think it does.

Here are the four major money-losing mistakes that Savings Bond investors make:

★ losing earnings by holding stinkers (bonds that have stopped earning interest), either in a futile attempt to avoid income tax or out of sheer ignorance that some of their holdings have a distinct aroma

★ missing maximum returns by buying the wrong bonds, by redeeming the wrong bonds, or by redeeming the right bonds at the wrong time

★ paying too much income tax by filling out tax forms incorrectly and by not having a plan to minimize taxes

★ paying large and totally unnecessary legal fees and state death taxes when passing bonds to heirs

The more Savings Bonds you have, the larger and more costly these mistakes become. But it's not hard to avoid them. This book tells you how.

Do-it-yourself Savings Bond investors who know what they're doing easily earn more than their commission-paying neighbors. Savings Bonds are an excellent choice for the low-risk foundation of your investment portfolio.

Do you want to know a secret?

About 55 million individuals own Savings Bonds. Since the U.S. population is now approaching 300 million, about five out of six Americans don't own a single Savings Bond.

For the most part, the five-out-of-six believe that Savings Bonds are a frumpy, old-fashioned investment. After all, we aren't bombarded with Savings Bond advertising as we are for investments that pay sales fees and commissions.

Unfortunately, many of the people who don't own Savings Bonds and who know little about them are the financial professionals who write books and offer personal advice.

If you're reading this page in a bookstore, look in the index of any of the books on the shelves in front of you. You'll discover that most financial advice books don't even have an index entry for Savings Bonds.

What's worse, many of these same advisors are certain they know how Savings Bonds work, but what they know hasn't been true for years (if was ever true at all).

Moreover, of the Americans who do own Savings Bonds, most have just one or two that they received as gifts or prizes. Often these bonds have more emotional than financial value. And these folks figure all other Savings Bond owners are just like them.

However, the total amount invested in Savings Bonds is over $200,000 million. Given the 80-20 rule, the 11 million Americans with the largest Savings Bond holdings are systematic savers who have, on average, an investment of over $14,500 each.

Here's the deal – although you hardly ever hear investment professionals talk about Savings Bonds; and when they do they're often spouting misinformation – Savings Bonds are the investment secret of millions and millions of American savers. You're in good company.

Getting the most from this book

You can use this book to learn about Savings Bonds by reading it straight through or you can use it as a reference tool.

Begin at the table of contents – the book has four parts:
★ Part I – Creating Your Investment
★ Part II – Managing Your Investment
★ Part III – Redeeming Your Investment
★ Part IV – Savings Bond Tables

This structure follows the phases of the investment cycle.

Information that's critical to those putting money into Savings Bonds is pretty different from the information that's critical to those who are managing a large Savings Bond investment, which is different from the information you'll need when you're ready to take money out.

This allows you to concentrate on the part of the book that concerns the phase of the investment cycle you're in.

The final section lists every issue of Savings Bond currently paying interest and many that aren't. You'll find current values, interest rates, and other information that's critical to managing your investment, including our exclusive Alert Recommendations.

The information in this part of the book can be used to track the value of your portfolio and to make sure you're cashing in your least valuable bonds and keeping your most valuable ones as you redeem portions of your investment.

Watch for notes in this part of the page. They will highlight or expand on the page's main idea and will often point you toward additional or more current information on our web site.

Getting the most from our web site

Centered at the bottom of every page of this book is the URL of our Savings Bond web site, ***www.Savings-Bond-Advisor.com***.

This URL brings up a page we refer to as our readers' clubhouse.

The book and the web site together will provide a better experience for you than either can alone.

For example, the Treasury changes Savings Bonds interest rates twice a year; rates of competing investments change daily. We always have current rates available on the web site.

Go to the web site now, add it to your Favorites or Bookmarks, and take a look around.

The link to *Book Notes* takes you to a page of links that are referenced in this book. You don't have to type in other URLs and if we make a mistake we can fix it. This is a good system!

While you're visiting the clubhouse, subscribe to our free Savings Bond email notification service. This allows you to be among the first to know when interest rates change or the Treasury makes other Savings Bonds announcements.

The clubhouse includes a link you can use to send us questions, comments, or feedback. We'll email a response to your questions.

After removing all information that would identify you, we post some of the questions we receive with our answers on the site. You can subscribe to our site's XML feed to keep up to date with new questions and answers.

Since this book comes out twice a year, we offer discounted upgrades to investors who already own a copy of the book. To take advantage of the discount, go to the clubhouse and look for the *Book Upgrades* link.

Don't miss our free email notification service. We don't bombard you with emails - we only send you something where there's news to report. Typically we send less than 12 issues a year. It's an easy way for you to get important updates on changes to the Savings Bond program.

Part 1 – Creating Your Investment

An introduction to Savings Bonds

Today's choices – Series I and Series EE

Electronic at TreasuryDirect or paper at your bank?

Naming the new baby – registration

Why Savings Bonds?

Chapter 1

An introduction to Savings Bonds

The top five misconceptions about Savings Bonds

Basic features of today's Savings Bonds

The top five misconceptions about Savings Bonds

Misconceptions and misinformation are the hallmark of discussions about Savings Bonds. Although they are an excellent choice for the low-risk portion of your investment portfolio, Savings Bonds aren't quite like any other investment.

As the word *savings* indicates, they have some features of bank savings accounts, such as they way they earn compound interest.

As the word *bonds* indicates, they have some features of corporate and government bonds, such as they way they are registered to specific owners.

They are also similar to bank certificates of deposit, in that they have early withdrawal penalties and that you can purchase and redeem them either at a brick and mortar bank or using an online account.

And like retirement savings plans such as 401Ks and IRAs, they allow you to defer income taxes on your earnings.

But while Savings Bonds share some features with other investment choices, in the end there's nothing else that works like a Savings Bond. This causes lots of misconceptions.

Let's begin by looking at the major misconceptions one by one, in Dave Letterman order:

#5 – You can't redeem a Savings Bond until it matures

While it's true that some competing investments can't be cashed until they mature, Savings Bonds can be cashed after one year.

There is a penalty of the most recent three months of interest if cashed before five years. All of the new bonds being issued today pay interest for 30 years. Depending on the Series, older Savings Bonds pay interest for 20, 30, or 40 years.

#4 – You earn interest on the face value of a Savings Bond, not on what it's worth

The paper Series EE Savings Bonds you buy at a bank are issued at half of their face value. This means you pay, for example, $50 for a bond that says $100 on it.

Most people think this means something, but in fact it means hardly anything at all. Even a broken clock is right twice a day, but when you learn to use the tables in the back of this book you'll discover there are no Series EE bonds that are worth exactly their face value.

These bonds, like all other Savings Bonds (none of which have this feature), are always worth:
- ★ what you invested, plus
- ★ what your investment has earned in interest, plus
- ★ what your accumulated interest has earned in interest

Series EE bonds are guaranteed to double in value in a certain number of years that changes as interest rates rise and fall. That's the source of the marketing gimmick of putting a value that's double your investment on the bonds.

But it's just a marketing gimmick. It has caused so much confusion the Treasury has stopped using it except on paper EE bonds.

#3 – You're better off holding Savings Bonds that have stopped earning interest than redeeming them and being forced to pay the income tax you owe

Savings Bonds come with a retirement-account-like tax-deferral feature – the IRS allows you to defer the interest you earn for tax purposes until you receive it in cash or your bond stops earning interest.

You earn interest on the amount you invested and your accumulated interest – no matter what series your bonds are; no matter if they are paper or electronic.

There are ways to minimize the income tax you pay. But these methods require attention to your investment and advance planning. In Chapter 15 I'll lead you through the tax issues and strategies of Savings Bonds.

But, as we'll see in Chapter 15, unless you have a low income and can take advantage of the Savings Bond education deduction, or unless you have a high income and are willing to give all your Savings Bond interest to a recognized charity, federal income tax on the interest you've earned will eventually be paid by either you or your heirs.

But some of us are so tax-averse that rather than paying the tax we owe, we hold on to Savings Bonds that have stopped earning interest. This is such a bad idea I've started calling these earnings-free bonds *stinker bonds*.

The Treasury actually has a small team of five people that tries to contact owners of these bonds to let them know their money hasn't been claimed.

The Treasury's unclaimed-bond team is so small and the amount of unclaimed bonds is so large they don't even try to contact people who have a common name or a small amount of unclaimed bonds.

Yet seven out of ten investors the team reaches say they don't want to cash the bonds because they'll have to pay income tax on the interest they've earned.

From a financial perspective, holding on to stinkers to avoid taxes is an appallingly bad decision. It costs far more money to hold stinkers than to pay the tax and reinvest what's left.

Either you or your heirs are going to pay the tax someday. The only alternative is to just let the Treasury have your investment in Savings Bonds forever, which is a lot more expensive than paying the tax you owe.

Stinker bonds aren't earning any interest. When you factor in inflation, they're losing money every month.

If your plan is to leave the taxes to your heirs, not only will you lose the interest you could have earned, their tax rate will probably be higher than yours, costing your family even more money.

And don't be fooled into thinking your heirs can avoid taxes by taking advantage of the *stepped-up-basis* rule (see Chapter 16). That rule applies only to capital gains; Savings Bonds earn interest and don't have capital gains.

But wait - there's more. The IRS says you actually owe the income tax in the year Savings Bonds stop earning interest – whether you cash them or not. By holding stinkers you're setting yourself up for an amended return for a previous year along with back taxes and penalties.

If you have Saving Bonds that have stopped earning interest, redeem them, pay your tax with some of the money, and use the rest to buy new bonds. Your family will end up with far more money than you'll ever get by holding on to dead and rotting stinkers.

And if you have Savings Bonds that aren't stinkers yet, let me give you an advance hint about what you'll learn in Chapter 15 – the best tax savings go to those who make a plan years in advance and redeem and reinvest their bonds over a multi-year period.

#2 – Savings Bonds earn lousy rates

There is no safer investment than Savings Bonds. Since the rate you earn is related to the amount of risk you're willing take, the interest rates that Savings Bonds pay are indeed lousy compared to what you get if you're lucky enough to actually get the top return of a riskier investment.

On the other hand, Savings Bond rates aren't lousy at all compared to what you get if you risk and lose, or even if you risk and come out even.

Compared to other low-risk investments, the Savings Bond rate is usually very competitive. However, since the Treasury puts a rate on Savings Bonds that's good for six months, while interest rates change every day, there are times when competitive investments have much better rates and times when they have much worse rates.

Overall, Savings Bonds earn solid, low-risk rates.

#1 – Good advice about Savings Bonds is easy to get

Traditionally, if you wanted to initiate a Savings Bond transaction, such as buying a bond or redeeming one, you went to a financial institution – a bank, savings and loan, or credit union.

Although there's now also an online alternative, which we'll discuss in Chapter 3, financial institutions are still the main place people initiate Savings Bond transactions today.

Consequently, people assume that bank tellers can advise them about Savings Bonds. And, in fact, a few bank tellers know Savings Bonds inside and out.

But because banks receive only a small handling fee from the Treasury for each Savings Bond transaction, they have no incentive to train their employees about Savings Bonds.

Banks can handle simple Savings Bond transactions, but they aren't trained to provide advice. Savings Bonds aren't a bank product. Your banker would rather see you invest in the bank's own certificates of deposit.

Savings Bonds are issued by the Savings Bond Division of the Bureau of Public Debt, which is a part of the U.S. Treasury. In this book we'll typically shorten all that to *the Treasury*.

It's also not unusual to find erroneous articles about Savings Bonds in newspapers, magazines, or on web sites. This is because reporters write articles by consulting experts.

But the typical expert sources for financial stories:

★ don't own Savings Bonds

★ don't have any incentive to learn about Savings Bonds, because they can't make a commission selling them

The Savings Bond Informer asked 400 banks five common questions about Savings Bonds. Only four banks (1%) answered all five questions correctly, although about half answered "boldly and inaccurately," as if they knew the correct answer.

★ think Savings Bonds are a simple, easily-understood investment, when in fact they have a wide variety of somewhat confusing characteristics, which depend on an individual bond's series and issue date.

Good advice about Savings Bonds is hard to get.

In addition to our book and web site, here are the other places you can get good information about Savings Bonds.

The Treasury has a Savings Bonds web site at *http://www.publicdebt.treas.gov/sav/sav.htm* that is the ultimate source for Savings Bond information. However, while the Treasury provides all the facts, ma'am, it doesn't provide much in the way of advice.

Daniel J. Pederson has written two books about Savings Bonds, *Savings Bonds: When to Hold, When to Fold and Everything In-Between* (1999) and *U.S. Savings Bonds: The Definitive Guide for Financial Professionals* (1999). Pederson's books were excellent when they were written and are still pretty good, but there have been a lot of changes to the Savings Bond program since 1999, such as TreasuryDirect, the demise of HH bonds, and the new fixed-rate Series EE bonds.

Brian J. Kurtz is the author of *Getting the Most Out of Your Savings Bonds: The Average Investor's Guide to U.S. Savings Bonds* (2004). Like Pederson, Kurtz has a lot of experience advising Savings Bond owners, which gives him a good perspective on the issues and problems readers are likely to encounter.

Newspaper and magazine reporters who use Pederson, Kurtz, Stephen Meyerhardt at the Bureau of Public Debt, or me(!) as a source for their stories are worth reading. The ones who use a local broker or investment counselor typically aren't.

Basic features of today's Savings Bonds

The Savings Bonds you can buy today have the following features. We'll spend as much as entire chapters discussing some of these features later, but for now you'll benefit from a high fly-over:

Guaranteed by the U.S. Treasury

All Savings Bonds are issued by the U.S. Treasury and backed by the full faith and credit of the U.S. government, making them among the safest of all investments.

No risk of capital loss

Unlike traditional corporate and government bonds, you can't get back less than you paid for Savings Bonds. The value of traditional bonds and bond mutual funds, on the other hand, goes down when interest rates go up.

Likewise, unfortunately, there is no possibility of capital gains when interest rates go down, as there is with traditional bonds and bond mutual funds.

Two series – Series I and Series EE

The Treasury's Savings Bond product line currently has two options, Series I and Series EE. We'll discuss the differences in the next chapter. Everything in this section applies to both Series.

Two types - paper and electronic

Most banks, credit unions, and similar financial institutions can process purchase and redemption transactions for the traditional paper (or *definitive*) Savings Bonds. Paper bonds are available in $50, $75, $100, $200, $500, $1,000, $5,000, and $10,000 denominations.

Electronic (or *book*) Savings Bonds can be purchased and redeemed online by opening an account with TreasuryDirect. You can invest any amount, to the penny, from $25 to $30,000.

Tax advantages

Federal income tax can be *deferred* on Savings Bond interest until you redeem the bond. Savings Bond interest is exempt from state and local income taxes. If you have higher education expenses, you may qualify to exclude your Savings Bond interest from your Federal income tax.

Purchase limits

Savings Bonds can be purchased for as little as $25. This compares to the minimum investment of $1,000 for most competing investments.

However, unlike other investments, there is a maximum limit on the amount you can invest in Savings Bonds in one calendar year.

The limit is $30,000 per person, per series, per type, which creates an effective maximum investment of $120,000 per person per year ($30,000 each in Series I electronic, Series I paper, Series EE electronic, Series EE paper – with the Series EE paper having a face value of $60,000).

Redemption limits and penalties

With one exception for Treasury-recognized disasters, Savings Bonds can't be redeemed at all for one year. If redeemed before five years, you forfeit the last three months of interest earned, disaster or not.

Large denomination paper bonds can be partially redeemed – you'll receive cash and your choice of smaller denomination bonds with the same Series and issue date. Electronic bonds can be partially redeemed in any amount of $25 or more.

In case of a significant disaster, the Treasury will allow Savings Bonds to be redeemed during the first year. We announce these exceptions in our Savings-Bond-Alert email notifications.

Final maturity after 30 years

Today's Savings Bonds stop earning interest after 30 years. All Series I and Series EE bonds that have ever been issued are currently earning interest.

Interest accrual and compounding

Interest on Savings Bonds is **compounded** twice a year and added to the value of the bond. This means interest earnings are calculated on both what you paid for the bond and the interest the bond has earned.

The most recent earnings are added to the compounding calculation every six months, starting from the first day of the month in which you purchased the Savings Bond.

Interest on today's Savings Bonds **accrues** monthly. This means when you redeem a bond, you receive the interest earned through the first day of the month of redemption.

The month and year in which you buy a Savings Bond determines its issue date. All interest calculations assume you purchased the bond on the first day of that month – no matter which day the Treasury actually got your money.

The Treasury bases its interest calculations on a hypothetical $12.50 investment for each issue date of each series. Your bond investment is essentially divided into a set of imaginary $12.50 bonds and you earn the calculated amount for each of them.

This typically causes any normal interest calculations to be too high or too low by a few cents. The Treasury's calculation method magnifies the normal rounding errors.

The Treasury does it this way to prevent large denomination bonds from earning a slightly different rate than small denomination bonds. Since the errors are randomly too high or too low, there's nothing unfair or underhanded about the Treasury's calculation method.

Bonds in older Savings Bond Series stop paying interest after 20, 30, or 40 years, depending on the Series and issue date.

Because Savings Bonds interest is always calculated as if you purchased the bond on the first day of the month, you can gain nearly an extra month's interest by timing your purchases to occur near the end of the month.

Likewise, when you redeem a bond, you should do it right after its value increases on the first day of the month. However, note that many older bonds accrue interest on a six-month schedule, rather than monthly. This creates a potential six-month redemption penalty. Find out how to avoid this penalty in Chapter 14.

Ownership registration

All Savings Bonds Series are registered securities and registration is conclusive of ownership. This means that possession of a bond is meaningless – all that really counts is the name in the Treasury's records in West Virginia.

Because of these characteristics, Savings Bonds can't be used for collateral on a loan and they can't be given to charities without first cashing them in and paying taxes on the interest.

Non-marketable

Registration also means you can't buy or sell Savings Bonds from anyone but the U.S. Treasury or its agents. As mentioned earlier, most banks and other financial institutions act as the Treasury's agents to help you buy and sell paper Savings Bonds, and the Treasury offers online Savings Bond accounts through TreasuryDirect.

Non-callable

The U.S. Treasury can't force you to redeem Savings Bonds before they stop paying interest at final maturity. Most interest-bearing investments work this way, but some fixed-rate bonds allow the issuer to call the bonds – which they typically do when interest rates fall.

No-load

Load refers to fees and commissions paid to those who sell you an investment. They are typically associated with mutual funds. There are never any fees for buying, selling, or holding Savings Bonds.

Zero-coupon

Coupon is a term that comes from the olden days, when corporate and government bonds were issued with tear-off coupons. Owners submitted the coupons to get their interest payments.

A zero-coupon bond is one in which interest payments are added to the value of the bond, rather than being paid in cash. This is how Savings Bonds and other investments that pay *compound interest* work.

Serial Numbers and face values

The first letter in a paper Savings Bond's serial number will match its denomination:

- ★ L - $50
- ★ K - $75
- ★ C - $100
- ★ R - $200
- ★ D - $500
- ★ M - $1,000
- ★ V - $5,000
- ★ X - $10,000

Chapter 2

Today's choices – Series I and Series EE

Historical overview of interest rates

Series I Savings Bonds feature inflation protection

Series EE Savings Bonds feature fixed rates

Series I versus Series EE

Historical overview of interest rates

Savings Bonds earn interest. As a Savings Bond investor, you will find it helpful to know about the historical swings in the level of interest rates and what caused these swings.

The primary force that moves interest rates up and down is inflation. We'll begin this section by looking at inflation, followed by interest rate levels, and we'll finish up by looking at *real interest rates* – the interest rate after removing inflation.

A long-term look at inflation

One of the longest series of economic statistics available today is the Consumer Price Index, for which we have over 200 years of data.

The Consumer Price Index is a measure of *inflation* and *deflation* – a general increase or decrease in the price of goods and services. During times of inflation, a dollar loses value, as it buys less and less. During times of deflation, on the other hand, it buys more and more.

The line in Figure 2-1 shows the annual percent change in the index. As you can see, prices have been quite volatile historically. However, periods of what television pundits like to call "skyrocketing" inflation have usually been associated with wars.

The vertical bars in Figures 2-1, 2-2, and 2-3 highlight the years 1812-1814 (War of 1812), 1861-1865 (Civil War), 1914-1919 (World War I), 1941-1945 (World War II), 1950-1953 (Korean War), 1965-1974 (Vietnam War), 1991 (Gulf War) and 2003-present (Iraq War).

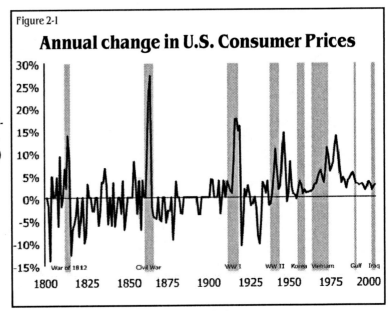

Figure 2-1

Annual change in U.S. Consumer Prices

As you can see, it is highly unusual for inflation rates to exceed 5 percent, except during wars. During the half-century between 1865 and 1915, inflation did not exceed 4 percent even once (1898's 10-week-long Spanish-American War notwithstanding).

Is inflation good or bad?

Investors and those who have lent money to others hate inflation. It means the dollars they get back when they are repaid aren't worth as much as the dollars they invested or loaned out. That's why interest rates go up with the inflation rate.

On the other hand, borrowers who have fixed-rate loans, such as home mortgages, love inflation, since they can pay back their loans with cheaper dollars. Whether inflation is good or bad depends on your perspective.

A long-term look at interest rates

Historical data on interest rates doesn't go back as far as price data. Figure 2-2 overlays the average annual long-term interest rate since 1871 on top of the graph in Figure 2-1.

Compared to the jittery line showing the annual change in consumer prices, interest rates had a history of being relatively steady until the late 1960s. During the 89-year stretch from 1879 to 1967, rates were consistently below six percent.

Perhaps the major lesson of Figure 2-2 is that although the "skyrocketing inflation" of the late 1970s was nothing new, the "skyrocketing interest rates" that followed were something we hadn't experienced before.

For the last 35 years, interest rates have followed

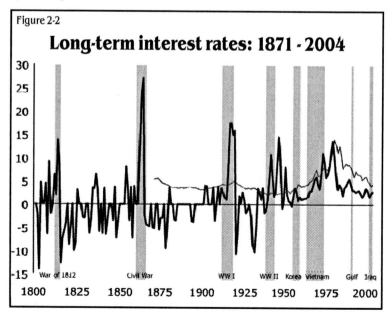

Figure 2-2

Long-term interest rates: 1871 - 2004

the inflation rate. In earlier years this didn't happen. From my perspective, this is because information about the inflation rate is more widely available and understood now than before, but I'm a journalist. Economists have different theories.

Inflation and real interest rates

Now consider this. Investors who earn six percent interest in a year when the inflation rate is six percent actually earn nothing at all. The interest payments they receive merely make their principle, which inflation has dwindled, whole again.

Likewise, borrowers who pay six percent interest in a year when the inflation rate is six percent actually pay no interest at all.

And borrowers who pay six percent interest in a year when the inflation rate is nine percent actually earn three percent interest on the amount they've borrowed! (At these rates investors lose three percent of their investment to inflation.)

When you subtract the inflation rate out of the interest rate, the result is what is known as the *real interest rate*.

Figure 2-3 keeps the thin interest rate line from Figure 2-2, but instead of the inflation rate, its thick line shows the real interest rate in the U.S. since 1871.

You might remember my earlier observation about inflation being associated with wars. Since high inflation causes low real interest rates, we again can see World War I, World War II, and the end of the Vietnam war, but now they show up as the real interest rate dropping under the zero line of Figure 2-3.

During these times investors earned less than the inflation rate and were losing money.

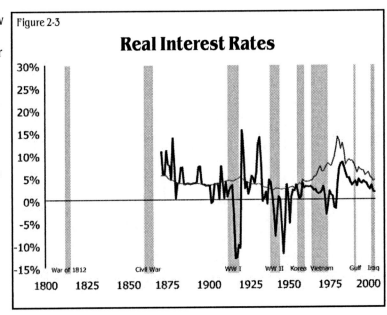

Figure 2-3

Real Interest Rates

When real interest rates are below zero, investors are suffering and borrowers are getting rich. Wars tend to be bad times for investors and good times for borrowers.

What causes inflation?

Economists attribute inflation to "too much money chasing too few goods." The amount of money in circulation is controlled by a country's central bank – in the case of the U.S. that's the Federal Reserve.

There's no need to go into the details of how it all works here, it's just important to understand that inflation isn't random but starts with the actions of the Federal Reserve.

At the same time, you have to recognize that the controls that the Federal Reserve has to steer inflation don't work like a rudder. It's more like paddling a canoe with your spouse in the back and the kids fighting in the middle than piloting a cabin cruiser.

Given all that, what we want to know as investors is where the Federal Reserve will try to dock inflation in the years ahead.

It seems like a simple answer to me. Just remember that borrowers love inflation and the that U.S. is in debt in every imaginable way.

At a time when the government should be running budget surpluses to save up for the future expense of Medicare and Social Security, it's running ever-larger deficits. Personal debt and foreign debt are out of control.

Where will the money come from to pay back these debts? Politically speaking, it's a lot easier to let the inflation rate go up a percentage point or two than it is to raise the equivalent amount by reducing benefits or by raising taxes.

Hang on to your life jackets.

Series I Savings Bonds feature inflation protection

Series I Savings Bonds have been issued since September 1998 under a single set of rules. In addition to the basic features mentioned in the previous chapter:

★ Series I bonds earn a composite of a fixed rate, which is set for the life of the bond at issue, and the current inflation rate, which is updated every six months.

 ★ There's no formula for setting the fixed rate component, but it's related to average 5-year market rate for Treasury Inflation Protected Securities (TIPS). The fixed rate component for Series I bonds has ranged from a low of 1.0% to a high of 3.60%.

 ★ The Treasury uses the *Consumer Price Index for All Urban Consumers,* (CPI-U) published by the Bureau of Labor Statistics, to determine the inflation rate to apply to I bond earnings.

  ★ The inflation percentage the Treasury uses doesn't appear in the CPI-U report. Instead, the Treasury calculates the percentage difference between the unadjusted March and September CPI-U indices every six months.

  ★ Since I bonds were introduced in September 1998, the annual rate of the inflation rate component has ranged from a low of 0.56% to a high of 3.81%.

 ★ In the event that the inflation rate is negative, which would happen if the U.S. economy entered a period of deflation, it is possible for the inflation component to cancel out all or part of the fixed rate component, leaving an I bond composite rate that is lower than the fixed rate. However, the Treasury has guaranteed that the composite rate will never go below zero.

For example, the initial Series I Savings Bonds issued in September 1998 have a fixed base-rate of 3.4%. In addition to that rate they also earn the current rate of inflation.

I bonds issued in May 2005, on the other hand, have a fixed base-rate of 1.20%. There's a table of all I bond fixed base-rates in Chapter 7.

Series EE Savings Bonds feature fixed rates

Series EE Savings Bonds were first issued in January 1980. The rules governing these bonds has changed several times, most recently in May 2005. Each bond follows the rules in effect when it was issued, so how interest rates are calculated for any specific bond depend on its issue date.

The May 2005 rule change was significant. Series EE bonds issued before May 2005 earn interest rates that are adjusted every six months. Now Series EE bonds earn a fixed rate of interest.

We'll discuss the rules for older series EE and E bonds in Chapter 6. The rules for Series EE bonds being issued now are:

★ The interest rate is fixed at the time of issue and will not change until the bond doubles in value. The Treasury reserves the right to change the rate at that time. The new rate would be good for ten years, at which time the rate could be changed again.

★ The fixed rate is based on the 10-year Treasury Note yield during the six months before rates are set, but there's no specific formula for setting the rate.

★ Paper Series EE bonds are sold at half face value. You pay $50 for a $100 Savings Bond. As mentioned earlier, this marketing gimmick has caused Savings Bonds owners, winners, and gift recipients waves of confusion. Electronic EE bonds and both paper and electronic I bonds don't have this feature.

★ Tied to the half-face-value gimmick, Series EE bonds have an *original maturity guarantee* that promises they will double in value in 20 years. Under the May 2005 Series EE rules, this guarantee is meaningless when the fixed rate is 3.5% or more. At that rate and higher the bond will double in value in 20 years or less anyhow.

Series I versus Series EE

So which one should you buy, Series I or Series EE? My advice? I like the I.

The arguments against the I bond

Let's begin, however, by looking at the two primary objections investors have to the Series I bond – its low fixed base-rate and taxes on inflation.

The I bond's low fixed base-rate

The first objection most people have to the I bond is its low fixed rate. This thinking goes something like this , "I can't hit my investment goals with a growth rate of 1.20% above inflation. I have to have an investment that pays more."

If you find yourself going down this line of thinking, my caution to you is to remember:

★ Savings Bonds are for the *low-risk* portion of your investment portfolio. Your investment goal here is to create savings that you can liquidate in an emergency with a low risk of loss. I bonds guarantee that your money won't be diminished, not even by inflation. ***No other investment comes with this guarantee.***

★ 1.20% above inflation seems meager, but what are your options? The 3.5% EE bond will have a real return of -0.08% during it's first six months (3.5% less the 3.58% inflation component of the I bond), and 1.20% looks great compared to that.

What you have to remember is that just because Series EE doesn't have an inflation component doesn't mean inflation isn't eating away your returns. The Series I bond protects from this, so it's base rate is lower. But will you really earn more, after inflation, with Series EE?

Paying income tax on inflation

In his 1999 book, *Savings Bonds: When to Hold, When to Fold and Everything In-Between*, Dan Pederson of the Savings Bond Informer, asked, "Hey, where's the protection?"

Pederson rightly points out that since you have to pay income tax on I bond interest, and I bond interest includes an inflation component, I bond owners end up paying income tax on inflation.

Pederson says to compare your marginal tax rate (see Chapter 12) to the proportion of the I bond composite rate that comes from its inflation component.

For example, when the I bond fixed-base rate is 1.2% and the inflation component is .4%, the inflation component makes up 25% of the I bond's composite 1.6% rate.

If your tax bracket is higher than 25%, you are paying more in taxes on your Savings Bond interest than you receive in inflation protection.

Pederson is right about the math, but ignores that you'd be even worse off with an EE bond that didn't keep up with inflation. The logical end to this argument is to put your money in the mattress and earn 0.00%. You won't pay any taxes on inflation, but you won't be better off, either.

There are some investments in which inflation creates capital gains (a price increase on something you own) rather than ordinary income (interest or dividends).

Capital gains are taxed at a lower rate for some people. But these investments aren't low-risk. And part of the risk is that the value of the investment won't keep up with inflation – a risk you avoid with I bonds.

The arguments in favor of the I bond

There are three reasons I like Series I bonds over the current Series EE – historical results, inflation projections, and the choices other investors are making.

Historical results

In his book, which was published shortly after I bonds were introduced, Pederson suggested that unless the I bond's fixed base-rate was over 3.25%, the EE bond would be the better investment.

By 2004, Pederson was quoted by newspaper reporters saying that 2.00% was the cutoff. At the same time, in the first edition of this book, I said that even Series I bonds with the then all-time-low fixed base-rate of 1.00% were the better investment.

Table 2-1

Series I versus Series EE results
(as of end of May – Oct 2005 rate period)

Issue Date	Series EE redemption value per $ invested	Series I redemption value per $ invested	% difference	Series I fixed base-rate
Sep 98 – Oct 98	1.3368	1.5080	12.81%	3.40%
Nov 98 – Apr 99	1.3176	1.5000	13.84%	3.30%
May 99 – Oct 99	1.2896	1.4620	13.37%	3.30%
Nov 99 – Apr 00	1.2616	1.4340	13.67%	3.40%
May 00 – Oct 00	1.2312	1.4008	13.78%	3.60%
Nov 00 – Apr 01	1.1952	1.3372	11.88%	3.40%
May 01 – Oct 01	1.1544	1.2520	8.45%	3.00%
Nov 01 – Apr 02	1.1272	1.1716	3.94%	2.00%
May 02 – Oct 02	1.1064	1.1460	3.58%	2.00%
Nov 02 – Apr 03	1.0840	1.1196	3.28%	1.60%
May 03 – Oct 03	1.0672	1.0848	1.65%	1.10%
Nov 03 – Apr 04	1.0528	1.0600	0.68%	1.10%
May 04 – Oct 04	1.0400	1.0476	0.73%	1.00%
Nov 04 – Apr 05	1.0248	1.0300	0.51%	1.00%
May 05 – Oct 05	1.0088	1.0120	0.32%	1.20%

So what have been the actual results Savings Bond investors have experienced?

The second and third columns of Table 2-1 show the redemption value, per dollar invested, of all Series EE and I bonds issued since I bonds were introduced. The value is calculated as of the end of the May–October 2005 rate period.

The fourth column shows that I bonds have always been the better investment. The early I bonds, in particular, have typically earned over 10% more than EE bonds issued the same month.

So far, Series I have always earned more than Series EE. Nonetheless, the degree to which I bonds are the better investment has become less and less as their fixed base-rates, which are shown in the final column, have declined.

In all but the bottom line of Table 2-1, I bonds are competing with the older adjustable-rate EE bonds. These older adjustable-rate bonds may be able to overtake I bonds if interest rates go up and inflation goes down. But the probability of that particular combination of events happening is somewhat low.

Inflation projections

There's another way to look at the choice today's Savings Bond investors have. To decide which is better, look at the difference between the Series EE rate, currently 3.50%, and the fixed-rate portion of the Series I rate, currently 1.20%. This difference is 2.30 percentage points.

If inflation is higher than this difference during the period you hold the bond, the Series I bonds will earn more. If inflation is less, Series EE bonds will earn more.

Since no one can predict the future, no one can tell you for sure which Series is the better choice. One reasonable strategy for investors who don't want to guess the future is to invest in both Series of bonds.

However, the history of inflation does give us some probabilities.

Earlier in this chapter we looked at long-term inflation rates. Now we're going to look at the same data in a slightly different way.

The exact Consumer Price Index data that the Treasury uses to determine the I bond inflation component is available going back 92 years to 1913. Figure 2-4 shows what the I bond inflation component would have been had I bonds been available during this entire period.

If you compare this data the to the comparable data in Figure 2-1, one difference

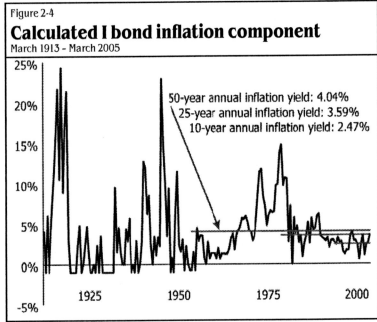

Figure 2-4

Calculated I bond inflation component

March 1913 – March 2005

50-year annual inflation yield: 4.04%
25-year annual inflation yield: 3.59%
10-year annual inflation yield: 2.47%

you'll notice is that the large deflationary dips in Figure 2-1 stop at just under 0% in this figure.

That's because of the way the I bond rate is set in deflationary times. A negative inflation component can wipe out an I bond's fixed base-rate, but it can't go lower than that.

The three horizontal lines at the right side of Figure 2-4 show you the annual yield of the I Bond inflation component over the last 50, 25, and 10 years.

The inflation yield for the entire 93-year period is 3.91%, about the same as the 50-year line. And the inflation yield for just the last five years is 2.46%, almost exactly the same as the 10-year line.

Since the difference between the Series EE fixed rate and the I bond's fixed base-rate is 2.30%, inflation during the period you hold your bond would have to dip below the average of the last five to ten years to make the Series EE bond the better investment.

On the other hand, if inflation hugs the level it's been at the last five to ten years, you'll do better with the I bond.

And if inflation looks more like it has over the last 25 to 50 (to 93) years during the period you hold the bond, the I bond's inflation component yield will make I bonds by far the better investment.

Now let's look at the Series EE versus Series I choice in an entirely different way.

Collective Genius

In 2004, James Surowiecki's book, *The Wisdom of Crowds* developed the theory of unconscious collective intelligence. It holds that the average decision of large groups of people acting independently is usually the right one.

If you think this theory might work, then you'd like to see some data on how others view the Series I or EE question.

Unfortunately, because of the May 2005 change in rules for Series EE, we don't have any apples-to-apples data to look at yet.

However, we do know that Series I bonds have outsold the adjustable-rate Series EE bonds since 2001. In 2003, over two-thirds of the Savings Bonds purchased were in Series I.

Figure 2-3 shows the relative sales of Series I and EE Savings Bonds since Series I bonds were introduced. The left side of the graph has annual data from fiscal year (Oct-Sep) 1999 to fiscal year 2005.

The 2005 number is the annualized sales for the first half of the fiscal year, since that was the only data available when this figure was drawn.

The right side of the figure has monthly data for fiscal year 2005.

The figure says nothing about total sales of Savings Bonds, but simply shows the EE (dark bars) versus I (light bars) proportions.

I update Figure 2-5 quarterly. To see the latest version, go to my web site, click on Book Notes, and pick Note 2-1.

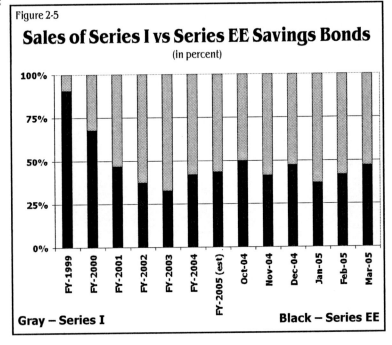

Figure 2-5

Sales of Series I vs Series EE Savings Bonds

(in percent)

Gray – Series I   Black – Series EE

Chapter 3

Electronic at TreasuryDirect or paper at your bank?

The where, who, when, and how much of Savings Bonds

What to expect when you buy paper Savings Bonds

Paper versus electronic

How to open a new TreasuryDirect account

Using your TreasuryDirect Account

TreasuryDirect payroll savings option

How to convert paper bonds to electronic bonds

The where, who, when, and how much of Savings Bonds

Where to buy Savings Bonds

The best way to buy Savings Bonds is online. To do this you'll need to open a **TreasuryDirect** account. Electronic bonds can be purchased and redeemed online. Money for the bonds is withdrawn from or deposited into the bank account you specify.

Alternatively, paper Savings Bonds can be purchased and redeemed at more than 40,000 financial institutions in the U.S., probably including your local bank. If you have an online account with your bank, you may also be able to buy paper bonds online through that account.

Systematic Investments

While most Savings Bonds are purchased at financial institutions, many are sold automatically on a scheduled basis, such as every two weeks or every month, through:

★ **TreasuryDirect** – you can set up any schedule you like to buy Savings Bonds and have the funds automatically deducted from your bank account.

★ **TreasuryDirect Deposits** – employers, pension funds, and others can deposit funds into your TreasuryDirect account. For more information, see the section *TreasuryDirect Deposit Option* later in this chapter.

★ **Payroll Savings Plans** – your employer deducts the amount you specify from your paycheck. The deduction can buy paper bonds.

★ **Bond-a-Month Plans** – your bank deducts the amount you specify from your account on whatever schedule you specify.

The Treasury keeps a list of banks that offer Savings Bonds online. Go to our web site, click on Book Notes, and see note 3-1.

Who can buy Savings Bonds?

Anyone who is a resident of the U.S. or its territories and who has a Social Security Number, without regard to citizenship or age, may purchase either electronic or paper Savings Bonds. The same applies to U.S. citizens living abroad. In addition:

★ Civilian employees of the U.S. government and members of its armed forces who have a Social Security Number, as well as residents of Canada or Mexico who work in the U.S. and have a Social Security Number, may buy Savings Bonds through a Payroll Savings Plan.

★ Anyone, without regard to residency, citizenship, or age – with the exception of those living in a few countries restricted by the U.S. Treasury – may be registered as the **co-owner** or **beneficiary** of a Savings Bond. In the event of the death of the bond's owner, the co-owner or beneficiary will become the bond's owner.

★ Series I Savings Bonds may be issued in the names of certain fiduciaries, including guardians and similar representatives of minors' and other living individuals' estates, as well as in the name of trustees of living owners' personal trust estates.

★ In addition to the registrations for I bonds, Series EE bonds may be registered in the names of companies, organizations, associations, public bodies, and additional types of trusts.

When to buy Savings Bonds

No matter when you buy a Savings Bond, you will earn interest from the first day of that month. Consequently, it makes sense to buy your Savings Bonds near the end of the month.

If you are buying paper bonds from a bank, the bond's issue month is determined by the day you complete the transaction at the bank.

For a list of the restricted countries, go to our web site, click on Book Notes, and see note 3-2.

A person who can't manage his or her affairs may be named as the owner, co-owner or beneficiary of a Savings Bond only if there's been a representative appointed for the estate. If the incompetent person's funds are used to purchase the Savings Bonds, another individual may not be named as co-owner or beneficiary. The Savings Bond registration must include appropriate reference to the guardianship or similar fiduciary arrangement.

If you are buying through TreasuryDirect, on the other hand, the bond's issue month depends on the day the Treasury receives the fund transfer from your bank, so the last day of the month is too late.

How much you can invest

Minimum Investment

Compared to other types of interest-bearing investments, Savings Bonds, which can be purchased for as little as $25, have a very low purchase limit. This makes them suitable for entry-level investors and those who want to invest smaller sums on a scheduled basis.

TreasuryDirect users can buy Series I and EE bonds in any amount, to the penny, from $25 to $30,000.

Paper Series I and EE bonds, on the other hand, are only available with the following face values: $50, $75, $100, $200, $500, $1,000, $5,000, and $10,000.

Maximum Annual Investment

Although Savings Bonds have a low purchase limit, unlike other investments they also have an annual maximum purchase limit of $30,000 per series per type per person per year.

This basically amounts to no limit at all. For example, in one year you can buy $30,000 worth of I bonds from TreasuryDirect, another $30,000 in paper I bonds. You can do the same with Series EE. Your spouse can do the same. So far we're up to $240,000.

Moreover, there's no penalty for going over the limit. However, if you invested through TreasuryDirect, the Treasury will figure it out and the overage will be refunded to you.

TreasuryDirect bonds don't have a denomination or face value. Paper Series I bonds are sold at their full face value; paper EE bonds are sold at one-half their face value – for example, you pay $25 for a $50 paper EE bond.

In all cases you earn interest on the amount you have invested – not on the face value.

What to expect when you buy paper Savings Bonds

You can buy paper Series I and Series EE Savings Bonds from most banks, credit unions, or savings institutions.

However, you don't receive your bond immediately. The bank will take your money and forward your order to a Federal Reserve Bank for you. The bonds will be mailed to the address you specify. You should receive them within 15 business days.

Remember that paper Series I bonds are sold at full face value (a $100 bond costs $100), but Series EE bonds are sold at half face value (a $100 bond costs $50).

Buying Savings Bonds to use as gifts

Because of the three-week delay, you have to either plan ahead when you buy a Savings Bond as a gift, or you can ask the bank teller for a free Savings Bond Gift Certificate. The Treasury provides these to banks, but banks don't always have them at hand. You can also download and customize them online – go to our web site, click on Book Notes, then see note 3-10.

The Federal Reserve will mail the gift bond either to you or to the recipient – it's your choice. You specify the address when you buy the bond.

If the Savings Bonds don't arrive

If your bonds don't arrive within 15 business days, contact the institution where you ordered the bonds. They'll work with you and the Federal Reserve to either find the missing bonds or get you replacements.

If you end up signing a form to get a replacement bond, the replacement should be delivered within 15 business days.

If paper bonds you bought through your employer's Payroll Savings Plan don't arrive, work with your payroll office to get them replaced.

While it's best to provide the Social Security Number of the recipient of the bond, if you don't have it you can use your own number. It's not used for tax purposes.

However, the number you give will be printed on the bond and will be used for identification purposes if the bond needs to be replaced. Your gift recipient probably won't think to give your number when trying to replace a lost or destroyed bond. That's why it's best to use the recipient's number.

Paper versus Electronic

Electronic Savings Bonds purchased through TreasuryDirect have these differences compared to paper Savings Bonds.

★ Electronic bonds are safe from fire, floods, and other disasters; you can close that safety deposit box .

★ You can determine the current interest rate and current value of electronic bonds simply by logging in to your TreasuryDirect account .

★ TreasuryDirect transfers money out of or into the bank account you specify – no checks to get lost.

★ Your employer or pension fund can deposit funds in TreasuryDirect as a deduction from your paycheck.

★ You can easily and quickly set up or change systematic investments inside TreasuryDirect.

★ Unlike paper bonds, which have fixed amounts, electronic bonds can be purchased in any amount, to the penny, from $25 to $30,000.

★ Electronic bonds can be partially redeemed. Electronic redemptions must be for at least $25 and the issue month you are cashing in must have a remaining balance of at least $25. Although paper Savings Bonds can also be partially redeemed, it's a hassle and the fixed denominations of paper bonds aren't as flexible.

★ You can transfer your own Savings Bond funds in partial amounts to anyone else who has a TreasuryDirect account. (This will be a taxable event, however.)

★ You can buy electronic Savings Bonds as gifts and either keep them in your account or transfer them to the recipient's account.

★ You can convert paper Savings Bonds to electronic Savings Bonds but you can't convert electronic to paper and you can't buy paper bonds with TreasuryDirect.

You can use the TreasuryDirect partial withdrawal feature to obtain interest payments from Series EE or Series I Savings Bonds. This gives them the **current income feature** that was formerly reserved for Series H and HH Savings Bonds, which are no longer issued.

★ Electronic bonds can only be registered in the names of individuals, not trusts or other types of organizations, as with paper bonds.

★ Co-ownership is weaker with electronic bonds. In TreasuryDirect the registration says *account holder* WITH *co-owner*, rather than OR as on paper bonds. The account holder must grant the co-owner view or transact rights before the co-owner can see the bonds in the **Shared Securities** area of their own TreasuryDirect account. This isn't even possible, obviously, unless the co-owner has a TreasuryDirect account. In any case, the owner isn't obligated to grant either kind of right.

★ At redemption, the 1099-INT tax form reporting the interest earned is issued in the Social Security Number of the TreasuryDirect account holder who **purchased** the bond. With paper bonds, it's issued in the Social Security Number of the co-owner who **cashed** the bonds. Electronic bonds more closely adhere to IRS regulations.

★ Electronic bonds have no paper trail. If something happens to you, there will be no sign that you own electronic Savings Bonds unless you print out what appears on your computer screen when you're in your TreasuryDirect account and file it.

★ In the case of the death of the owner, the person entitled to electronic bonds must send an email to TreasuryDirect referencing the owner's TreasuryDirect account number to begin the process of transferring ownership of the bonds. With paper bonds, this is handled by a bank.

See Book Note 3-11 for the email address of TreasuryDirect.

★ Paper Savings Bonds require that a bank officer certify the identity of bond holders. With electronic bonds, knowledge of a TreasuryDirect account number and password is considered proof of identity. Consequently, anyone with the password is effectively a "co-owner", although their name isn't on the registration. ***This is the case even when the password is obtained fraudulently! You must handle your account number and password with great care.***

How to open a new TreasuryDirect account

The U.S. Treasury offers two distinct online services that are both called **TreasuryDirect**. One is for Savings Bonds. The other is for marketable Treasury securities (T-Bills, T-Notes, TIPS). Although you'll always know which one we're talking about here, other information sources sometimes confuse the two.

In order to open an account, you need the following six pieces of information. Note that there are no citizenship requirements:

★ Social Security Number

★ Address in the United States

★ Driver's license – or, if don't drive, a state ID

★ Account (checking or savings) at a bank in the United States – you'll need to know the routing numbers to your account

★ Email address

★ Web browser that supports 128-bit encryption

There's more on bank routing numbers and on web browsers coming up.

The process for opening a TreasuryDirect account is to enter your personal information, such as name and address, as well as the information listed above. You will also select a password, a password reminder, and additional authentication information. You will also have an opportunity to read the TreasuryDirect terms and conditions and privacy and legal notices.

After you submit this information, the Treasury will email the account number of your new account to you. You will need the account number and the password you selected to log in to your new account.

The URL is **www.TreasuryDirect.gov**

Will your browser work with TreasuryDirect?

Most current browsers support the level of encryption needed to use TreasuryDirect.

In fact, if your browser doesn't support this level of encryption, it may be difficult for you to upgrade, because the latest

Or you can go to our web site, click on Book Notes, and see:

Note 3-3: Terms and conditions
Note 3-4: Privacy and legal notices
Note 3-5: Open an account

browsers may require a newer operating system than you have on your computer.

To determine what version of browser you have:

★ **Windows**: Select the bottom item in the list that drops down from your browser's *Help* menu

★ **Macintosh**: With your browser open and active, select the first item in the list that drops down from your *Apple* menu (look in the top-left corner of your screen)

In either case, the window that opens will give you the browser's version number. It may also tell you the level of **encryption cipher strength** supported – you need 128-bit or higher. The following versions support this level of encryption:

★ **Internet Explorer** – version 5.01 or newer

★ **Netscape** – version 6.2 or newer

★ **Mozilla Firefox** - version 1.0 or newer

TreasuryDirect uses a security certificate from a company called Entrust, which keeps a detailed list of supported browsers and their security vulnerabilities.

For Internet Explorer upgrades, go to our web site, click on Book Notes, and see note 3-6.

For Netscape and Mozilla Firefox upgrades see note 3-7.

For Entrust's list of supported browsers, see note 3-8.

Bank Routing Numbers

You can always call your bank and ask for the routing numbers to your account, but if you have a check or deposit slip, just look at the funny numbers at the bottom.

The first group of numbers will begin and end with a character that looks like a vertical line followed by two dots, one on top of the other. The numbers in between these characters are your bank routing number.

The second group begins and ends with a character that looks like two vertical lines followed by a single dot. The numbers between these characters are your bank account number.

Checks may have a third group of characters, which give the check number. (And cancelled checks will have a fourth group of numbers, which is the amount of the check). You can ignore these.

Using your TreasuryDirect account

Once you have opened an account, you can log into it from anywhere and:

★ buy new bonds

★ schedule future one-time or periodic purchases

★ redeem the electronic bonds you own

★ buy gift bonds and transfer them to accounts belonging to others

★ change the beneficiary on your bonds

★ set up accounts for specific purposes, such as an education or wedding fund for your kids, that are linked to your main account

★ check up on the current interest rate and current value of your bonds.

WARNING: if you receive an email that appears to be from the Treasury asking for your account number and password, **do not provide it**. Instead, log into TreasuryDirect by typing in the URL and use the *Contact Us* link to report the fraudulent email. The Treasury will never send you an email like this.

To access your account, go to **www.TreasuryDirect.gov**.

If you've forgotten your account number or password, there are links on the login page to help your recover it.

Or go to our web site, click on Book Notes, and see note 3-9.

TreasuryDirect deposit option

Your employer, pension fund, or anyone else who sends you money regularly can deposit a part of the money into TreasuryDirect.

Once inside your TreasuryDirect account, the deposits appear in what the Treasury calls a *Zero-Percent Certificate of Indebtedness*. Think of this as a holding area for your money inside TreasuryDirect.

From within TreasuryDirect, you can put additional money into your holding area by creating an electronic withdrawal from your bank account or by redeeming Savings Bonds you already have.

You can take money out of your holding account either by creating an electronic deposit into your bank account or buying Savings Bonds.

To receive deposits into your account, give your payroll office or financial institution the following information:

★ TreasuryDirect's Routing Number: 051736158

★ Your ten-digit TreasuryDirect account number

★ Account type: savings

★ The amount to be deducted

★ The frequency for the deduction

As you can tell from the name, a *Zero-Percent Certificate of Indebtedness* doesn't earn interest, so make sure you set up transactions in TreasuryDirect to move the money into Savings Bonds.

How to convert paper bonds to electronic bonds

If you have both a TreasuryDirect account and paper bonds, you can put your paper bonds in your TreasuryDirect account, which will convert them to electronic bonds.

The first step is to sort your paper Savings Bonds into groups based on how they're registered. Bonds that have different co-owners or beneficiaries should go into separate groups.

Next, logon to your TreasuryDirect account and click on *Manage My Conversions*.

On that page. click on *Create my registration list* and enter the registration information for each of the groups you've created.

After you've created your list of registrations, enter each of your bonds. You'll select the registration on the bond from the list you've created and enter the series, denomination, and serial number. You will also be able to enter comments, such as a note about a name change or misspelling.

When you've finished entering your bonds, click the button labeled *Create a Manifest*. This will display a list of all the bonds you've entered. You'll need to print this, sign it, and mail it with the bonds to the address shown on the manifest. You can put up to 50 bonds on one manifest, and you can have as many manifests as you need.

The bonds will be listed in your TreasuryDirect account, where you'll be able to see their current value and interest rate. You'll also be able to check on the status of your conversions to see if processing is proceeding normally or if a problem has occurred.

Chapter 4

Naming the new baby: registration

Whose name goes on the bond?

What it means to be a registered security

Whose name goes on the bond?

The issue that probably gets the least thought when purchasing new bonds is how the bond is registered. It's more important than that.

Owner

All Savings Bonds must have a registered owner. This must be a single individual or, in rarer cases that we'll discuss in a moment, a single legal entity.

Unless a Savings Bond owner dies, changing the registered owner almost always creates a taxable event..

In addition to the owner, Savings Bonds can optionally list a second registered name. The second name can be either a co-owner or a beneficiary. Three names aren't allowed, so you can't have both.

Co-owner

In the bond's registration, a co-owner's name is preceded by the word OR on paper bonds; by the word WITH on electronic bonds.

Either an owner or a co-owner can redeem a paper Savings Bond without the knowledge or consent of the other.

Changing the co-owner of a Savings Bond can create a taxable event, although there are several exceptions.

We discuss the exceptions in which changing the owner or co-owner doesn't create a taxable event in Chapter 11.

Beneficiary

In the bond's registration, a beneficiary's name is preceded by the initials POD ("payable on death").

A beneficiary has no rights to a Savings Bond unless the owner has died. In that case, the beneficiary must present the owner's death certificate to redeem a bond or have it reissued.

With bonds available today you can change the beneficiary at any time without creating a taxable event or getting the permission of the current beneficiary.

Registration and estate planning issues

Legally, Savings Bond co-owner and beneficiary designations overrule your Last Will and Testament. The funds are available to your heirs immediately, rather than after certification of your Will by a Probate Court, which typically takes six months or more.

If you want your Will to determine distribution of the proceeds of your Savings Bonds, don't add a co-owner or beneficiary. For example, if your Will states that you want to divide your possessions among two children evenly, but half of your estate is in Savings Bonds and you've made one child the beneficiary on all of them because you want that child to be Executor of your estate, that child can legally keep all your Savings Bonds and one-half of the rest of your estate. Your other child could receive much less than you intended.

★ At the death of a registered owner of a Savings Bond, the bond belongs to the co-owner or beneficiary, if the bond has one. If not, the bond becomes part of the owner's estate and is distributed according to the owner's Will, if there is one, or according to state law.

★ If both the registered owner and the co-owner or beneficiary of a Savings Bond die, the bond becomes the property of the estate of the person who died last.

Other forms of registration

As mentioned in the previous chapter, Series I bonds may be registered only in the names of individuals and, in some cases, fiduciaries, such as trusts. Uniform Gifts to Minors Act registrations are not allowed.

In addition to the registrations allowed for Series I, Series EE bonds may be registered in the names of companies, organizations, associations, and public bodies.

With older Series E or H bonds, changing the beneficiary requires the permission of the current beneficiary.

Want to make a gift to your country? The U.S. Treasury may be listed on Savings Bonds as the beneficiary, but not as the co-owner.

What it means to be a registered security

Savings Bonds are registered securities. With registered securities, *registration is conclusive of ownership.*

This means that possession of a Savings Bond, or the source of the funds used to buy a Savings Bond, cannot be used to establish ownership. All that counts is the name on the bond.

Registration is what prevents Savings Bonds from being marketable – you can't sell a Savings Bond to someone or use it as collateral on a loan because possession of a Savings Bond is meaningless – only those named on the bond itself can redeem it.

However...

Although non-owners aren't supposed to be able to redeem a Savings Bond, banks handling Savings Bonds have been known to mistakenly redeem Savings Bonds to named beneficiaries and others.

Although possession of a Savings Bond is supposed to be meaningless, it's best to keep them where thieves can't find them and your heirs can't miss them. This is also true for TreasuryDirect account numbers and passwords.

At TreasuryDirect, knowing the account number and password is considered proof of identity. Carefully review our advice about password protection in the previous chapter.

The Treasury handles these issues on a case-by-case basis. If one of your Savings Bonds is redeemed by someone who isn't entitled to it, notify the Treasury by email at:

Savbonds@bpd.treas.gov

or by regular mail at:

Savings Bond Operations
Bureau of the Public Debt
P. O. Box 1328
Parkersburg, WV 26106-1328

Chapter 5

Why Savings Bonds?

Why save?

First stop paying interest, then start earning it

Anchor your portfolio with low-risk investments

Low-risk investment options

Low-risk investment rates of return

What's a marketable Treasury security?

Risks of Savings Bonds

Why save?

There are two primary reasons to save:

★ So that you can buy the things you want with money you already have rather than borrowing and paying interest.

★ So that you can even out your level of consumption over your lifetime.

Avoiding interest payments

Let me tell you about a very powerful financial technique – it's the foundation of the banking industry.

Banks lend money at a higher interest rates than they pay savers. The business doesn't amount to much more than borrow low, lend high, but it's huge.

Except for a home mortgage, you should avoid paying interest, unless you can get a very low interest, fixed-rate loan.

Sock away a significant portion of your income every month, buy what you want with the money you already have, and avoid paying interest whenever possible.

You'll come out way ahead of your friends and relatives who borrow freely and end up spending a large part of their income on interest. How useless is that?

Leveling out your standard of living

The second reason to save is to avoid large dips in your standard of living over your lifetime. Most want to avoid having to make large reductions in our level of consumption. The only way to avoid this, particularly when your salary income drops after you retire, is through saving.

Calculating how much to save for retirement is a lot more complicated than the investment sales literature would have you believe.

Because Social Security will make up a larger proportion of their after-retirement income, those with relatively low incomes actually need to save a lower proportion of their income than those with higher incomes.

For a detailed analysis, we recommend **The Coming Generational Storm** by Lawrence J. Kotlikoff and Scott Burns. See Book Note 5-1 on our web site for an Amazon link to this book.

Kotlikoff and his colleagues have also written a software program that will help you answer the "how much to save for retirement" question. See our Book Note 5-2 for a link to his web site.

First stop paying interest, then start earning it

The way to get started is by saving back a significant part of your income each month.

If you aren't paying off your credit card bills in full, that is the best place to invest the money you're saving back. It doesn't make any sense to save money at an interest rate that's lower than what you're paying on your credit cards.

Once you've stopped contributing to the profits of the credit card companies, it's time to start putting the amount you're holding back into low-risk savings.

Don't be tempted at this point by investments that advertise high rates. The higher the rate, the higher the risk. As a beginning saver, you need to stick with low-risk investments.

In general, the smaller your investment portfolio, the higher the proportion that you should keep in low-risk investments.

The low-risk portion should be able to replace your income long enough to give you a satisfactory comfort level – financial counselors typically recommend at least six months.

So until you have half your annual salary safely saved, it doesn't make sense to even consider higher-risk investment options.

Anchor your portfolio with low-risk investments

No matter how large your investment portfolio and no matter how high your tolerance for risk, you should have a portion of your financial portfolio devoted to liquid, low-risk investments.

Liquidity means the *ability to quickly turn your investment into cash.* **Low-risk** means *no chance your investment will ever be worth less than what you've put into it.*

Although higher-risk investments have historically earned a better return over long time spans, sometimes you need access to your funds when the markets are down. In these situations you are forced to sell at a loss, which devastates your returns.

Figure 5-1 tracks the value of a investment made on January 1, 1998. The slowly rising line represents an investment in a Series EE Savings Bond. The jagged line shows an investment in the stock market – represented here by the relative value of an investment in Vanguard's 500 Index Fund - one of the best and most widely-owned stock market investments.

I update Figure 5-1 quarterly. To see the latest version, go to my web site, click on Book Notes, and pick Note 5-3.

The Vanguard 500 line includes growth both from price changes and from reinvestment of all dividends.

This figure shows that you can predict that the value of a Savings Bond will always go up, but you can't predict what the stock market or other high-risk investments like mutual funds or real estate will do.

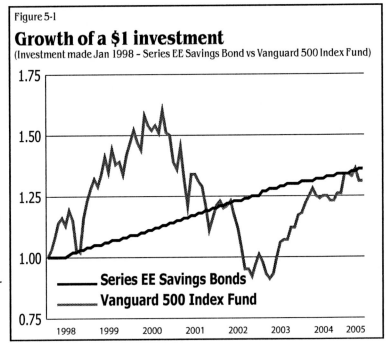

Figure 5-1

Growth of a $1 investment
(Investment made Jan 1998 – Series EE Savings Bond vs Vanguard 500 Index Fund)

Series EE Savings Bonds
Vanguard 500 Index Fund

If you needed your money during late 2002 or early 2003, the 500 Index Fund investment would not only have given you back less than you'd have gotten with a Savings Bond, you'd actually have gotten back less than you invested!

And since early 2002, you'd have gotten back less than if you had invested in Savings Bonds back in 1998.

If you have the time to ride out their dips, high-risk investments can be good to you. But when you can't wait – when you need the money now for a down payment on a house, for a daughter's wedding, or to tide you through a layoff – you have to face the possibility of getting back less than you paid.

The best investment portfolios are diversified. Unless you have a working crystal ball and know how markets are going to perform in the future, your best bet is to split up your portfolio into investments with a variety of risk and reward levels.

Beginning investors should start with the low-risk anchor and move into building the higher-risk portions of their portfolios only after they have at least half a year of income covered.

Advanced investors should base their diversification strategy on their tolerance for risk. As we've seen in the last 10 years, many investments can lose value drastically, but the value of Savings Bonds always goes up.

Low-risk investment options

Let's take a quick look at the world of low-risk investment options.

Banks, Savings and Loans, and Credit Unions – which we'll refer to in this discussion as just *banks* – offer Savings Accounts, Money Market Accounts, and Certificates of Deposit.

Mutual fund companies offer Money Market Funds and various types of bond funds, only some of which are low-risk.

Table 5-1

Comparison of U.S. Savings Bonds with other low-risk investments

	Safe from borrower default	Safe from capital loss	Safe from inflation	Rates	Redemption limits	No fee	Tax advantages
Bank Savings Accounts	FDIC or equivalent insurance to $100,000 per account	Yes	No	Adjustable	No	Yes	No
Bank Money Market Accounts	FDIC or equivalent insurance to $100,000 per account	Yes	No	Adjustable	No	Yes	No
Bank Certificates of Deposit	FDIC or equivalent insurance to $100,000 per account	Yes	No	Fixed	Early withdrawal penalty	Yes	No
Money Market Mutual Funds	Minimal risk	Yes	No	Adjustable	No	No	No
Bond Mutual Funds	Depends on fund	No	No	Fixed	No	No	No
Insurance Policies and Annuities	Depends on policy	Yes	Depends on policy	Depends on policy	Yes	No	Yes
Marketable Treasury Securities	Guaranteed by the US Government	No	Yes, with TIPS	Fixed	No with commission	When bought at auction	No
Series EE Savings Bonds	Guaranteed by the US Government	Yes	No	Fixed	1-year limit Early redemption penalty	Yes	Yes
Series I Savings Bonds	Guaranteed by the US Government	Yes	Yes	Fixed base-rate plus inflation adjustment	1-year limit Early redemption penalty	Yes	Yes

Insurance companies offer life-insurance policies and annuities that offer low-risk at a high price.

In addition to Savings Bonds, the U.S. Treasury offers marketable Treasury Securities, such as T-Bills, T-Notes, and Treasury Inflation Protected Securities, or TIPS.

Table 5-1 compares the basic features of these options.

Safety – default, capital loss, inflation

Safety is the defining characteristic of low-risk investments. If an investment isn't safe, it isn't low-risk. There are several dimensions on which you can measure the safety of an investment.

Risk of default refers to the possibility that the institution you've loaned your money to won't be able to pay you back.
- ★ Treasury securities, including Savings Bonds, are guaranteed by the Federal government, which is as safe as you can get
- ★ Bank products have government insurance up to $100,000 per account, which is the next level of safety.
- ★ Money market mutual funds aren't insured, but are considered to be at the next level of safety because they invest on very short terms
- ★ The safety of corporate bonds, bond mutual funds, and insurance products depends entirely on the company and the product and varies widely

Risk of capital loss refers to the possibility that the value of your investment could drop below what you paid for it.

The value of traditional corporate and government bonds and bond mutual funds drops as interest rates rise. The effect is minimal in short term funds but exaggerated in long term funds.

For example, if a bond's maturity is 20 years away, it's value drops roughly 10 percent for each 1 percentage point rise in the prevailing level of interest rates being paid for similar bonds.

Risk of inflation refers to the possibility that the value of your investment could be melt away because of inflation, as we've discussed in earlier chapters.

Series I Savings Bonds offer inflation protection, as do Treasury Inflation Protected Securities (TIPS). TIPS are the Treasury's big-boy version of Series I bonds. The rules for TIPS, however, are different from the rules for I bonds; they carry the risk of capital loss.

Fixed-rate investments, on the other hand, including Series EE bonds, standard government and corporate bonds, and bank certificates of deposit, have no inflation protection. Severe inflation would reduce the value of these investments with no hope of recovery.

Redemption Limits

The ease with which you can turn your investment into cash is called liquidity. Savings Bonds aren't liquid at all for the first year, they are liquid with a three-month interest penalty after the first year and until five years, and they are totally liquid after that.

* ★ Bank savings accounts and bank and mutual fund money market accounts are the most liquid low-risk investment, but they also pay the lowest rates
* ★ Bank certificates of deposit, like Savings Bonds, have early redemption penalties
* ★ Insurance products are typically not liquid for many years and even then have significant withdrawal penalties
* ★ Marketable Treasury securities are liquid, but you will have to pay a commission to a security broker to handle the sales transaction for you.
* ★ The liquidity of other corporate and government bonds varies, although bond mutual funds are very liquid

Sales and management fees

Sales and management fees are a huge drawback to insurance products. All mutual funds have management fees. Buying and selling mutual funds and marketable Treasury securities can involve broker's commissions, although if you buy directly from the mutual fund company or the Treasury you can avoid those.

Tax advantages

Traditional IRAs, retirement accounts such as 401Ks, and insurance products have tax advantages that are somewhat like Savings Bonds – you don't pay tax on your earnings until you withdraw your money.

However an important difference is that income tax on your initial investment is also deferred with retirement accounts, while with Savings Bonds it's not. Instead, with Savings Bonds you pay tax only on the interest you've earned; with traditional retirement accounts you pay tax on your total withdrawal.

Roth IRAs have the best tax advantages – you don't pay any tax at all on the money you earn.

Municipal bonds and bond funds are free of federal income tax. Federal securities are free of state and local income tax. There are some money market mutual funds that invest in municipal bonds of a single state that are totally free of federal, state, and city taxes for residents of that state.

Low-risk investment rates of return

Table 5-2 shows the comparative levels of interest rates for most of the low-risk investments we've been talking about as reported by Bankrate.com for May 3, 2005. These rates change daily, so if you're interested in a true comparison, go to our web site, click on Book Notes, and see Note 5-4.

Table 5-2

Rates of low-risk investments

Investment	Rate	Fixed/ Adjustable
Bank Savings Accounts	2.55%	Adjustable
Money Market Funds and Accounts	2.19%	
Certificate of Deposit – 1 year	3.27%	Fixed
Certificate of Deposit – 2 years	3.63%	
Certificate of Deposit – 3 years	3.78%	
Certificate of Deposit – 5 years	4.14%	
Jumbo CD – 1 year	3.52%	
Jumbo CD – 2 years	3.89%	
Jumbo CD – 3 years	4.16%	
Jumbo CD – 5 years	4.31%	
Series EE Savings Bonds	3.50%	Adjustable
Series I Savings Bonds	4.80%	

Banks usually require an minimum investment of $1,000 for a Certificate of Deposit. A Jumbo CD usually requires an investment of at least $100,000.

To compare Savings Bonds with CDs that have terms less than five years, remember that you pay a three-month interest penalty if you redeem a Savings Bond before it's five years old.

If you want to compare the Savings Bond rate to a one-year CD, multiply the Savings Bond rate by 0.75 (if you redeem at 12 months, you'll receive three-fourths of a year's interest). For two years use 0.875, for three use 0.916.

A version of Table 5-2 is updated daily on our web site. To see the most recent version, click on Book Notes, then on Note 5-4.

Figure 5-2 is a way of looking at these calculations in terms of a *yield curve*. A yield curve is simple graph showing the interest rate of a specific type of investment at various terms.

For example, you could do a yield curve for certificates of deposit by graphing the rates offered for 1-year, 2-year, 3-year, and 5-year CDs. On this graph, the line labeled *Marketable Treasury Securities* is their actual yield curve on May 2, 2005.

Note that the *Marketable Treasury Securities* line has pretty much the same slope as the Series EE line for the first five years, then in goes up.

Keep in mind that the Series EE yield curve won't change for six months, while the Treasury and CD yield curves change every day. When prevailing market rates decline, Savings Bonds sometimes end up with a higher rate than 1-, 2-, 3, and even 5-year marketable Treasury securities, *even after paying the penalty for redeeming before five years.*

We update Figure 5-2 quarterly. To see the latest version, go to our web site, click on Book Notes, and pick Note 5-5.

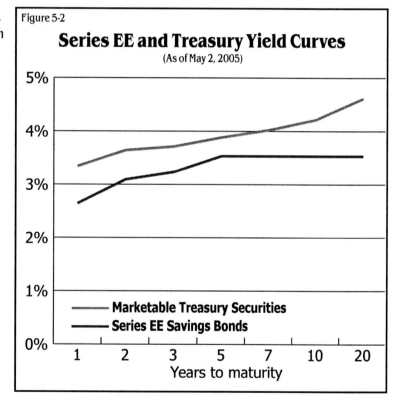

Figure 5-2

Series EE and Treasury Yield Curves
(As of May 2, 2005)

Marketable Treasury Securities
Series EE Savings Bonds

Years to maturity

What's a marketable Treasury security?

In this chapter we've mentioned marketable Treasury securities several times. Let's take a quick look and make sure we all know what these are.

In addition to Savings Bonds, the U.S. Treasury sells investors – by auction – Treasury Bills (T-Bills), Treasury Notes (T-Notes), and Treasury Inflation Protected Securities (TIPS).

Because T-Bills, T-Notes, and TIPS can all be bought and sold in the open market after they are issued, as a group they are known as marketable Treasury securities.

Like Savings Bonds, marketable Treasury securities are backed by the full faith and credit of the U.S. Federal government.

Table 5-3

Savings Bonds versus Marketable Treasury Securities

Feature	Savings Bonds	Marketable Treasury Securities
Form	Paper (definitive) or Electronic (book)	Electronic only
Minimum Investment	$25	$1,000
Increments above Minimum	Paper – $25 Electronic – $0.01	$1,000 increments only
Maximum Annual Investment	$30,000 per series per type per year	No limit
Systematic Investments?	Yes, several types	No
Income tax on interest earnings can be deferred?	Yes	No
Capital gains and losses?	No	Yes
Maturities	30 years; can be redeemed after 1 year; 3-month interest penalty when redeemed before 5 years; never a redemption fee	2, 3, 5, 10, 20, and less than 1 year maturities; can be purchased at auction and held to maturity with no fees or purchased or redeemed at any time in the open market with the help of a broker
Inflation protection?	Yes, with Series I	Yes, with TIPS

To buy marketable Treasury securities in the open market rather than directly from the Treasury at its auction, you would contact a broker, who will charge you a commission.

To get them when the Treasury issues them at auction without paying a fee (it's not as complicated as it sounds), you open an online account using a separate version of TreasuryDirect.

Table 5-3 compares the major features of Savings Bonds and marketable Treasury securities.

As you can tell by scanning the table, marketable Treasury securities are the big-boy version of Savings Bonds. The minimum and maximum investment levels are very different, Savings Bonds are tax deferred, can be purchased and redeemed at any time (after one year), and support systematic investing.

Compared to Savings Bonds, marketable Treasury securities earn higher rates and have the potential for capital gains and losses.

They can be purchased and redeemed an any time through a broker, but they are only available from the Treasury on certain auction dates. To avoid a broker's fee on redemption, you have to hold them until final maturity.

Types of marketable Treasury securities

Treasury Bills have a maturity of one year or less. They typically mature in 2-, 4-, 13- or 26-weeks. Because Savings Bonds have to be held one year before they can be redeemed, they don't compete with short-term T-Bills.

The Treasury hasn't consistently offered a one-year T-Bill, but when it does, Savings Bonds sometimes offer competitive rates, even after paying the early redemption penalty of three-month's interest.

Treasury Notes are issued in 2-, 3-, 5-, and 10-year maturities. The Series EE rate is based on the average rate for 10-year Treasury Notes, but not using a specific formula.

Check the current Yield Curve as shown in Figure 5-2 and Book Note 5-5 to get a clear picture of the current relationship between one-year T-Bill and Savings Bond rates.

Treasury Inflation Protected Securities – The Treasury issues these in 5-, 10-, and 20-year maturities. Like Series I Savings Bonds, they have a fixed base-rate of interest that doesn't change during the life of the security.

Unlike Series I Savings Bonds, however, the fixed portion of TIPS interest payments isn't added to the value of the security, but is paid to you every six months.

The inflation adjustment portion of TIPS, on the other hand, is added to the TIPS principal amount, which is also how it works with a Series I bond.

When deflation occurs, that is also applied to the TIPS principal amount. With Series I Savings Bond, deflation adjustments are limited to zeroing out the fixed base-rate. There is no limit to the size of the TIPS inflation adjustment, which gives an advantage to Savings Bonds.

Another advantage to Series I bonds is that there's no risk of capital loss if the level of the TIPS base rate rises.

Moreover, TIPS don't have the deferred-tax feature of Savings Bonds. Consequently, you have to pay income tax on the inflation adjustments each year – even though you receive no cash to pay it with!

Unless a large difference develops between their fixed base-rates, Series I Savings Bonds are always the better choice for individual investors.

To make a comparison based on today's rates, go to our web site and click on Book Notes. Note 5-6 will show you the current Series I fixed rate and note 5-7 will link you to the current open-market rates for TIPS at 5, 7, and 10-year maturities.

If you're interested in investigating marketable Treasury securities further, see the following links on our web site. Click on Book Notes, then on the note shown here:

5-8 – Open a TreasuryDirect account for marketable Treasury securities.

5-9 – The U.S. Treasury's web site for T-Bills, T-Notes, and TIPS.

5-10 – Tentative schedule of upcoming Treasury auctions.

Risks of Savings Bonds

Although Savings Bonds have few risks, they aren't entirely riskless. However, their largest risk is one that may surprise you.

Over 5% of the Savings Bonds outstanding have stopped earning interest. This means that the largest risk you face with an investment in Savings Bonds is that you'll forget you have them, or that you'll die and your heirs won't find them.

If you're going to invest in Savings Bonds, you need to make sure this doesn't happen to you.

In Chapter 10, we'll give you some additional information about how to find out if you – or those who have left you an inheritance – own forgotten Savings Bonds.

We'll also give you additional information in Chapter 15 about how to keep track the Savings Bonds you own, and how to make sure your heirs know you have them.

The only other significant risk of Savings Bonds concerns the electronic bonds at TreasuryDirect. If someone obtains the password to your account, they effectively have control of your money.

While the technical level of security of TreasuryDirect is unsurpassed, other financial institutions do a better job than the Treasury does of letting you know about transactions and changes occurring to your account.

The result is that someone could steal your password and you wouldn't realize it until months later when you received a 1099-INT telling you that you owe income tax on money that's been stolen from you.

Finally, as we mentioned earlier, while the registration feature of Savings Bonds keeps others from cashing your bonds, banks sometimes make mistakes. It's best to keep your Savings Bonds where thieves can't find them and your heirs can't miss them.

Part II –
Managing your investment

Savings Bond A, B, Cs

Current interest rates paid by all Savings Bonds

How much are my Savings Bonds worth?

Keeping track of your Savings Bond inventory

Lost and stolen Savings Bonds

Changing the registration

Managing the deferred-tax time bomb

Is tax-deferral better than higher rates?

Chapter 6

Savings Bond A, B, Cs

Before I and EE came A, B, C, D....

Series E and EE Savings Bonds issued before May 2005

Reaching face value: the original maturity guarantee

The guaranteed rate feature of older Savings Bonds

Series H and HH feature current income

Before I and EE came A, B, C, D....

Like New York City subway lines, Savings Bonds use letters to identify their series. Bonds in Series A, B, C, D, F, G, J, and K are not only no longer sold - they no longer earn interest and should be cashed in.

The one Savings Bond Series that doesn't have a letter - bonds in this series are sometimes called *Savings Notes* and sometimes *Freedom Shares* - has also stopped earning interest and should be cashed in.

You may also hear the term *Patriot Bond*, however, this isn't an official Savings Bond series. Since December 11, 2001, all paper Series EE bonds purchased at financial institutions - but not those purchased through Payroll Savings Plans - have been called Patriot Bonds. These bonds are identical to other Series EE bonds except that the words Patriot Bond are printed on the top half of the bond between the social security number and issue date.

The Patriot Bond is just a standard Series EE bond with the Patriot Bond wording on the front.

The only two series of Savings Bonds that the Treasury makes available for purchase today are Series I and Series EE. We described the current features of the Series I and EE bonds in the first part of this book.

Older issues of Series EE bonds have a few different rules and features. In addition, there are three series of Savings Bonds - Series E, H, and HH - that are no longer issued but still have some issue dates earning interest. We'll describe the older E and EE bonds first, then the H and HH bonds.

Series E and EE Savings Bonds issued before May 2005

Unlike the fixed rates of the current Series EE, older Series EE and Series E Savings Bonds pay interest rates that adjust every six months based on the prevailing level of interest rates in the bond market.

However, the exact method of determining this adjustable rate depends on when a bond was issued.

May 1997 through April 2005 issue dates

The Series EE Savings Bonds issued during this eight-year period have the following differences from bonds issued now:

★ The interest rate paid by these bonds changes every six months.

★ The interest rate for each six-month rate period is 90% of the average yield for five-year Treasury securities during the previous six months.

★ These bonds have a working *original maturity guarantee.*
   ★ Bonds issued from June 2003 to April 2005 are guaranteed to double in value in 20 years, which creates an annual yield of 3.5% for bonds held that long.
   ★ Bonds issued from May 1997 to May 2003 are guaranteed to double in value in 17 years, which creates an annual yield of 4.12%.

May 1995 through April 1997 issue dates

The Series EE Savings Bonds issued during this two-year period have the following differences from bonds issued previously:

★ The interest rate for each six-month rate period is 85% (rather than 90%) of the average yield for five-year Treasury securities.

★ Interest accrues (is added to the bond's value for redemption calculations) twice a year rather than monthly. The accrual dates are the first business day of the bond's issue month and six months later. For example, a bond issued in January jumps in value on January 1 and July 1.

★ The original maturity guarantee on these bonds is 17 years or 4.12%.

Issue dates prior to May 1995

Series E and Series EE Savings Bonds issued before May 1995 have the following differences from bonds issued previously:

★ Interest rates are calculated two different ways. At redemption, the method that provides the highest return is used to calculate the value of the bond.

    ★ The first method is based on *guaranteed rates* during the life of the bond.

    ★ The second method is based on the average of the market-based rates (85% of the average yield for 5-year Treasury securities) published during the life of the bond.

★ Consequently, the interest earned during any particular month depends on which of the two methods will give the bond the highest value.

    ★ If the first method is best, the bond will earn whatever rate is required to make its value reach the guaranteed rates in effect during its life.

    ★ If the second method is best, the bond will earn whatever rate is required to make its value reach the average of the market-based rates published during its life.

★ Interest accrues (is added to the bond's value for redemption calculations) twice a year. See Table 14-1 in Chapter 14 for the exact payment dates.

★ The original maturity guarantee on these bonds is complete – the bonds have already reached face value – except for

---

All Savings Bonds issued before May 1997 accrue interest semiannually. While many accrue interest in their issue month and six months later, some Series E bonds don't even follow that pattern.

This creates a potential **redemption penalty of up to six-months interest** that most people don't know about. We discuss how to avoid this penalty in Chapter 14.

bonds issued in April 1995 and before that are less than 18 years old. These bonds double in value in 18 years, which creates a yield guarantee of 3.89%.

★ Stops earning interest:
  ★ Series E issued before Dec 1965 – 40 years
  ★ Series EE and Series E issued Dec 1965 and since – 30 years

★ Purchase price:
  ★ Series E – sold at 75% of face value (you paid $75 for a $100 bond)
  ★ Series EE – sold at 50% of face value (you paid $50 for a $100 bond)

★ Issue Dates:
  ★ Series E – first issued in May 1941, last issued in June 1980
  ★ Series EE – first issued in January 1980 – note the six-month overlap with Series E issue dates in the first half of 1980

Reaching face value: the original maturity guarantee

All Series EE bonds, including electronic EE bonds, are guaranteed to double the value of your investment within a certain number of years.

The number of years, which varies by issue date, is called the *original maturity* period. This guarantee is related to the *sold at half of face value* marketing gimmick.

If the interest rates paid by the bonds haven't doubled your investment in the guaranteed number of years, the Treasury boosts the bond's value on its 20th anniversary.

Because the Treasury lengthened the original maturity period by six years in March 1993, the next time one of these boosts could occur is in March 2011.

Series I bonds don't have an original maturity guarantee.

Table 6-1 lists all EE bonds that are still within their original maturity period. The table shows issue dates, how long the period is, and the effective interest rate the original maturity guarantee creates.

Table 6-1
Original Maturity Guarantee

Issue Date	Original Term	Interest Rate
Mar 93 – Apr 95	18 years	3.89%
May 95 – May 03	17 years	4.12%
Jun 03 – present	20 years	3.50%

The guaranteed rate feature of older bonds

As we've seen, Series E and EE bonds issued prior to May 1995 have a feature called guaranteed rates. Most of these bonds are actually earning their guaranteed rate, so let's look at this feature in more detail.

In addition to *rate periods*, which we've mentioned several times (there's a complete explanation of rate periods in the Appendix), Savings Bonds also have *maturity periods*.

A bond's first maturity period is called the original maturity period, and, as we've just seen, is related to how long it takes your investment to double in value. The guaranteed rate during the original maturity period will always accomplish that.

After the original maturity period, these older bonds enter one or more *extended maturity periods*, each lasting ten years. After that, they enter their *final maturity period*, which lasts until the bond stops earning interest.

As these older bonds move from one maturity period to the next, the Treasury can adjust their guaranteed rate.

The Treasury's guaranteed rate for a bond moving into a new maturity period has been 4% since March 1993. Since that's over ten years ago, all of the older bonds that are in an extended or final maturity period currently have a guaranteed rate of 4%.

However, note that these bonds won't necessarily earn the guaranteed rate in each of their six-month rate periods. The rate guarantees apply to what a bond earns over its entire life, not to each six-month piece of it.

Consequently, bonds that earn more than their guaranteed rates early in their life can pay less than their guaranteed rates later in their life and still meet the guarantee over the bond's life as a whole.

This is why some Savings Bonds are earning less than their guaranteed rate in specific rate periods, as you can see in the tables in Chapter 17.

Because the Treasury has held the guaranteed rate for Savings Bonds moving into new maturity periods at 4%, most bonds issued prior to May 1995 - but not all of the them - are earning a higher rate than new bonds.

Series H and HH feature current income

Series HH Savings Bonds, as well as the older Series H bonds, are no longer issued. They are substantially different from Series I and EE bonds in that their interest is sent to you – typically by direct deposit into your bank account – rather than added to the value of the bond, as with all other Savings Bonds.

The payment is made in the issue month of the bond and six months later. If you have moved, changed banks, or inherited Series H or HH bonds, it's possible that you're not receiving interest payments that are owed to you. We'll discuss how to solve this problem in a moment.

When they were available, the only way to obtain H / HH bonds was in exchange for E / EE bonds or matured H /HH bonds.

Income tax on the interest earned by the E / EE bonds that were exchanged for the H / HH bonds is deferred until the H / HH bonds are redeemed or until they reach final maturity and stop earning interest.

On the face of an HH bond you'll see an entry called *deferred interest*. This is the amount of interest that you will have to pay income tax on when the bond is redeemed or matures.

On the other hand, unlike other Savings Bonds, you pay income tax on the interest earned by these bonds in the year in which you receive it.

The redemption value of these bonds is always their face value. Although there was a minimum holding period for HH bonds, it's long past and all H and HH bonds are redeemable.

H and HH bonds have 10 year maturity periods. The rate paid by a new bond was set for the first ten years when it was issued and is reset at the end of each ten-year period to the then-current rate, which is currently a meager 1.5%.

If you have a large investment in Series E / EE or H / HH bonds that will stop paying interest in the next few years, you are sitting on a **deferred-tax time bomb**. See Chapter 12.

All H / HH bonds have a **hidden interest-rate penalty** you can easily avoid if you understand when to redeem your bonds. See Chapter 14.

Series H / HH bonds were issued at full face value (you paid $500 for a $500 bond) and came in four denominations: $500, $1,000, $5,000, and $10,000.

Series H bonds were first issued in June 1952 and earn interest for 30 years. They were replaced by Series HH Savings Bonds in January 1980. Series HH bonds earn interest for 20 years.

Inheriting Series H and HH Savings Bonds

Chapter 16 discusses the forms to use to have Savings Bonds reregistered when you inherit them or are Executor of the estate of a Savings Bond owner. The same forms are used for Series H and HH Savings Bonds.

However, timely reregistration is more important if the deceased person owned Series H or HH bonds. That's because the semiannual interest payments are being deposited in his or her bank account, which you will be closing.

In order to get the payments going to the correct account, follow the reregistration instructions in Chapter 16.

Missing interest payments

If you aren't receiving interest payments on an H or HH Savings Bond, notify the following office in writing, including your HH bond registration information, face values, and serial numbers and they will work with you to correct the situation:

H / HH Assistance Branch
Bureau of the Public Debt
PO Box 2186
Parkersburg WV 26106-2186

Direct deposit of interest payments

If you are receiving your Series H / HH interest payments by check, you can use the Treasury's **Public Debt Form 5396 – *Direct Deposit Sign-Up Form* –** to sign up for direct deposit.

For the Direct Deposit sign up form, see the Appendix or go to our web site, click on Book Notes, and see note 6-1.

Treasury web site for Series HH Savings Bonds

The Treasury has an internet site for Series H / HH Savings Bond owners. You can access the site using the Social Security Number and the Serial Number on one of your H / HH bonds. The site allows you to:

★   view your accounts

★   change your address

★   request tax information

We have a link to this site at Book Note 6-2 on our web site. The H / HH site is available:

★   Monday-Friday, 8 am to 8 pm Eastern time

★   Saturday, 7 am to 2:30 pm Eastern time

★   (excluding federal holidays)

To link to the Treasury's web site for Series H / HH bonds, go to our web site, click on Book Notes, and see note 6-2.

Chapter 7

Current interest rates paid by all Savings Bonds

Series I interest rates

Series EE interest rates

Series E interest rates

Series H / HH interest rates

Series I interest rates

Series I Savings Bonds earn a composite interest rate that is the sum of:

★   the bond's fixed base-rate, which is set at issue
★   the current inflation rate
★   an inflation adjustment to the fixed base-rate (the fixed rate times the inflation rate divided by two)

Because the composite rate includes both a component related to the bond's issue date and a component related to the current inflation rate, Series I bonds pay a wide variety of interest rates.

Table 7-1 shows the fixed base-rate for all I bonds since their introduction in September 1998, as well as the composite rate these bonds will earn during their two rate most recent six-month rate periods.

Table 7-1 **Series I Rates**				
Issue Date	**Months Spanned**	**Fixed Base-rate**	**Interest rate for rate periods beginning Nov 04 – Apr 05**	**Interest rate for rate periods beginning May 05 – Oct 05**
Inflation rate			2.66%	3.58%
Sep 98 – Oct 98	2	3.40%	6.11%	7.04%
Nov 98 – Oct 99	12	3.30%	6.00%	6.94%
Nov 99 – Apr 00	6	3.40%	6.11%	7.04%
May 00 – Oct 00	6	3.60%	6.31%	7.24%
Nov 00 – Apr 01	6	3.40%	6.11%	7.04%
May 01 – Oct 01	6	3.00%	5.70%	6.63%
Nov 01 – Oct 02	12	2.00%	4.69%	5.62%
Nov 02 – Apr 03	6	1.60%	4.28%	5.21%
May 03 – Apr 04	12	1.10%	3.77%	4.70%
May 04 – Apr 05	12	1.00%	3.67%	4.60%
May 05 – Oct 05	6	1.20%	---	4.80%

Series EE interest rates

As we saw in the previous chapter, Series EE bonds earn interest rates under different rules. Table 7-2 shows EE bond interest rates for the two most recent six-month rate periods.

Note that the only bonds that pay the current rate announced by the Treasury in May and November are those in the bottom three rows (issue dates of May 1997 and since).

Table 7-2

Series EE Rates

Issue date	Number of issues	Interest rate for rate periods beginning Nov 04 – Apr 05	Interest rate for rate periods beginning May 05 – Oct 05	Original Maturity Guarantee
Jan 80 – Feb 83	38	4.00%	4.00%	(complete)
Mar 83 – Apr 83	2	3.32%	3.32%	
May 83 – Oct 83	6	2.83%	2.83%	
Nov 83 – Apr 84	6	3.26%	3.26%	
May 84 – Oct 84	6	3.23%	3.23%	
Nov 84 – Apr 92	90	4.00%	4.00%	
May 92 – Oct 92	6	4.00%	4.00%	
Nov 92 – Feb 93	4	4.00%	4.00%	
Mar 93 – Apr 93	2	3.03%	3.03%	3.89%
May 93 – Oct 93	6	3.06%	3.06%	
Nov 93 – Apr 94	6	3.10%	3.10%	
May 94 – Oct 94	6	2.97%	2.97%	
Nov 94 – Apr 95	6	3.03%	3.03%	
May 95 – Apr 97	24	3.07%	3.07%	4.12%
May 97 – May 03	73	3.25%	3.42%	
Jun 03 – Apr 05	23	3.25%	3.42%	3.50%
May 05 – Oct 05	6	---	3.50%	

Series E interest rates

The Series E bonds that are still earning interest are earning several different rates.

During 2005, Series E bonds issued in 1965 and 1975 will stop earning interest on the first day of their issue month.

By November 2005, all of the Series E bonds that were issued with 40 year maturities will have stopped earning interest.

Table 7-3 summarizes what E bonds will earn during the two most recent six-month rate periods.

Table 7-3

Series E Rates

Issue Date	Months Spanned	Interest rate for rate periods beginning Nov 04 — Apr 05	Interest rate for rate periods beginning May 05 — Oct 05
May 41 — Apr 65	288	0.00% *	
May 65	6	4.00%	0.00% *
Jun 65 — Jul 65	2	6.00%	0.00% *
Aug 65	1	5.94%	0.00% *
Sep 65 — Oct 65	2	3.32%	0.00% *
Nov 65	1	3.32%	%
Dec 65 — Apr 75	112	0.00% *	
May 75 — Oct 75	6	4.00%	0.00% *
Nov 75 — Feb 78	27	4.00%	
Mar 78 — Apr 78	2	3.32%	%
May 78 — Jun 80	26	4.00%	
* no longer earning interest			

Series H / HH interest rates

During 2005, on the first day of their issue month, Series H bonds issued in 1975 will stop earning interest, as will Series HH bonds issued in 1985.

Series HH bonds that entered a new maturity period in December 2002 or before are earning 4%; those that entered a new maturity period in January 2003 or after are earning 1.5%.

Table 7-4

Series H / HH Rates

Issue Date	Series	Months Spanned	Interest rate for rate periods beginning Nov 04 – Apr 05	Interest rate for rate periods beginning May 05 – Oct 05
Jun 52 – Apr 75	H	275	0.00% *	
May 75 – Oct 75		6	4.00%	0.00% *
Nov 75 – Dec 79		50	4.00%	
Jan 80 – Apr 85	HH	64	0.00% *	
May 85 – Oct 85		6	4.00%	0.00% *
Nov 85 – Dec 92		86	4.00%	
Jan 93 – Apr 95		28	1.50%	
May 95 – Oct 95		6	4.00%	1.50%
Nov 95 – Dec 02		86	4.00%	
Jan 03 – Aug 04		20	1.50%	
* no longer earning interest				

www.Savings-Bond-Advisor.com

Chapter 8

How much are my Savings Bonds worth?

Looking up a bond's value using our tables

Values in TreasuryDirect

Savings Bond Calculator

Savings Bond Wizard

Looking up a bond's value using our tables

The quick and easy way for you to look up the value of a Savings Bond is to use the tables in Chapter 17 of this book. First find your bond's series, then its issue date.

If the bond is still earning interest, each issue month has its own row. You'll see a set of seven columns that show the interest rate and redemption value of your bond on a month-by-month basis.

If the bond is no longer earning interest, rows represent issue years and the columns issue months. Only the redemption value is shown.

In both cases, I give you the redemption value per $1 of your bond's face value (FV). If you have a $100, $1,000, or $10,000 bond, you can calculate its value in your head simply by moving the decimal point.

For other face values, multiply the face value of your bond by the number we give you.

If the redemption month you're interested in is later than those shown in this book, our web site has information about how you can get this book upgraded with current information.

How can it be, you will ask, that the number for some bonds is less than 1.0000?

Don't forget that paper Series EE bonds are sold at half of face value. So they won't reach face value, or 1.0000, until you've owned them a number of years. You invested $50 to receive a $100 paper EE bond, so the number we show for a new bond is 0.5000. Multiply that times the $100 face value, and you get the $50 the bond is worth.

Values in TreasuryDirect

TreasuryDirect provides a summary of your Savings Bond holdings and their current value. Once you've logged in to TreasuryDirect, click on the *Current Holdings* button and you'll see a page that looks like Figure 8-1.

The value shown in the **Amount** column is how much you've invested and the value in the **Current Value** column is what your investment is worth now.

If you click on one of the radio buttons shown in the top figure and then on *Submit*, you'll see a **Current Holdings >> Summary** page, as shown in Figure 8-2.

This page shows you not only how much you've invested (**Amount**) and the **Current Value** of your investment, it also shows you the issue dates and current interest rate for each of your holdings.

Don't forget you can now convert you paper bonds to electronic and track all your Savings Bonds in TreasuryDirect. See Chapter 3 for complete information.

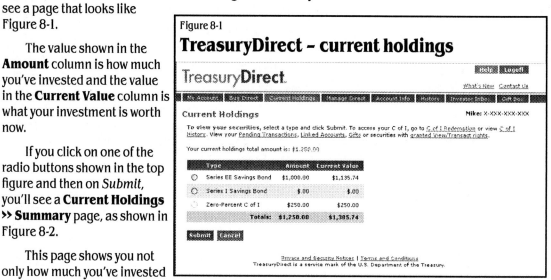

Figure 8-1

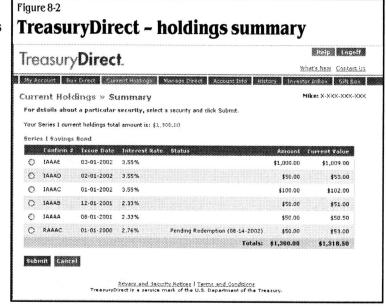

Figure 8-2

Savings Bond Calculator

The Treasury provides two free ways to find out the value of your paper Savings Bonds – the *Savings Bond Calculator* and the *Savings Bond Wizard*.

The Savings Bond Calculator is your best choice if you have internet access, don't want to be bothered with downloading and installing a program, or if you have a Macintosh or Linux system.

If you have a Windows computer and the ability and willingness to install new software, the Savings Bond Wizard is your best choice. We'll talk more about it in a minute here.

Savings Bond Calculator Feature Overview

The Savings Bond Calculator is an online program you access using your internet browser. Figure 8-3 shows you what it will look like the first time you link to it.

Note there are two sections, each with its own tab. The uppermost tab says **Value As Of** and the lower tab says **Bond Info**.

When you link to the actual Savings Bond Calculator, you may also see a survey under it, which you can safely ignore until you are familiar with the tool.

It's easy to enter your bonds in the Savings Bond Calculator, but you will find these three tips helpful:

★ **Serial Number**: This field is optional. Leave it blank unless your goal is to create and save a complete permanent record of your Savings Bonds. That's because it's hard to edit this field later, but I'll have more info for you on that in a moment. What you enter here doesn't have to be the bond's serial number – you can actually enter anything you like, up to 13 characters.

If you are a Linux user, **GBonds** is a free downloadable program you can use. For more info, go to our web site, click on Book Notes, and see Note 8-1.

Figure 8-3

Savings Bond Calculator with no entries

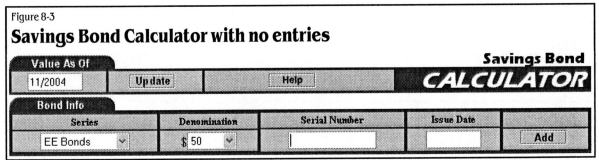

- ★ **Issue Date**: Enter the month as a one- or two-digit number and the year as a two- or four-digit number. Use the slash (/) or hyphen (-) to separate the month from the year. For example, all these formats work: 2/02, 02-02, 02/2002

- ★ **Keyboard Add**: Right after you've entered the Issue Date, pressing the *Enter* key on your keyboard does the same thing as clicking the *Add* button with your mouse.

Ready to play? OK, but come back here to learn how to save the bonds and other tricks before you enter more than one or two. To link to the Savings Bond Calculator, go to our web site, click on Book Notes, and see Note 8-2.

Tips for Using the Savings Bonds Calculator

Figure 8-4 shows the Savings Bonds Calculator after three bonds have been entered. Compare this image with the first one and you'll see two new tabbed sections, **Results** and **Legend**.

To run the Treasury's Savings Bond Calculator, go to our web site, click on Book Notes, and see note 8-2.

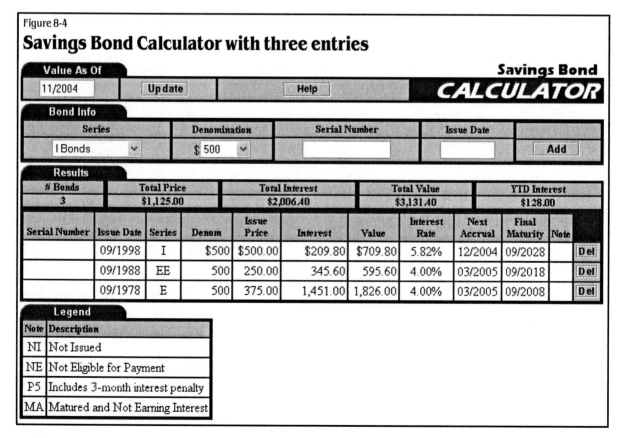

Figure 8-4

Savings Bond Calculator with three entries

Value As Of
11/2004

Update   Help

Savings Bond CALCULATOR

Bond Info

Series	Denomination	Serial Number	Issue Date	
I Bonds	$ 500			Add

Results

# Bonds	Total Price	Total Interest	Total Value	YTD Interest
3	$1,125.00	$2,006.40	$3,131.40	$128.00

Serial Number	Issue Date	Series	Denom	Issue Price	Interest	Value	Interest Rate	Next Accrual	Final Maturity	Note	
	09/1998	I	$500	$500.00	$209.80	$709.80	5.82%	12/2004	09/2028		Del
	09/1988	EE	500	250.00	345.60	595.60	4.00%	03/2005	09/2018		Del
	09/1978	E	500	375.00	1,451.00	1,826.00	4.00%	03/2005	09/2008		Del

Legend

Note	Description
NI	Not Issued
NE	Not Eligible for Payment
P5	Includes 3-month interest penalty
MA	Matured and Not Earning Interest

The **Results** tab is split into two sections. The upper section, shown in Figure 8-5, summarizes your holdings; the lower section, shown in Figures 8-6 and 8-7, gives details about each bond you've entered.

In the upper section of the **Results** tab you'll see:
* ★ the total number of bonds you've entered in the calculator
* ★ the total amount you paid for these bonds
* ★ the total interest you've earned
* ★ the total value (what you paid plus the interest)
* ★ the year-to-date interest

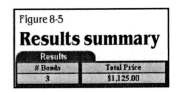

Figure 8-5

Results summary

# Bonds	Total Price
3	$1,125.00

In the lower section of the **Results** tab, in addition to the data you entered, for each bond you own you'll see:
* ★ the amount you invested (referred to as the *Issue Price* – 50% of the face value of EE bonds, 75% of the face value of E bonds, 100% of the face value of I bonds; see Figure 8-6)
* ★ the interest earned so far by this bond
* ★ the total value of the bond (what you paid plus the interest)
* ★ the current interest rate (see Figure 8-7)
* ★ the next accrual date (the date interest will be paid – if you're thinking about cashing in older bonds, you need to know this to avoid a potential six-month interest penalty)
* ★ the final maturity date (when the bond will stop earning interest)
* ★ a note section – any notes here are explained in the Legend (see next paragraph)
* ★ a *Delete* button – Unless you're an HTML hotshot, once you enter a bond, there's no way to make corrections (such as adding the serial number), other than to use the *Delete* button to remove the bond and re-enter it.

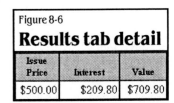

Figure 8-6

Results tab detail

Issue Price	Interest	Value
$500.00	$209.80	$709.80

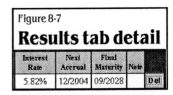

Figure 8-7

Results tab detail

Interest Rate	Next Accrual	Final Maturity	Note	
5.82%	12/2004	09/2028		Del

If you're thinking about cashing in older bonds, you need to know the accrual date to avoid a potential six-month interest penalty. See Chapter 14.

The Savings Bonds Calculator **Legend** tab has short, cryptic descriptions of what the notes mean. Here's what they really mean:

- ★ **NI – Not Issued** – you've entered a bond with a future issue date
- ★ **NE – Not Eligible for Payment** – bonds have to be a year old before you can redeem them
- ★ **P5 – Includes 3-month interest penalty** – the interest amount shown here is what you'll get if you redeem the bond today. Since you've held the bond less than five years, you will be charged a three month interest penalty, which has already been deducted from the interest shown.
- ★ **MA – Matured** – This is a stinker bond that is no longer earning interest. Cash it in, pay your taxes, and reinvest in a new bond.

You can use the Savings Bonds Calculator **Value As Of** tab shown in Figure 8-8 to see what interest amounts had been earned at points in the past back to January 1996. It will also show a few months into the future, but beyond that interest rates are unknown. To see values for a different month, change the date to the month you are interested in and click the *Update* button.

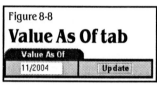

Figure 8-8

Value As Of tab

If you enter more than 10 bonds, a button will appear at the bottom of the **Results** tab, as shown in Figure 8-9, that will let you either view them all your bonds at once or view them 10 at a time. I think View All is the more useful setting.

Figure 8-9

View All button

How to Save Saving Bond Calculator Data in a File on Your Own Computer

If you'd like to check up on your Savings Bonds regularly, you can save the bond data you've entered using the Savings Bond Calculator on your own computer. This saved data can also be loaded into the Windows-based Savings Bond Wizard, should you decide to switch to it in the future.

Here's how to save your data:
- ★ Select the **Save As...** command from your browser's **File** menu.

To run the Treasury's Savings Bond Calculator, go to our web site, click on Book Notes, and see note 8-2.

★ If you get a message that says the page may not save correctly, ignore it.
★ In the box that pops up, make sure **Save as Type** is set to *Web* or *HTML*.
★ Pick a folder and filename you will remember and save the file.
★ In your browser, select the **Open** command from your browser's **File** menu.
★ Find the file you just saved and open it.
★ Immediately create a bookmark to this file, so you can easily find it next time you want to use it.

OK, now here's the hard part. When you open this file again six months from now, you have to remember these two things:
★ After you open file, change the date in the **Value As Of** tab and click update.
★ If you add additional bonds, you have to save the file again. After you forget to do this a time or two you'll reconsider whether this is really the tool you want to use.

If you want to save data on several different portfolios of Savings Bonds (for example, your own and your parent's), just save the data with different filenames.

To run the Treasury's Savings Bond Calculator, go to our web site, click on Book Notes, and see note 8-2.

Savings Bond Calculator Info For HTML Hotshots

If you know how to edit an HTML file, you can edit Savings Bond Calculator entries. The data is in a set of hidden fields near the beginning of the file.

Use your browser's **View Source** command to capture the calculator's HTML code. Skip past the head and body tags and you'll find a section that looks like this:

```
<!-- *** Inventory *** -->
<input type="hidden" name="SerialNumList" value=" ; ; ;">
<input type="hidden" name="IssueDateList" value="001;608;705;">
```

```
<input type="hidden" name="SeriesList" value="E;EE;I;">
<input type="hidden" name="DenominationList" value="500;100;75;">
```

There are additional hidden fields after these four, but they will all be updated, based on what's in these, when you click the Savings Bond Calculator's **Update** button. You have to do that in any case to get the calculator to use your changed data.

Note that in each hidden field the values are separated with semicolons. The first value in each hidden field all refer to the same bond. The second value in each hidden field all refer to your second bond, and so on.

In the sample HTML above, the hidden field for serial numbers has blanks between the semicolons because nothing was entered in the serial number field.

Issue Dates are encoded in three digit numbers with 001 equal to May, 1941 and every month after that one unit higher (January 2000 is 705).

It's possible, of course, to enter bad data in all sorts of ways – for example, to have an I bond with an issue date before I bonds existed. Also keep in mind that the Savings Bond Calculator doesn't support Series H or HH bonds. Zeros and NAs in the data for a bond indicates you've entered something weird like this.

To run the Treasury's Savings Bond Calculator, go to our web site, click on Book Notes, and see note 8-2.

Savings Bond Wizard

The first time you run the Treasury's free Savings Bond Wizard, it will look something like the display in Figure 8-10.

Like any standard Windows program you've used before, there is an outer program window and an inner file window. You can have several files open at once if you are working with bonds registered to different owners.

As shown in Figure 8-11, the program window has three menu bars – the top one is the standard drop-down menu bar you're

If you are a Linux user, **GBonds** is a free alternative to the Savings Bond Wizard. For more info, go to our web site, click on Book Notes, and see Note 8-1.

Figure 8-10

Savings Bond Wizard – initial display

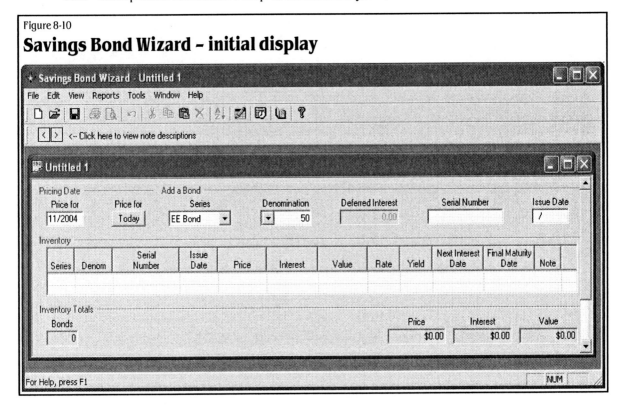

used to; the middle one is a standard icon-based menu bar; the bottom one is unique to the Wizard. It displays simple definitions of the contents of the Notes field for each bond, which we'll get to in a second here.

The file window has four sections.

The **Pricing Date** feature shown in Figure 8-12 allows you to look up the value of your bonds as of any date between January 1996 and as many months into the future as can be calculated (none to six). If the **Today** button is dim, the date is already set to the current month.

Figure 8-11

Savings Bond Wizard – program window

Figure 8-12

File window: Pricing Date

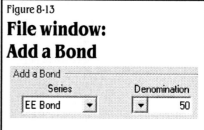

Figure 8-13

File window: Add a Bond

The **Add a Bond** feature shown in Figure 8-13 provides a way to add bonds to the file one at a time. The Wizard also has an *Easy Inventory Builder* feature that gives you a one-step way to add bonds you've purchased on a schedule, such as a Payroll Savings Plan, which we'll describe in complete detail soon.

The Wizard can inventory I, E, EE, H, and HH bonds, as well as Savings Notes. (If you actually have any Savings Notes, however, they've stopped earning interest and you'd be better off redeeming them than entering them.)

The *Deferred Interest* field is active only if you're entering an H or HH bond.

The *Serial Number* field holds any 13 characters. Unlike the Savings Bond Calculator, the Wizard allows you to edit this field.

The *Issue Date* field wants you to enter a two-digit month and a four-digit year – don't try to enter the slash. You can use a leading zero or a leading or trailing space to enter the months from January to September. The bond is automatically added to the inventory when you complete the date – there's no **Add** button as with the Savings Bond Calculator.

The Inventory section summarizes the information you've entered for each bond. In addition to what you've entered, which is shown in Figure 8-14, this section also shows you (you can see these fields in Figure 8-10):

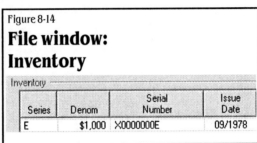

Figure 8-14

File window: Inventory

Series	Denom	Serial Number	Issue Date
E	$1,000	X0000000E	09/1978

Figure 8-15

File window: Totals

Inventory Totals

Bonds

5

★ the *Price* of the bond (your initial investment)
★ the *Interest* it has earned as of the pricing date you've selected
★ the bond's total *Value* (investment price plus interest earned) on the pricing date
★ the interest *Rate* for the current rate period
★ the bond's annual *Yield* from its issue date to its last interest payment date
★ the *Next Interest Date*, which is important to avoid up to a six-month interest penalty when you redeem older bonds
★ the *Final Maturity Date*, which is when the bond stops earning interest
★ any *Notes* about this bond

The Inventory Totals feature, which is shown in Figure 8-15, is at the bottom of the file window. It shows you how many bonds are in this file, including any that are marked cashed or exchanged, as well as:

★ the total *Deferred Interest* from H or HH bonds, if any, as of the pricing date

* the total *Price* you invested in the bonds that hadn't been cashed as of the pricing date
* the total *Interest* earned by the bonds that hadn't been cashed as of the pricing date
* the total *Value* of the bonds that hadn't been cashed as of the pricing date

If you double click on a specific bond in the file window, an *Edit Detail* window will open for that bond, which is shown in Figure 8-16.

Using this window you can correct any errors you made when you entered your bonds.

You can also mark bonds as cashed in or exchanged for HH bonds in this window.

The Savings Bond Wizard needs to download updated information on interest rates and values every six months. While your computer is connected to the internet, select **Redemption Values** from the **Tools** menu, then click the *Automatic Update* button. The Wizard will grab the latest files for you.

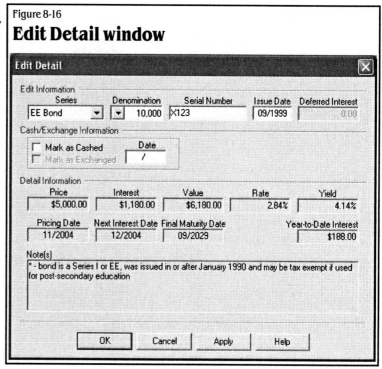

Figure 8-16
Edit Detail window

The Wizard also imports and exports files in Savings Bond Calculator format and in a specific Microsoft Excel format (see the Wizard's help file for details on this format).

If you have data files from an older version of Wizard, don't try to import them – just open them using the **Open...** command in the **File** menu.

Downloading and Installing the Savings Bond Wizard

The current version of the Savings Bond Wizard is 4.10. If you've downloaded the Wizard before, you can see if you have the current version by selecting **About the Wizard...** from the **Help** menu.

The Savings Bond Wizard runs on any Windows-based computer except very old models that use a system prior to Windows 95. The Wizard requires less than 3 megabytes of disk space.

The Wizard is free. To download it, go to our web site, click on Book Notes, and select Note 8-3. The download link on our web site will link you to the web site of the Bureau of Public Debt at the U.S. Treasury. You will download the file from their site, not ours.

When you follow the link, you will see a standard *Save Dialog Window* – create a new folder or select an existing one to save the file – **sbwsetup.exe** - on your own computer.

After you have downloaded the file, select the **Run...** command from your **Start** menu. Click on the *Browse* button, find the file you just downloaded, select it, then click the *OK* button. If you have administrative rights to install software on your computer, you'll be seconds away from using the Wizard.

The installation process will put a link to the Savings Bond Wizard in your **Start** menu. When the installation process is complete, find the Wizard in your **Start** menu and crank it up.

> To download the Savings Bond Wizard, go to our web site, click on Book Notes, and select Note 8-3.

Tips for using the Savings Bond Wizard

Right after you get the Wizard started for the first time, click on the *Maximize* button (the middle one of the three shown in Figure 8-17) in the inner *File* window. This will change the look of the Savings Bond Wizard a bit, as you can see in Figure 8-18. Note that you can also *Maximize* the *Program* window, or resize it by dragging the right or bottom edge (or better yet, the right-bottom corner).

Figure 8-17
Maximize button

Figure 8-18

Savings Bond Wizard – File window maximized

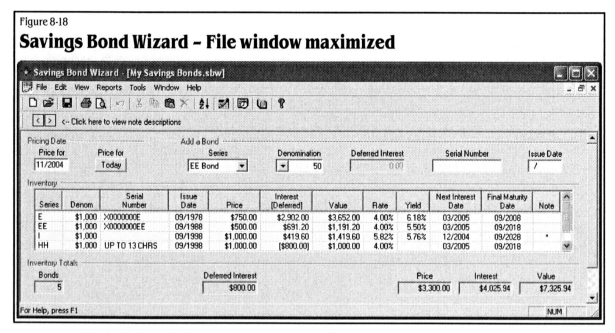

Next, select the **Options...** command on the **Tools** menu and change the *Startup* selection to *Last Closed Inventory*, as shown in Figure 8-19.

Also make sure the box in front of *Show "Current Date" notice when opening file* is checked. When you close the Savings Bond Wizard (by selecting **Exit** from the **File** menu), these settings – as well as the window sizes – will be saved and used next time you run the Wizard.

If you don't see all three of the menu bars, pull down the **View** menu, as shown in Figure 8-20, and put checks in the *Toolbar* and *Note Descriptions* boxes. There's no reason to hide either of these menu bars. The *Status Bar* is at the very bottom of the Wizard window – there's no reason to bother hiding it, either.

It's possible to make your *file window* seem to completely disappear by accidentally clicking on its *Minimize* button (the

Figure 8-19

Options

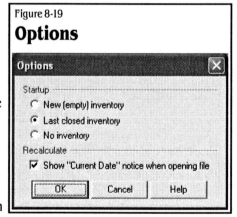

Figure 8-20

View

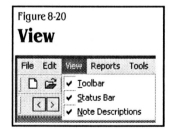

button on the left in Figure 8-17). If this happens to you, drop down the **Window** menu and select the file, which will listed at the bottom of the dropdown.

The *Easy Inventory Builder* is a cool feature for those who have purchased bonds on a scheduled basis. You enter the Series and Denomination (face value) of the bonds you've purchased, the starting and ending months, and whether you made weekly, biweekly, or monthly purchases.

You can also choose whether to add this series of bonds to your current inventory file or to create a new file. Then click *OK* and the *Easy Inventory Builder* does all that typing for you.

You can get to this feature from the **Tools** menu or by clicking on the *Easy Inventory Builder* toolbar icon (the one that looks like a large pencil on top of a small notebook).

There are two ways to sort your inventory list. The easy one is to simply click on the title at the head of a column. This will sort the list by that column. If you click a second time, the Wizard will resort the list, on the same column, in the opposite order (low to high, then high to low).

If you want to Sort on multiple columns at once, use the **Sort...** command in the **Tools** menu.

If you Right-Click on a bond in your inventory, you'll get the pop-up menu shown in Figure 8-22. The three selections at the bottom open the bond *Edit Detail* window or allow you to mark bonds as cashed in or exchanged for HH bonds.

You can also copy a bond and duplicate it with the paste command. Since you can't select an empty line in the inventory list, you may be concerned that paste will overwrite another bond, but it doesn't – it always creates a new bond.

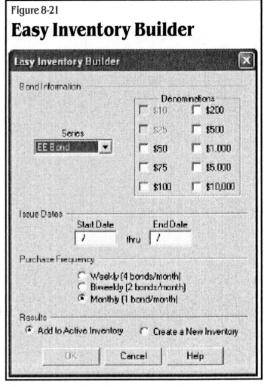

Figure 8-21
Easy Inventory Builder

Figure 8-22
Right-click menu

Chapter 9

Keeping track of your Savings Bond inventory

Controlling the biggest risk of Savings Bonds

Simple ways to keep an inventory

Commercial tracking and valuation services

Controlling the biggest risk of Savings Bonds

As discussed elsewhere in this book, Savings Bonds are a very safe investment. However, they carry one risk few other investments share – ***the risk that you'll forget you own them***.

As impossible as this sounds, over 5% of all Savings Bonds outstanding are no longer earning interest and haven't been redeemed. In other words, their owners have forgotten about them.

You can't depend on the Treasury to notify you when your Savings Bonds stop earning interest. The Treasury only has a very small team that initiates communications with holders of Savings Bonds that have stopped earning interest.

Even TreasuryDirect doesn't send automated emails confirming transactions or other changes to your account.

When you own stocks, mutual funds, or other investments, you receive at least an annual report reminding you – and your heirs, after you're gone – of those assets. The Treasury doesn't provide anything like this for Savings Bonds.

In this chapter we'll look at some ways you can control this risk by keeping records of the Savings Bonds you've purchased and redeemed.

Simple ways to keep an inventory

Here are three simple ways to keep an inventory of your Savings Bonds.

The photocopy method

This one's really simple if you only have paper bonds – just photocopy each of your bonds on a separate piece of paper and put all the photocopies in a folder. If you're the paperless type, you can scan the bonds and keep the images in a computer file.

The big advantage of this method is that you will capture all the data about each bond – registration, face value, issue date, and serial number. There's no chance of typographical or transcription errors.

It's easy to add new bonds to your inventory by slipping a new photocopy into your folder.

When you redeem bonds, rather than removing the photocopy of that bond, keep it. Just make a note in writing on that sheet that you've redeemed the bond. This will keep you from wondering someday whether you cashed it or not.

You can use the blank space on each sheet to write in things such as current values, interest rates, when the bond will stop earning interest, best days for redemption, and bond rating – all of which you can get from the tables in the back of this book.

The disadvantage of this method is that it doesn't summarize the total value of the inventory for you. But you can combine it with others methods, such as,...

The spreadsheet method

You can use just a pencil and blank sheet of paper to write down all the important information on your Savings Bonds, but if you have Microsoft Excel, we've created a simple spreadsheet you can download (go to our web site, click on Book Notes, and select Note 9-1).

If you want to stick with paper, lay out 15 columns on the sheet. Here are the titles to use for the 15 columns (the spreadsheet template has an extra column which calculates the current value for you after you enter the *Value per $* from our tables):

- ★ First Owner
- ★ OR or POD
- ★ Second Owner or Beneficiary
- ★ Social Security Number
- ★ Serial Number
- ★ Type (paper or TreasuryDirect)
- ★ Series
- ★ Issue Date
- ★ Face Value
- ★ Deferred Interest (H and HH only)
- ★ Current interest rate (from tables)
- ★ Current Value (face values times *Value per $* from tables later in this book)
- ★ To avoid rate penalty, redeem (from tables)
- ★ Lifetime APY (from tables)
- ★ Alert Recommendation (from tables)
- ★ Stops paying interest (from tables)

The advantage of this method is that you will develop a familiarity with your bonds. The disadvantage, of course, is that it's a lot of work.

A Savings Bond Wizard inventory

If you're using the Savings Bond Wizard, you'll want to check out its **Reports** menu. This menu lists a wide variety of reports you can run and print out. Reports are a feature that the Savings Bond Wizard provides but the online Savings Bond Calculator doesn't.

You can read all about the Savings Bond Wizard in Chapter 8.

Reports that would come up empty are dim in the menu – for example, if you haven't marked any bonds as cashed in, the *Bonds Cashed In* report will be dim and you won't be able to select it.

One of the most useful reports provided by the Savings Bond Wizard is the *Active Inventory* report, shown in Figure 9-1. This report lists all of your bonds, including their serial numbers, if you have entered them. One disadvantage of this report, which you can overcome with handwritten notes or a photocopy inventory, is that it doesn't include any of the registration information on your bonds.

Find a safe place to keep your inventory

No matter which of these methods you use, it's important to keep your inventory and your actual Savings Bonds in different locations. Some of the risk of losing your Savings Bonds comes from disasters like fire and storms. If everything is in one location you can lose both at the same time.

One idea for a second safe place for your actual bonds is a bank safe deposit box. These are typically somewhat expensive just for storing Savings Bonds. However, many people already have one for storing other documents. If you don't already have a safe deposit box, there are other solutions.

For example, you can keep the Savings Bonds in a safe place in your home and keep the photocopies at work. Or ask a relative or lawyer to keep the photocopies for you. If you have registered the Savings Bonds with a co-owner or beneficiary who doesn't live with you, it would be good to give him or her a copy.

In any case, make sure that your heirs know you own Savings Bonds and that they'll be able to find an up-to-date inventory of your holdings with your other financial paperwork.

Figure 9-1

Savings Bond Wizard – Active Inventory Report

Inventory Report
Active Inventory

Print Date: 09/03/2004
File Pricing Date: 11/2004

Bonds:

No.	Series	Denom	Serial Number	Issue Date	Price	Interest [Deferred]	Value	Rate	Yield	Next Interest Date	Final Maturity Date	Note
1	E	$1,000	X0000000E	09/1978	$750.00	$2,902.00	$3,652.00	4.00%	6.18%	03/2005	09/2008	
2	EE	1,000	X0000000EE	09/1988	500.00	691.20	1,191.20	4.00%	5.50%	03/2005	09/2018	
3	I	1,000		09/1998	1,000.00	419.60	1,419.60	5.82%	5.76%	12/2004	09/2028	*
4	HH	1,000	UP TO 13 CHRS	09/1998	1,000.00	[800.00]	1,000.00	4.00%		03/2005	09/2018	
5	I	50		10/2000	50.00	13.14	63.14	6.02%	5.80%	12/2004	10/2030	P5*

Inventory Totals:

Bonds	Deferred Interest	Price	Interest	Value
5	$800.00	$3,300.00	$4,025.94	$7,325.94

Commercial tracking and valuation services

In addition to the inventory tracking methods mentioned previously, another option is to use a commercial, fee-based service.

The services that are available typically add additional features that the free Savings Bond Calculator and Savings Bond Wizard don't provide, such as data safe-keeping, automatic updating, reports that are emailed to you, and so on.

For a list of these services, go to our web site, click on Book Notes, and see note 9-2.

Chapter 10

Lost and stolen Savings Bonds

Finding forgotten Savings Bonds

Treasury Hunt

Savings Bonds never received

Destroyed, stolen, and lost Savings Bonds

Finding forgotten Savings Bonds

There are two flavors of forgotten Savings Bonds.

Sometimes you'll have some kind of documentation that you or your bequestors held Savings Bonds, but you can't find the bonds. They may have been redeemed, but you don't know for sure. Would you like to get confirmation of their status?

In the other case, you don't even have documentation about the bonds, but just a memory, or a question. Did we lose them in that last move? How many Savings Bonds did Aunt Jean give Sally when she was a kid?

In either case you can write a letter to the Treasury's Bureau of the Public Debt and ask them either:

★ to give you the redemption status of bonds for which you have documentation

★ to search the Treasury's records for bonds you can neither find nor document.

In return you'll receive a printout of unredeemed bond holdings, including series, issue date, face value, and serial number – note that Savings Bonds you have already redeemed will not be on the list. If some of the bonds on the list are indeed lost, we'll tell you how to get them replaced in a minute here.

In your letter, you should provide as much information as you can. At a minimum you must provide your name, current address, and social security number. But the Treasury's ability to search improves as you provide additional information, such as:

- ★ the serial numbers on the bonds
- ★ the serial numbers of any other bonds you own
- ★ the name of co-owners or beneficiaries on the missing bonds
- ★ the series and denomination
- ★ the issue date – even if only approximate
- ★ your name and address at the time of issue
- ★ and, if the bond was a gift to you, the giver's
  - ★ name
  - ★ address, and
  - ★ social security number

If the owner of the bonds has died and you're the representative of his or her estate, provide documentation of your status and a copy of the death certificate of the owner.

Sign your request and send it to:

Bureau of the Public Debt
Accrual Securities Branch
P. O. Box 1328
Parkersburg, WV 26106-1328

Treasury Hunt

A simpler way to search for bonds that have stopped earning interest or that were returned to the Treasury by the Post Office is to use an online system called Treasury Hunt. Treasury Hunt allows you to enter your:

★ First Name
★ Middle Name or Initial
★ Last Name
★ Social Security Number (with or without dashes)
★ City
★ State

Note that for bonds you received as gifts, you should also try the name, SSN, city, and state of the giver.

Some of the records in the data base have both name and Social Security Number, other records have one but not the other. The system looks for matches on any field you enter rather than matches on all fields at the same time.

The data you enter must match the data on a registered Treasury security (marketable Treasury securities and Savings Bonds are both in the system) that:

★ Has stopped earning interest (however, the oldest Savings Bonds that have stopped earning interest aren't in the system)

★ Was returned as undeliverable in 1996 or later (each year, the Post Office returns over 15,000 Savings Bonds and 25,000 interest payments to the Treasury undelivered) The Treasury suggests you try spelling your name different ways, since a misspelling could be why a bond wasn't delivered.

The system contains a small subset of all Savings Bonds. In particular, it won't find "lost" Savings Bonds if they were delivered correctly and are still earning interest.

Ready? To get to Treasury Hunt, go to our web site, click on Book Notes, and go to Note 10-1.

Savings Bonds never received

When you buy a Savings Bond at a bank or through your Payroll Savings Plan, it should arrive within three calendar weeks. If you don't receive the bond by then, contact your bank or payroll office, which will work with the federal office that issues Savings Bonds to find the missing bond or get you a replacement.

Destroyed, stolen, and lost Savings Bonds

If you know that a Savings Bond has been lost, stolen, or destroyed, you can have it replaced without a fee. To do so, you'll need a copy **Public Debt Form 1048** – *Claim for lost, stolen, or destroyed United States Savings Bonds.*

You can download a copy of this form from our web site. Click on Book Notes, then on Note 10-2. Start by reading the instructions on the last page of the form, which include the address where you should mail the form after completing it.

If you don't have internet access, you can order a copy of this form by mail. See the Appendix for complete instructions.

You can provide approximate issues dates and you can enter "unknown" for denominations and serial numbers, but you must provide complete registration information – the name of the owner and the address and Social Security Number that appeared on the bond (if the bond was a gift, the address and SSN could be those of the giver rather than those of the bond's owner).

The Treasury will establish the existence of the bonds and that they haven't already been cashed. On the form, you can ask to have the bonds replaced (they'll have the original issue date), or you can ask for the funds.

A claim that a bond was improperly redeemed requires a higher level of information that may involve police reports or other legal documents.

If you haven't lost your Savings Bonds yet, reading this chapter should give you some incentive to go back to Chapter 9 and create an inventory of your Savings Bonds as soon as you can.

Chapter 11

Changing the registration

Why change the registration?

When all the registrants are still living

Adding a co-owner or changing the beneficiary

Changing the owner or co-owner

Changing the owner to a trust

Why change the registration?

In Chapter 4, I discussed Savings Bond registration from the point of view of someone making an investment in Savings Bonds.

That chapter has basic information about Savings Bonds registration that you'll need before attacking this chapter. It includes a discussion of why you might want to register Savings Bonds one way or another for estate planning purposes.

For an overview of information about Savings Bond registrations, see Chapter 4.

The Treasury won't reissue bonds to fix minor spelling errors if the registration information is sufficient to establish ownership.

Neither will it update the delivery address or Social Security Number (SSN), or split a large bond into smaller denominations.

Neither the delivery address, which may include a name, nor the SSN can be changed. Neither represents a right to the bond. The delivery address is simply where the Treasury mailed the paper bond when it was issued. Like the SSN, it's only used to track lost bonds, not for redemption or tax purposes.

The Treasury says you don't need to have a bond reissued to update a name changed by marriage, but the forms will allow you to do so.

When you send bonds in to have the registration changed there's no need to sign the back of the bonds. In fact, signing the back of the bonds is a signal to the Treasury that you want redemption, not reissue, so things can get confused if you sign bonds you want reissued.

When all the registrants are still living

If you want to change a Savings Bond's registration because one of the registrants has died, the information you need is in Chapter 16, *Inheriting and passing on Savings Bonds*.

There are two ways to change a Savings Bond's registration. One is to have the bond reissued with the new registration; the other is to redeem the original bond and buy a new one with the desired registration.

Cashing in the old bond and buying a new one is preferable surprisingly often, particularly if having the bond reissued to change the registration will cause a taxable event anyhow.

A taxable event means a status change in a Savings Bond that causes a 1099-INT IRS form to be issued to the original owner, forcing income tax to be paid on the bond's earnings to date, as if the bond was redeemed.

Adding a co-owner to a registration that doesn't already have one never creates a taxable event. Neither does adding, changing, or removing a beneficiary.

Changing a living owner or co-owner, on the other hand, always creates a taxable event, except in a few special cases we'll get to in a moment.

Adding a co-owner or changing the beneficiary

To add a co-owner or to add, remove, or change a beneficiary you'll need copies of one or both of the following forms. See the sidebar on this page for information on how to obtain copies.

Print out and follow the instructions that come with the forms. In addition, there are a few warnings and cautions to be aware of:

★ Forms:
  ★ For electronic bonds at TreasuryDirect, you can manage the registrations online. You don't really edit the old registration, however. You add a new registration to your list of possible registrations in the system, then switch your bonds one-by-one from the old registration to the new one.
  ★ For paper Series I bonds, use **Public Debt Form 5387** – *Request for Reissue of Series I United States Savings Bonds*
  ★ For paper bonds in any other series use **Public Debt Form 4000** – *Request to Reissue United States Savings Bonds*

★ Warnings and Cautions:
  ★ your signature on the form must be certified by a bank representative; there's no need to sign the back of the bonds themselves
  ★ the Treasury won't reissue paper bonds to update an address, SSN, or to change denominations
  ★ changing the beneficiary on the older and no longer issued Series E or Series H bonds requires the consent of the current beneficiary
  ★ keep in mind that a Savings Bond registration can have only a co-owner or a beneficiary, not both; you can remove a beneficiary and add a co-owner (but not vice-versa) without creating a taxable event

If you don't have internet access, you can order a copy of these forms by mail. See the Appendix for complete instructions.

Otherwise, go to our web site, click on Book Notes, and see Notes 11-1 and 11-2.

Changing the owner or co-owner

Having a Savings Bond reissued to change the registration can be preferable to redeeming a bond and buying a new one when the original bond pays a higher rate of interest than new bonds or when it's to your advantage to continue deferring income tax on the original bond.

However, preferable or not, changing the owner or co-owner of a Savings Bond will create a taxable event and end tax deferral except in the case of the death of a registrant or a few other special cases. These exceptions include:

★ Removing a co-owner who didn't put up any of the money used to buy the bond.

★ When bonds that you and a co-owner bought jointly are reissued to each of you separately in the same proportion as your contribution to the purchase price.

★ Transfer of bonds between spouses or as part of a divorce, except in community property states.

★ Transfer to a trust, but only when you are considered the owner of the trust and the increase in value both before and after the transfer continues to be taxable to you.

For official documentation on these exceptions, see IRS Publication 550, *Investment Income and Expenses*.

There's a link to this IRS document at Book Note 11-4.

If you're going to create a taxable event anyhow, or if higher rates on a new bond overcome the disadvantages of losing tax-deferral on the original bond, then you're better off just redeeming the old bond and buying a new one.

The redemption-repurchase route to changing the registration on your Savings Bonds has the following advantages and disadvantages:

★ Advantages:
   ★ no forms to fill out
   ★ provides an opportunity to switch from one series to another, from paper bonds to TreasuryDirect, or to change denominations
   ★ restarts the 30-year maturity clock
   ★ no limitations on whose name can be on the new bond

- ★ if reissue would create a taxable event, redemption-repurchase avoids the *double-taxation trap* (see Chapter 12)
- ★ if the new owner has a higher tax rate than the current owner, it's better to create a taxable event and pay income tax at the current owner's lower rate
- ★ new bonds pay higher interest rates than some older bonds (see Chapter 7)

★ Disadvantages:
- ★ if the bonds are H or HH bonds, you won't be able to get a replacement in that series
- ★ if Series EE or I bonds are less than one year old, you can't redeem them
- ★ if Series EE or I bonds are less than five years old, there's a three-month interest penalty on redemption
- ★ the $30,000 maximum annual purchase limit could prevent repurchase of a large amount of Savings Bonds
- ★ redemption-repurchase will always create a taxable event for the original owner
- ★ redemption-repurchase loses any ongoing advantages of tax deferral, as does a taxable event
- ★ some older bonds pay higher interest rates than new bonds (see Chapter 7)

If you decide it's to your benefit to have the bonds reissued to change the registration, here's how to proceed:

If you have electronic bonds at TreasuryDirect, just transfer your bonds to the TreasuryDirect account of the new owner. This is always a taxable event.

To have paper Savings Bonds reissued, print out and follow the directions on these forms (see the sidebar on the next page for information on obtaining the forms you'll need):

Forms:
- ★ For paper Series I bonds, use **Public Debt Form 5387** – *Request for Reissue of Series I United States Savings Bonds*

See Book Note 11-1

- ★ For paper bonds in any other series:
    - ★ to remove or change the owner or co-owner, use
        Public Debt Form 1938 – *Request for Reissue of United States Savings Bonds to Remove Name of One or More Living Registrants*

See Book Note 11-3.

- ★ Warnings and Cautions:
    - ★ unless you are eligible for one of the taxable-event exceptions mentioned earlier (death of a registrant, court order related to a divorce, removing a co-owner who didn't invest, split between co-owners in the proportion in which they invested, transfer between spouses outside community property states, transfer to a trust without change in tax status), changing the owner or co-owner will set you up for the *double-taxation trap* (see the next chapter). Make sure you give the new owner a copy of your next tax return as proof that you've already paid some of the tax on the bond.
    - ★ read the Tax Liability section on the first page of **Form 1938** carefully. If you are eligible for an exception to creation of a taxable event, include a separate page with the form explaining why. The form is usually processed as a taxable event unless it's clear why it shouldn't be.
    - ★ except in the cases of the death of the registrant or a court order related to a divorce:
        - ★ changing or removing an owner or co-owner requires the signatures of both the owner and co-owner
        - ★ any new owner or co-owner must be someone related to you by blood or marriage or a trust that benefits you or an eligible person. In particular, it can't be a charitable organization.
    - ★ your signature on the form must be certified by a bank representative; there's no need to sign the back of the bonds themselves

If you don't have internet access, you can order a copy of these forms by mail. See the Appendix for complete instructions.

Changing the owner to a trust

New Savings Bonds can be registered in the name of a trust and old Savings Bonds can be reissued to change the registration to a trust.

As before, if changing the registration is going to cause a taxable event anyhow, you should consider the option of just cashing in your old bonds and buying new ones in the name of the trust.

The form for requesting reissue to a trust is **Public Debt Form 1851**, *Request to Reissue United States Savings Bonds to a Personal Trust.*

See Book Note 11-5.

When you complete this form, you are required to check one of two boxes that basically ask whether the trust will provide you a way to get out of paying the tax on the bonds.

If the trust treats you in a way that will force you to pay the tax on the Savings Bond interest when the bonds are redeemed, you can have the bonds reissued without creating a taxable event.

If you don't have internet access, you can order a copy of this form by mail. See the Appendix for complete instructions.

Otherwise you have to check the other box, in which case you'll receive by return mail the reissued bond and a 1099-INT for the interest earned to date.

The instructions on the form go into detail about what provisions are related to each kind of trust. It also has an IRS address you can write to for a ruling if you still have a question about a particular kind of trust after reading the information in the form's instructions.

Chapter 12

Managing the deferred-tax time bomb

Your marginal tax rate

The tax-deferral feature of Savings Bonds

What is the deferred-tax time bomb?

When your tax rate is headed up, avoid tax deferral

Your Marginal Tax Rate

Before we can discuss the tax-deferral feature of Savings Bonds in the depth it deserves, we have to make sure that you understand what marginal tax rates are and that you know what yours is.

In the United States, income tax rates are graduated. The higher your income, the higher your tax rate. The graduated scales have many fewer steps and lower rates now than they used to, however.

Your top rate is called your *marginal* rate because you pay it only on the part of your income that exceeds the threshold for that rate. In other words, everyone pays the same percentage on lower levels of income – the higher rates apply only to the portion of your income that exceeds the threshold amount for that rate.

This means that when you are in a situation where you can move income from one year to another, you will pay the least in taxes if you move your income to the year in which you are in the lowest tax bracket and have the lowest marginal tax rate.

The tax-deferral feature of Savings Bonds gives you this kind of flexibility. Within the range of the 30-year life of a Savings Bond, you can choose when to redeem the bond and pay the income tax on the interest you've earned. You don't even have to redeem your bond to pay the accumulated tax, as I'll explain in a minute here.

Table 12-1 will help you determine your tax bracket or marginal tax rate. You need to know your filing status and your taxable income.

Your taxable income is not the same as your total income, but is your income after deductions and exemptions. Look for the line on your tax return labeled *Taxable Income.*

The US Tax Rates shown in Table 12-1 are from IRS Publication 505, Tax Withholding and Estimated Tax.

When the table for 2006 is released, we'll have it our web site. Click on Book Notes and go to Note 12-1.

Table 12-1

2005 US Tax Rates

When your taxable income is over:				Your marginal tax rate is:
Single	Married Joint Return	Married Separate Return	Head of Household	
$0	$0	$0	$0	10%
$7,300	$14,600	$7,300	$10,450	15%
$29,700	$59,400	$29,700	$39,800	25%
$71,950	$119,950	$59,975	$102,800	28%
$150,150	$182,800	$91,400	$166,450	33%
$326,450	$326,450	$163,225	$326,450	35%

The tax-deferral feature of Savings Bonds

Savings Bonds are tax-deferred investments. This means that rather than paying income tax on the interest you earn each year, you don't owe any income tax on the interest until you redeem the bond.

This feature gives Savings Bonds two advantages most other investments lack. First, it gives you the opportunity to move income into years in which your tax rate is lower.

Secondly, rather than giving up part of your interest each year to pay income tax, the Treasury "loans" you the tax amount and lets you earn interest on it. This is what makes tax-deferred investments like free money.

In addition to allowing you to earn interest on this tax loan, tax-deferred investments are particularly profitable when your tax rate drops between the time you would have otherwise paid your taxes and when you actually do pay your taxes.

However, keep in mind that while there are benefits to tax-deferred investments, there can be even bigger benefits to earning a higher interest rate to begin with. We have a great example of this in our analysis of 1.5% HH bonds, which we'll tell you about in the next chapter.

Figure 12-1 shows how much of a Savings Bond's value is a tax-deferred investment. The proportion of your bond's total value that is your deferred-tax loan – as opposed to the part you'd keep if you redeemed the bond and paid your taxes – depends on two things:

★   the percentage of the bond's value that is interest earned, rather than what you paid for the bond

★   your marginal tax rate

According to the IRS, tax-deferral is only available to those use cash-basis accounting, which includes almost all individuals. Businesses, on the other hand, often use accrual accounting. Those who use accrual accounting should report Savings Bond interest to the IRS annually.

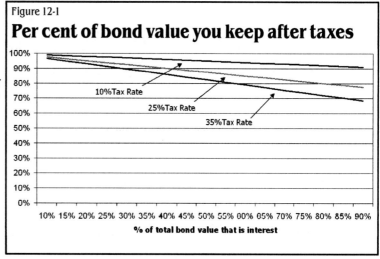

Figure 12-1

Per cent of bond value you keep after taxes

10%Tax Rate

25%Tax Rate

35%Tax Rate

% of total bond value that is interest

In Figure 12-1 (repeated on this page), the numbers running left-to-right represent how much of your bond's value is tax-deferred interest.

For example, at the point at which an EE bond reaches face value, interest makes up 50% of what it's worth. What you originally paid for the bond makes up the other half.

For Series EE bonds, the highest this percentage goes is just over 80%. For Series E bonds that paid interest for 40 years, this percentage can go as high as just over 90%.

But these are the extremes. The percentage on your own bonds is almost certainly lower – you can look up the percentage for your bonds in the tables in Chapter 17 (use the *% interest* column).

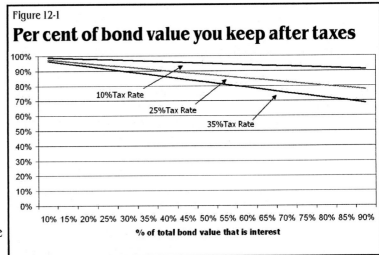

Figure 12-1

Per cent of bond value you keep after taxes

In Figure 12-1, the percentages running up and down represent how much of the bond's value you'd keep if you cashed in the bond and paid your income tax. You keep the proportion below your tax line and the IRS gets the proportion above your tax line.

The upper line represents the lowest income tax rate, which is 10%; the bottom line represents the highest income tax rate, which is 35%.

Find the line in the figure that is closest to your current tax rate. The space between this line and the top of the graph – the 100% line – represents the value of the tax-deferred loan on which you're earning interest.

Now find the line in the figure that is closest to the tax rate you expect to have when you cash in your bonds. The space between this line and the line indicating your current tax rate represents the benefit (free money) you'll receive from being able to defer your tax until you have a lower tax rate.

As you can see, the advantages of the deferred-tax feature of Savings Bonds is worth the most when:

★ the value of your Saving Bonds is primarily interest
★ you are in a high tax bracket
★ you expect to be in a lower tax bracket when you redeem your bonds.

If none of these are true, the deferred-tax feature of Savings Bonds is of minimal value to you.

You can keep deferring taxes with Savings Bonds until they reach final maturity and stop paying interest.

The IRS says you owe income tax in the year a bonds stops earning interest whether you redeem it or not. If you cash the bond in a year or two later, the 1099-INT is issued for the year in which the bond matured. You'll have to file an amended return for that year. If additional taxes are due, there will be a penalty.

Table 12-2 shows how long each series of Savings Bonds pays interest.

Table 12-2

How long Savings Bonds pay interest

Series	First Issued	Last Issued	Years until interest stops	Bonds issued in this year stop paying interest in 2005
E	May 1941	Nov 1965	40	1965
E	Dec 1965	Jun 1980	30	1975
EE	Jan 1980	---	30	---
I	Sep 1998	---	30	---
H	Jun 1952	Dec 1979	30	1975
HH	Jan 1980	Aug 2004	20	1985

What is the deferred-tax time-bomb?

As wonderful as tax-deferral sounds, it will blow up on you if you cash in a large Saving Bond investment all at once.

If you have participated in a Payroll Savings Plan or otherwise invested heavily in Savings Bonds, you've made regular, scheduled purchases. To avoid the deferred-tax time bomb, you need to cash them in the same way – on a regular schedule spanning multiple years.

The worst thing you can do is to follow the advice of an unqualified financial consultant who tells you to "just cash them all in".

The reason that cashing them all in is a bad idea is that the boatload of tax-deferred interest you'll receive could push you into a higher tax bracket or cause you to pay tax on Social Security income you otherwise wouldn't have to pay.

You need to be particularly careful about this if you are near retirement and someone is trying to get you to convert your Savings Bond investment into an annuity. Many people make the mistake of cashing in all their Savings Bonds just before they retire, when they're already in the highest tax bracket of their lives.

The best strategy is to let the bonds quietly earn tax-deferred interest while you're in a high tax bracket, then cash them in year-by-year after you retire and are in a lower tax bracket. This gives you a do-it-yourself annuity with none of the fees and sales commissions that the let-the-pros-do-it-for-you annuities have.

On the other hand, if all of your Savings Bonds were purchased in the same year or two, they will all mature in the same year or two as well. In this case, you have to plan ahead – cash some of the bonds well before final maturity to spread out the interest income over a multi-year period.

No matter how many bonds you cash, always make sure you hold back enough money to pay the income tax you'll owe on the interest you've earned. How much you'll need depends on your tax bracket. If it's over several thousand dollars, you may avoid a penalty by having some of the interest withheld when you cash in your bonds or by sending in an estimated tax payment.

When your tax rate is headed up, avoid tax deferral

You aren't required to accept the tax deferral feature of Savings Bonds – the IRS will allow you to pay the income tax on your Savings Bond interest every year.

You can get automatic permission to do this from the IRS – the details are under the Savings Bond topic of the Interest Income section of IRS Publication 17, *Your Federal Income Tax for Individuals*. Go to our web site, click on Book Notes, and Note 12-2 will take you directly to this publication.

In general, we don't recommend this because:
* ★ you are setting yourself up for the double-taxation trap (see Chapter 15)
* ★ you will cancel out the normally advantageous tax-deferral benefit
* ★ if you select this option, you have to do it for every Savings Bond you own
* ★ if you have a large investment in Savings Bonds, selecting this option will explode the deferred-tax time-bomb

However, if you are in a much lower tax-bracket now than you will be when you cash the bond, it can make sense to pay your tax as you go.

Consider this example: you buy bonds on a scheduled basis and register them in your child's name. Depending on how much interest the bonds earn, you may want to let the tax defer until the child is 14. (Before age 14 the IRS taxes the interest at the parent's rate if the child has more than $1,600 in investment income a year.)

When your child reaches 14, you ask the IRS for automatic permission for your child to switch to the annual reporting method. You'll pay the tax on all the interest earned up to that point at the very low tax rate the typical 14-year-old has. You then continue to declare the interest annually. If your child earns less than $800 in interest a year and has no other sources of income, you won't even have to file a tax return.

Your child can pay for college with these bonds – since you have been paying the tax on the interest all along, there's no deferred-tax time-bomb or education deduction to deal with. The tax you pay in the years the bonds are cashed will be only on the interest earned annually and should be low to nothing.

But most importantly, you won't have to worry about whether you'll be able to meet any of the many limitations of the regular Savings Bond college education deduction. And if your child ends up not going to college, you still receive both your entire investment and the tax benefits.

There's more information on the Savings Bond college education deduction in Chapter 15.

The tricky part of this is:
- ★ Remembering from year to year what you're doing
- ★ Figuring out how much interest the bonds earn each year, which is why we provide this information in the tables in Chapter 17 (use the second column on the right-hand pages – *Interest per $FV*)
- ★ Making sure your child doesn't get caught in the double-taxation trap and end up paying income tax on the bonds a second time when they are cashed in, just because the 1099-INT says to. Instead, declare the full amount of interest shown on the 1099, but under it add a line that says *U.S. Savings Bond interest previously reported* and subtract the appropriate amount

Double-taxation trap? See Chapter 15.

Chapter 13

Is tax-deferral better than higher rates?

Why 1.5% Series HH Savings Bonds are a bad choice for almost everyone

Results when your tax rate is steady or goes up

Results when your tax rate goes down

What if you need the current income of Series HH Savings Bonds?

What if you hold 4% Series H / HH Savings Bonds?

Why 1.5% Series HH Savings Bonds are a bad choice for almost everyone

As the Treasury's August 31, 2004 deadline on issuing new Series HH Savings Bonds was approaching, many people exchanged their Series E and EE Savings Bonds for Series HH Savings Bonds who shouldn't have.

Because of the low 1.5% interest rate paid by Series HH Savings Bonds, the conversion only made sense when:

★ The Series E or EE bonds were close to final maturity – that is, they were about to stop paying interest

★ The owner's tax rate would drop after the E or EE bonds had stopped paying interest

If you were among those who made the conversion, it's not too late to consider switching back to Series EE or Series I Savings Bonds. Making this switch would mean that you would have to pay income tax on the deferred interest from the Series E or EE bonds you exchanged for the HH bonds.

However, if by making the switch you'll end up with more money, why wouldn't you?

The following analysis applies only to Series H and HH bonds paying 1.5%. There are some that pay 4%; we'll talk more about those later in this chapter.

Figure 13-1 compares two options. Option one is to keep your 1.5% Series HH bond. The alternative option is to redeem the Series HH bond and reinvest the proceeds in a new Series EE or I bond.

To make the comparison equal, we have to assume that under the reinvest in Series EE or I bond option, you would withdraw the same interest amount every six months as the Treasury would have sent you had you invested in Series HH bonds. With TreasuryDirect's electronic bonds, you're allowed to make this kind of partial withdrawal after your electronic bond is a year old.

In the graph, the left-to-right axis indicates how many more years you would hold the bonds.

The front-to-back axis is what proportion of your HH bond's value is deferred interest. For example, if the face value of your HH bond is $500, and the deferred interest entry on the front of the bond says $250, 50% of your HH bond's value is deferred interest.

In the up-and-down axis, zero is in the middle and represents no difference between the two options. The farther the result dips or rises from zero, the better that option is. Positive results favor keeping the 1.5% Series HH Savings Bonds; negative numbers favor switching to Series EE or I bonds. The difference in the two options is calculated at the point at which all bonds have been cashed and all taxes have been paid.

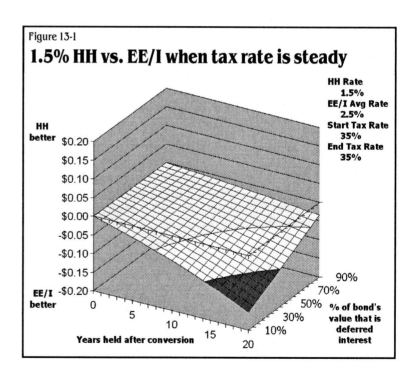

Figure 13-1

1.5% HH vs. EE/I when tax rate is steady

Results when your tax rate is steady or goes up

Figure 13-1 was drawn with the following settings:
* ★ HH bond rate is 1.5%
* ★ EE / I bond rate averages 2.5%
* ★ Income tax rate is the maximum 35% and doesn't change before your final redemption

What the graph clearly shows is that if your tax rate isn't going to change and the Series EE or I bond rate averages at least 2.5%, switching back is always the better option compared to keeping the HH bonds.

The 2.5% Series EE or I bond rate used in the graph was selected to show you the results at an extreme limit – if you exchange for Series EE now you'll get 3.5%, which makes this option an even better choice.

If your tax rate isn't going to drop, you should redeem your 1.5% HH bonds (you may need to redeem them over a period of several years to avoid the deferred-tax time bomb we discussed in the last chapter), pay the income tax on the interest you've earned, and reinvest in new Series EE or I bonds. It never makes sense to keep 1.5% Series HH bonds as long as your tax rate is holding steady into the future.

If your tax rate is lower than the maximum 35% shown in the graph, the results hold but the cost of a bad decision is less. If your tax rate goes up, on the other hand, the results hold but the cost of a bad decision is more than what is shown in the graph.

Results when your tax rate goes down

If you're not sure what your income tax rate is and how it will change in the years ahead, now's the time to figure that out. While it's impossible to predict how Congress might change our tax laws in the future, it's easier to predict what your own total income will be.

You can look up your tax rate in our tax rates tables at the beginning of Chapter 12. The table will give you a good idea of where your rate is now and how it might change in the future.

Figure 13-2 was drawn with the following settings:
* HH bond rate is 1.5%
* EE / I bond rate averages 2.5%
* Income tax rate drops to 28% from 35%

In this graph you can see that the feature of Series HH Savings Bonds that allows you to continue to defer taxes until your rate goes down can have a significant impact. Keeping your Series HH bonds is the better choice when your tax rate will go down relatively soon, when the value of your original Series E or EE bonds was primarily interest, and when you expect Series EE/I bonds to pay relatively low interest rates.

Figure 13-3 on the next page is what Figure 13-2 looks like when you view it from the top. From this view it's easier to see the exact curve that separates the two options. The option of keeping HH bonds is better in the upper-left area (dark color); the option of switching back to Series EE/I bonds is better in the lower-left (lighter color) area.

For example, if 50% of the value of your HH bonds was

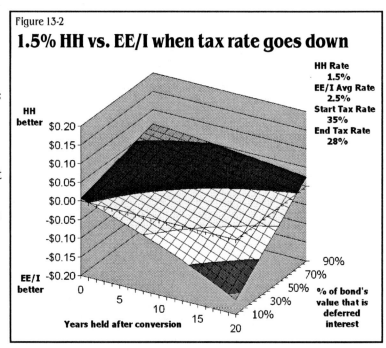

Figure 13-2

1.5% HH vs. EE/I when tax rate goes down

HH Rate
1.5%
EE/I Avg Rate
2.5%
Start Tax Rate
35%
End Tax Rate
28%

deferred interest and you expected your tax rate to change in 10 years, you could find the intersection of 50% and 10 years in Figure 13-3, see it's in the light area, and decide it would be better to cash in your HH bonds now, pay the tax on the deferred interest, and buy Series EE or I bonds.

However, keep in mind that Figures 13-2 and 13-3 also assume that the EE/I bonds will average just 2.5% and that your tax rate will drop from 35% to 28%.

To help you find the best action for other tax rate changes, the following figures show the effect of a variety of drops in your tax rate under three different assumptions:

★ Figure 13-4 – the new Series EE or I bond you reinvest in pays an historically-low average rate of 2.5%

★ Figure 13-5 – the new bond pays an historically-middling average rate of 4.5%

★ Figure 14-6 – the new bond pays an historically-high average rate of 6.5%

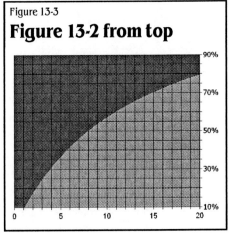

Figure 13-3

Figure 13-2 from top

As you can see from the graphs, keeping 1.5% Series HH bonds almost never makes sense. If it does make sense, it's because:

    ★ Your tax rate will fall drastically while you hold the Series HH bonds

    ★ Your tax rate will fall sooner rather than later

    ★ The value of the bonds you hold now is primarily interest

    ★ The Series EE/I bond interest rate remains at historically low levels

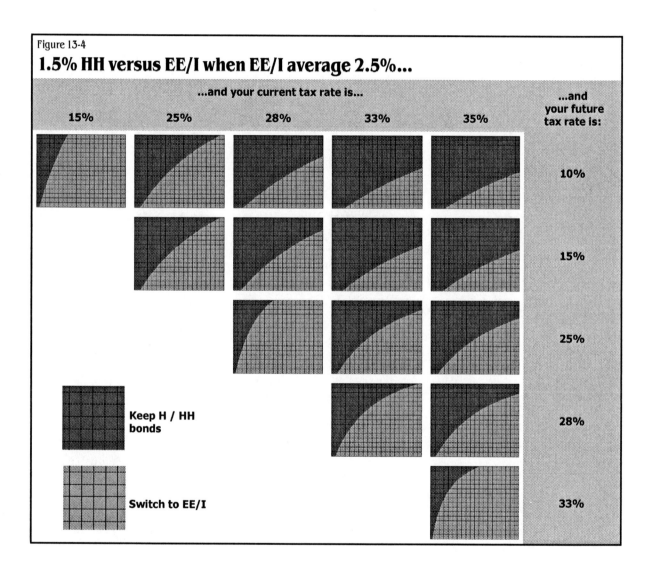

Figure 13-4

1.5% HH versus EE/I when EE/I average 2.5%...

...and your current tax rate is...

| 15% | 25% | 28% | 33% | 35% | ...and your future tax rate is: |

10%

15%

25%

Keep H / HH bonds

28%

Switch to EE/I

33%

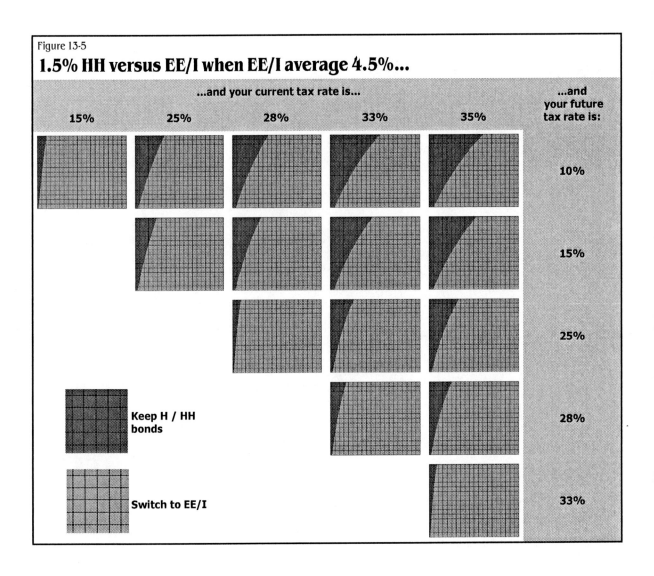

Figure 13-5

1.5% HH versus EE/I when EE/I average 4.5%...

...and your current tax rate is...

...and your future tax rate is:

15% 25% 28% 33% 35%

10%

15%

25%

Keep H / HH bonds

28%

Switch to EE/I

33%

Figure 13-6

1.5% HH versus EE/I when EE/I average 6.5%...

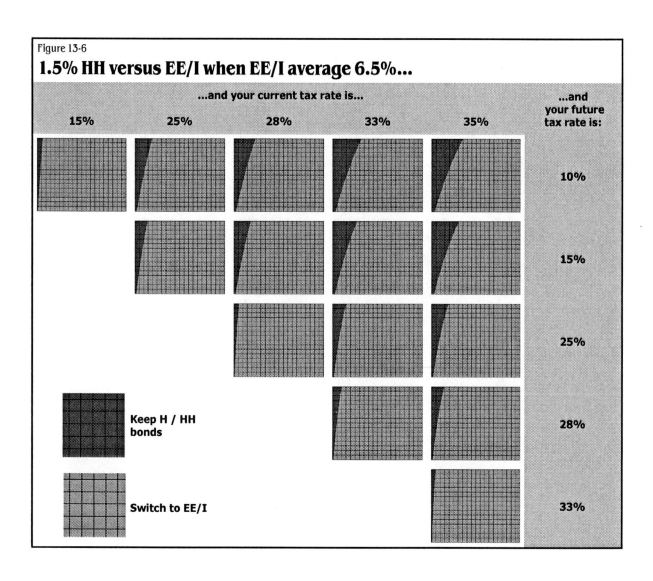

...and your current tax rate is...

...and your future tax rate is:

15%	25%	28%	33%	35%	
					10%
					15%
					25%
					28%
					33%

Keep H / HH bonds

Switch to EE/I

What if you need the current income of Series HH bonds?

Before TreasuryDirect, there was no way to get current income from Series I or EE Savings Bonds. If you owned Series HH bonds, on the other hand, the Treasury would deposit the interest you'd earned in your bank account every six months.

Now you can get current income from Series I or EE bonds by using TreasuryDirect's partial withdrawal feature. As long as you withdraw $25 or more and the issue month you're withdrawing from has a remaining balance of at least $25, there are no limits on TreasuryDirect's partial electronic withdrawals.

Note, however, that you can't make withdrawals during the first year and there is a three-month interest penalty on withdrawals made before five years.

Series HH bonds have the same hidden interest-rate penalty as older Series E and EE bonds, so you'll want to redeem them right after you receive an interest payment.

If you have a large investment in HH bonds, you should redeem them over a period of several years. The deferred taxes they carry from the Series E or EE bonds you used to purchase them can create a deferred-tax time-bomb if your tax rate is already low.

What if you hold 4% Series H or HH Savings Bonds?

If you now hold Series H or HH Savings Bonds, you're probably actually earning 4% rather than 1.5%. All Series H bonds that are still paying interest and all Series HH bonds pay 4% except:

★   HH bonds issued since January 2003

★   HH bonds that have turned 10 years old since January 2003

As long as Series I and EE bonds are paying less than 4%, you should keep the H / HH bonds.

When Series I and EE rates rise above 4%, on the other hand, your choice is between the 4% guarantee on your H and HH bonds and the higher, but adjustable, rates on Series EE or I.

As we've seen in this analysis, you'll do better with the HH bonds when:

★   Interest rates on Series EE and I are historically low
★   Your tax rate will go down – the sooner the better
★   Your bonds carry a high proportion of tax-deferred interest

Part III –
Redeeming your investment

Basics of Savings Bond redemption

How to minimize the income tax bite

Inheriting and passing on Savings Bonds

Chapter 14

Basics of Savings Bond redemption

How to cash in a Savings Bond

Avoiding hidden interest-rate penalties

How much do I hold back for taxes?

Redemption tips for Series I Savings Bonds

Redemption tips for Series E / EE Savings Bonds

Redemption tips for Series H / HH Savings Bonds

How to cash in a Savings Bond

The simplest way to redeem a paper Savings Bond is to take it to a financial institution that handles Savings Bond transactions. This includes most banks, savings and loan associations, and credit unions, but it's best to call ahead to make sure.

The basic process is similar to cashing a check. A bank representative will ask you for identification. Then you will sign your name on the back of the bond and the bank representative will certify your signature.

Remember that you must be the owner or co-owner of the bond to redeem it. For example, a parent can't sign for a child if the child is the owner of the bond.

In some cases you won't receive your money immediately from the bank, but the bank begin the transaction for you.

Electronic Savings Bonds can be redeemed online through your TreasuryDirect account. The proceeds are deposited into the bank account you specify.

Both paper and electronic Savings Bonds can be partially redeemed. For TreasuryDirect's electronic Savings Bonds, you must redeem at least $25 and you must leave at least $25 in the account for that specific issue date. For paper Savings Bonds you must redeem in an amount that can be split between what you receive in cash and a bond with a smaller denomination.

Don't forget that you can pay hidden interest-rate penalties when you cash in Savings Bonds.

The information in this chapter will help you avoid making that mistake ever again.

Special case redemption form

If you want to redeem a large number of bonds or if you have any difficulty redeeming a Savings Bond at a local bank (for example, if you aren't a US citizen and have no plans to come to the US), you can submit **Public Debt Form 1522**, *Special Form for Request of Payment of Unites States Savings and Retirement Securities Where Use of a Detached Request is Authorized.*

To get a copy of this form, go to our web site, click on Book Notes, and select Note 14-1.

If you don't have internet access, you can order a copy of this form by mail. See the Appendix for complete instructions.

Otherwise, go to our web site, click on Book Notes, and see Note 14-1.

With this form, you can provide a list of the bonds – the list must include serial numbers – and have your signature certified on the form rather than on the back of all of the bonds. In other cases the form and its instructions will provide a way to have your signature certified when that is otherwise a barrier.

Bonds less than a year old

In general, you cannot cash in Savings Bonds that are less than one year old. However, after a natural disaster, such as a flood, hurricane, or tornado, the Treasury sometimes allows those who have been impacted to redeem these newer bonds.

If you are in an area that has been affected by a disaster, you may be eligible. If you're a subscriber to the Savings-Bonds-Alert emails (subscriptions are free on our web site), we will notify you when the Treasury makes this option available.

Whether you've been in a disaster or not, you will pay a three-month interest penalty if you redeem a Series I or EE Savings Bond before it's five years old.

When everything is equal, you should redeem bonds that are more than five years old first. However, things are at times unequal – then it makes sense to keep older bonds that are paying a higher rate even if you have to pay the three-month penalty on newer, lower-rate bonds.

As a one-year investment, Savings Bonds sometimes pay higher rates than one-year bank CDs or Money Market Accounts and Funds, even after you pay the three-month interest penalty.

Fifth anniversary bump

Because of the three-month penalty, Savings Bonds have a much larger-than-usual increase in value when they arrive at their fifth anniversary. If you have a Saving Bond that is almost five years old, you should avoid redeeming it until its issue month if you can.

If a bond owner is unable to go to bank to have his or her signature certified, the owner can give a durable power of attorney to someone else who can. There's a link to a form, which the owner will still have to have signed by a notary public, on our web site. Click on Book Notes, then Note 14-2.

Avoiding hidden interest-rate penalties

As I just mentioned, when you redeem a Series EE or I Savings Bond before it's five years old, you lose the most recent three months interest the bond has earned.

However, you can lose up to six months interest on bonds older than five years by simply cashing them in on the wrong day.

All Series E bonds, all Series H and HH bonds, and Series EE bonds issued before May 1997 pay interest - and therefore increase in redemption value - just twice a year.

On the other hand, the newer Series EE bonds issued in May 1997 and since, and all Series I bonds, increase in redemption value monthly (however, for compounding purposes, the interest is still added to the value of the bond semiannually, not monthly).

When the redemption value of your bond increases just twice a year, you need to redeem the bond right after an increase . Otherwise you lose all interest from the day of the increase to the day you redeem the bond.

Every month, some Savings Bond holders unwittingly lose nearly six months worth of interest by redeeming right before their bond's value increases.

In general, the increase in value occurs on the first business day of the month in which the bond was issued and six months later. However, some Series E bonds pay interest on an unusual schedule.

Use Table 14-1 to determine when to redeem your Savings Bonds.

Redeem Saving Bonds on the first business day of the month in which interest is paid - otherwise you will lose the interest for the days between the first business day and the day you actually redeem the bond.

Purchase Savings Bonds, on the other hand, near the end of the month - you'll earn the same amount of interest no matter which day of the month you invest.

Table 14-1

When to redeem to avoid hidden penalties

Series I Series EE issued May 1997 and since	Redeem on the first business day of any month.
Series EE issued April 1997 and before Series E issued December 1965 and since Series H Series HH	Redeem on the first business day of the month of issue or of the month six months later.
Series E issued November 1965 and before	Redeem on the first business day of the month shown.

Issued in:	Redeem in:
Jan – July	Apr – Oct
Feb – Aug	May – Nov
Mar – Sep	Jun – Dec
Apr – Oct	Jan – Jul
May – Nov	Feb – Aug
Jun – Dec	Mar – Sep

How much do I hold back for taxes?

When you redeem a Savings Bond, the Treasury notifies the IRS of the amount of interest you have earned on a 1099-INT tax form. You'll receive a copy of this form – sometimes when you cash the bond, but usually the following January.

The interest earnings you receive in cash – the amount shown on the 1099-INT – are your pre-tax earnings. Your after-tax earnings will be less than this.

Many people either reinvest or spend the entire amount they receive when they cash a Savings Bond. When tax time comes the following April, they don't have any money to pay the tax bill with.

Don't make this mistake!

Back in Chapter 12, Table 12-1 gives you the percentage of your Savings Bond interest that you should reserve for your tax payment.

You can keep this amount in a bank account until tax time to earn a bit of interest or you can remit it immediately as an estimated tax payment.

At tax time, you will owe the IRS a penalty for underpayment if:

★   you owe more than $1,000 when you file your return and
★   your withholding and estimated tax payments are less than both 90% of your current-year taxes and 100% of your previous year taxes

Depending on how much Savings Bond interest you've earned, it can make sense to send what you'll owe on your Savings Bond interest to the IRS immediately as an estimated tax payment to avoid a tax penalty.

How to make an estimated tax payment

You can make an estimated tax payment by mailing the IRS a check and a Form 1040-ES payment voucher or by using the Electronic Federal Tax Payment System (EFTPS).

If you already file Form 1040-ES, just add the amount you'll owe for your Savings Bond interest to your next payment. On the other hand, if this is the first time you've filed Form 1040-ES, Book Note 14-4 will link you to the instructions and payment vouchers.

Book Note 14-4 is a link to IRS Form 1040-ES.

If the only thing you have to pay is the tax on your Savings Bond interest, you can skip the 1040-ES worksheet and go straight to the payment vouchers. There are four of them – the difference is the due date printed in the upper-right corner of the vouchers.

Pick the voucher that has the next upcoming due date, write in the amount of tax you'll owe (multiply the interest you've earned by your marginal tax rate from this book's Table 12-1), and send it in.

Book Note 14-5 is a link to EFTPS, which is shown in Figure 14-1.

The Form 1040-ES instructions will tell you where to send the voucher and your payment. It also has a version of the marginal tax rate table that our own Table 12-1 is based on.

Alternatively, you can enroll in EFTPS and have the money deducted from your bank account. Book Note 14-5 has a link to EFTPS.

On your first visit, click on the **Enrollment** button. After you have heard back by mail that your account is ready, just click on the **Make a Payment** button to initiate an estimated tax payment.

Figure 14-1

EFTPS online tax payment system

Redemption tips for Series I Savings Bonds

When you have to decide which Series I bonds you will redeem, keep the ones with the highest fixed interest rate. All of your I bonds earn the same inflation adjustment during each rate period – ignore that part of the composite rate when selecting bonds to sell.

On the other hand, there are significant differences in the fixed rate portion of Series I bond interest rates, as shown in Table 14-2 and in the tables in Chapter 17.

Table 14-2

Series I – Alert Recommendations

Issue Date	Months spanned	Fixed base-rate	Alert Recom- mendation
Sep 98 – Oct 98	2	3.40%	A+++
Nov 98 – Oct 99	12	3.30%	A++
Nov 99 – Apr 00	6	3.40%	A+++
May 00 – Oct 00	6	3.60%	A++++
Nov 00 – Apr 01	6	3.40%	A+++
May 01 – Oct 01	6	3.00%	A+
Nov 01 – Oct 02	12	2.00%	A
Nov 02 – Apr 03	6	1.60%	B+
May 03 – Apr 04	12	1.10%	B
May 04 – Apr 05	12	1.00%	B
May 05 - Oct 05	6	1.20%	B

Redemption tips for Series E / EE Savings Bonds

When you have to decide which Series E / EE bonds you will redeem, keep the ones that are paying the highest interest rates. There are significant differences in the rate paid by these bonds, depending on the issue date. Table 14-2 and the tables in Chapter 17 show our recommendations for which Series E / EE Savings Bonds to keep.

Table 14-3

Series E / EE – Alert Recommendations

Issue Date	Months spanned	Current rate	Alert Recommendation
1941 – 1964	276	0.0%	Interest stopped – stinker alert
1965 – 1966	24	4.00%, then 0.0%	Stops paying interest in 2005/2006 issue month
1967 – 1974	96	0.0%	Interest stopped – stinker alert
1975 – 1976	24	4.00%, then 0.0%	Stops paying interest in 2005/2006 issue month
1977 – Feb 78	14	4.00%	A
Mar 78 -Apr 78	2	3.32%	B
May 78 – Feb 83	57	4.00%	A
Mar 83 – Apr 83	2	3.32%	B
May 83 – Oct 83	6	2.83%	B-
Nov 83 – Oct 84	12	3.23% to 3.26%	B
Nov 84 – Feb 93	111	4.00%	A
Mar 93 – Apr 97	49	2.97% to 3.10%	B-
May 97 – Apr 05	96	3.42%	B
May 05 - Oct 05	6	3.5%	C

Redemption tips for Series H or HH Savings Bonds

Unlike other series of Savings Bonds, Series H and HH bonds don't have a three-month interest penalty when they are redeemed before five years. In addition, the minimum holding period for H and HH bonds is history so all are now redeemable.

On redemption, you will receive the face value of the bond. However, you will also receive a 1099-INT tax form showing you earned interest in the amount labeled *deferred interest* on the face of the bond. This is the deferred interest from the Series E or EE bonds that were converted into Series H or HH bonds.

Keep in mind that the deferred interest can create a deferred tax time bomb (see Chapter 12). It's best to redeem these bonds in amounts that don't raise your tax rate.

All Series H and HH bonds also have the hidden interest-rate penalty discussed in the first section of this chapter.

Financial institutions are sometimes reluctant to get involved in cashing Series H and Series HH bonds because they don't deal with them regularly. If this happens to you, print out a copy of **Public Debt Form 5396** – *Direct Deposit Sign Up Form*. Check the Redemption Payment box at the top of the form and fill out the section requesting your name and address.

If you don't have internet access, you can order a copy of this form by mail. See the Appendix for complete instructions.

Otherwise, go to our web site, click on Book Notes, and see Note 14-3.

Then take the form to your financial institution and have them help you fill in the bank routing section. Then ask them to certify your signature on the back of the bonds. Send the form and the certified bonds by registered mail to the nearest address in the instructions on the form.

When you have to decide which Series HH bonds you will redeem, consider the interest rate that each of your bonds is currently paying, how long each bond will pay that rate, and when each bond will mature. On the next page, in Table 14-3, you'll find our current recommendation for which Series H and HH Savings Bonds to keep.

Table 14-4

Series H / HH – Alert Recommendations

Issue Date	Months spanned	Current rate	Alert Recommendation
1952 - 1974	272	0%	Interest stopped – stinker alert
1975 – 1976	24	4.0%, then 0.0%	Stops paying interest in 2005/2006 issue month
1977 – 1979	36	4.0%	A
1980 – 1984	48	0.0%	Interest stopped – stinker alert
1985 – 1986	24	4.0%, then 0.0%	Stops paying interest in 2005/2006 issue month
1987 – 1992	60	4.0%	A
1993 - 1994	24	1.5%	D
1995 – 1996	24	4.0%, then 1.5%	Rate drops in 2005/2006 issue month
1997 – 2002	60	4.0%	A
2003 – 2004	20	1.5%	D

Chapter 15

How to minimize the income tax bite

The stinker bond penalty

The double-taxation trap

The state income tax deduction

The education deduction

Using a charitable deduction to avoid taxes

How to avoid the stinker bond penalty

The IRS says you have to pay income tax on a Savings Bond's interest in the earlier of these two years:

★ when your redeem your bond

★ when your bond stops earning interest

Many Savings Bond investors are under the impression that they can avoid income tax by simply not redeeming their bonds.

Or from a kinder, gentler point of view, they just forget about their bonds and don't realize they've stopped earning interest.

Over 5% of the Savings Bonds outstanding have stopped earning interest. As you know by now, I call these stinker bonds.

When you redeem a stinker bond that stopped paying interest in a previous year, you and the IRS receive a 1099-INT reporting the interest *for the previous year.*

So thanks to this stinker bond, now you're not just giving the Treasury an interest-free loan, but you're:

★ paying the tax you always owed anyway

★ filing an amended tax return for a previous year

★ paying a penalty for underpaying your taxes that year

You can avoid all this by redeeming your bonds before or when they mature.

Once you're tax rate is as low as it's going to get, you should be redeeming a few bonds and paying the tax owed every year. If you don't need the money, reinvest in new bonds.

This avoids not only the stinker bond penalty, but also the deferred tax time bomb I told you about in Chapter 12.

How to avoid the Savings Bond double-taxation trap

The 1099-INT tax form that you and the IRS will receive when you cash in a Savings Bond will always show how much interest the bond earned over its entire life.

This will be true whether income tax has already been paid on some of this interest or not. When the 1099-INT leads you to pay tax a second time, you've been caught in the double-taxation trap.

One situation in which tax on some of the interest may have been paid is when you cash a bond that was originally purchased by someone else. If the bond was a gift that was reissued in your name, the person who gave it to you received a 1099-INT for the interest earned up to the time of the gift.

Likewise, if you were named as the beneficiary on a bond, tax on the interest up to the time of the original owner's death may have been paid by the original owner's estate. Depending on how the estate was handled, sometimes it is but usually it's not.

The second situation in which tax on some of the interest may have been paid is when you have elected to include your Savings Bond interest on your tax return each year. There's only one good reason to do it this way, which we describe in the *When your tax rate is headed up* section of Chapter 12.

When you prepare your tax return, if you can demonstrate that some of the tax on a Savings Bond that you've cashed in has already been paid, report the entire interest amount shown on your 1099-INT with your other interest income. Then, as a final interest entry, write *US Savings Bond Interest Previously Reported* and subtract the amount of interest on which tax has already been paid.

If you are audited, you'll have to provide hard proof that the tax was paid. The best proof is a copy of the tax return when the tax was paid – but if you received the bond as a reissued gift or as a beneficiary, that will be someone else's return – and it might be difficult or impossible for you to get a copy.

The lesson is – if you inherit a Savings Bond or if a Savings Bond is reissued in your name as a gift, also ask for the gift of the tax return showing that tax has already been paid on part of the bond's interest earnings.

If you have paid a significant amount of double-tax within the last three years, you can file amended tax returns to get the money back.

How to avoid state and local income taxes on your Savings Bond interest

The interest you earn from a Savings Bond is exempt from both local and state income taxes.

However, there's nothing automatic about this exemption. To get it, depending on what state you live in, you'll probably have to fill out an extra form when you do your state income taxes. If you have your taxes prepared for you, make sure this happens.

Typically, state income tax forms begin with the adjusted gross income from your federal income tax form. Your Savings Bond interest will be included in this number.

Next, your state income tax form will allow you to enter modifications to the federal adjusted gross income. You will probably have to calculate your modifications on that extra state tax form.

On the extra state tax form, look for a line titled something like *Interest on U.S. Government Obligations* in the section on *Subtractions from Federal Adjusted Gross Income*. That's where you enter your Savings Bond interest. This removes the interest from your official state income so you don't pay tax on it.

But forget this detail, and your state income tax exemption is lost. You'll pay tax that you don't actually owe.

The fine print of the Savings Bond college education deduction

The federal government offers a large number of programs to help you get a college education deduction for yourself or a dependent.

The simple truth is that the ability to deduct Savings Bond interest from your income when it is spent on education is one of the least attractive options.

If you are in the planning stage of figuring out how to pay for college, please realize that books as big as this one are devoted to the subject. A good place to start is with IRS Publication 970, *Tax Benefits for Education*. Go to our web site, click on Book Notes, and see note 15-1 for a link to this publication.

The problem with the Savings Bond education interest deduction is that it comes with a large amount of fine print. It's actually impossible to even know whether you'll qualify for the deduction when you start investing.

One way to deal with this is to use your Savings Bonds to fund Coverdell and other qualified tuition-savings programs (QTPs) in years in which you know you qualify for the deduction. For many people, this is the best way to take advantage of the Savings Bond deduction.

We discussed another way to fund a college education with Savings Bonds – a method that doesn't even try to use this deduction – in the *When your tax rate is headed up* section of Chapter 12.

However, if you already own Savings Bonds and you have education expenses, you may be able to cash in a bond and deduct at least some of the interest you've earned from your income, if you can meet all of the following limitations:

★ You are the registered owner of the bond

★ If there is a co-owner, it is your spouse

★ Your bond is Series I or Series EE and was issued in January 1990 or later

Book Note 15-1 links to IRS Publication 970, **Tax Benefits for Education.**

★ You were at least 24 years old on the issue date of the bond (the first day of the issue month)

★ The education expenses are for you, your spouse, or a person you are claiming as a dependent on this same tax return

★ The education expenses are for:
  ★ tuition and fees (not room, board, or non-degree courses)
  ★ contributions to a qualified tuition program or QTP
  ★ contributions to a Coverdell education savings account (ESA – also known as an education IRA)

★ You haven't already used the above expenses for other income-tax related deductions on this return

★ Your modified adjusted gross income is within the limitations. In 2004, the deduction began to phase out at the lower end of the ranges shown here and was not available at all to those over the high end:
  ★ Married filing jointly or qualifying widow or widower: $89,750 – $119,750
  ★ Married filing separately – deduction not allowed
  ★ All other filing statuses: $59,850 – $74,850

The deduction also phases out if the amount of money you receive from cashing the bonds (not just the interest, mind you, but the total amount) is more than the eligible education expenses. This can be a particular problem if you happened to invest in bonds with high denominations – you will have to make a partial redemption for cash and a new bond with a lower value.

Because of this hassle, a new investment program aiming to take this deduction should be placed in TreasuryDirect's electronic bonds rather than paper bonds, because it's easy to make partial withdrawals from TreasuryDirect.

There are two tax forms you'll have to fill out to take the deduction. **Form 8815** calculates the two phase outs and **Form 8818** is an optional form for recording the data on the bonds you cashed in. We have links to these forms on our web site – see Book Note 15-2.

Book Note 15-2 links to IRS forms 8815 and 8818, which are needed to take the Savings Bond education deduction.

Using a charitable deduction to avoid taxes

I'm often asked if Savings Bonds can be reissued to charities. They cannot.

However, under certain conditions you can avoid the tax on your Savings Bond interest by donating it to an IRS recognized charity in the year you redeem the bond.

Basically, the way this technique works is that you declare the interest you've earned on your tax return. On the same return, you take a charitable deduction for your donation, which cancels out the Savings Bond interest income.

If you're interested in this technique, there are a few things you need to consider.

First, you can't take a charitable deduction that's more than 50% of your adjusted gross income in any year. If you donate more than that, you can carryover the excess to the following tax year, but there are several arcane rules associated with this.

Moreover, for some organizations, such as veterans organizations, fraternities, cemeteries, and some private foundations, the limit is 30% of your adjusted gross income rather than 50%.

There may also be associated tax issues, such as the Savings Bond interest income making your Social Security income taxable or snaring you in the Alternative Minimum Tax.

If you think this might work for you, see **IRS Publication 526**, *Charitable Contributions*. Then consult your tax advisor.

There's a link to this IRS publication at Book Note 15-3.

Chapter 16

Inheriting and passing on Savings Bonds

Inheriting Savings Bonds

Bequeathing Savings Bonds

Inheriting Savings Bonds

Remember that over 5% of all Savings Bonds outstanding have stopped earning interest but have never been cashed. In many cases, this is because the heirs who should have received the bonds didn't know about them and didn't look for them.

Finding the decedent's Savings Bonds

When someone close to you dies – particularly if you are Executor of the estate – it's essential to determine whether the person who died owned any Savings Bonds. You should look for paper bonds in safe deposit boxes, file cabinets, and other locations where the decedent kept financial records.

If you find some Savings Bonds, keep looking. Don't assume you'll find them all in one place. Many people buy Savings Bonds on a regular basis. Older bonds might be in a safe deposit box, while bonds received more recently might be in a file cabinet. In addition to actual Savings Bonds, you should look for documents that list Savings Bond holdings and documents related to a TreasuryDirect account.

Check any computers for the *Savings Bond Wizard*. You can do this by searching for a file called **SBWizard.exe**. If you find it, do a second search for data files that end with *.sbw* (put an asterisk before the file extension to create the search term **.sbw*, which will find any file that ends with *.sbw*). Open all the files you find by double clicking on them – they should provide a wealth of information.

If you can't find the *Savings Bond Wizard*, look for a file or folder that might contain Savings Bond data from the *Savings Bond Calculator*. This will be an HTML file. Use the search term **.htm** (note this one both begins and ends with an asterisk, so it will find files that end with either *.htm* or *.html*) and scan the long list of results you'll receive for a file that looks like it might contain Savings Bond data. If you find one, just double-click on it to open.

If you find documentation that the decedent owned Savings Bonds, but you can't find the bonds, you should ask the Treasury to determine whether the bonds have already been cashed or not. See the first section of Chapter 10, *Finding forgotten Savings Bonds*, to learn out how to do this.

If you find a TreasuryDirect account number, send an email that includes the number to **treasury.direct@bpd.treas.gov** notifying them of the death of the account owner. They will work with you to have the account's assets transferred to the new owner.

It can also be worthwhile to enter the decedent's name and Social Security Number in *Treasury Hunt* (see the second section of Chapter 10).

Who inherits the bonds?

On the bonds you do find, carefully check the name on the bonds. If the decedent's name is the only name on the bond, the bonds pass to the decedent's estate and are distributed according to the decedent's will.

On the other hand, if there are two names on the bond, look to see if the names are separated by OR or by POD.

★ the OR separator means that the second person is co-owner of the bonds and now has exclusive rights to them. If the co-owner has also died, the bonds go to the estate of the person who died last.

★ the POD (payable on death) separator means that the second person was the beneficiary of the bonds. Just as with a co-owner, if the beneficiary has also died, the bonds go to the estate of the person who died last.

Tax issues

Whether you inherit Savings Bonds through a Will or because you are named as co-owner or beneficiary, there are tax issues that you need to be aware of. Someone will have to pay the income tax on the interest earned by the bond.

When you inherit stocks, mutual funds, and other investments that can change in price, US tax law gives you a *stepped up basis* on the investments. This means that you will owe capital gains tax on any price increases only from the day your benefactor died, not from the day your benefactor bought the investment. The capital gains that occurred during your benefactor's life-time are ignored for tax purposes.

Savings Bonds, however, don't change in price – they earn interest. Savings Bonds don't have capital gains. Likewise, Savings Bonds don't receive a stepped-up basis.

Whether ownership of your benefactor's bonds transfers to you through a co-owner or beneficiary registration or through a Will, the Executor of your benefactor's estate has a choice. The estate can pass the deferred taxes on to you with the bonds or it can pay the deferred taxes on your benefactor's final tax return.

The only exception to this is if your benefactor has been paying income tax on the interest each year, rather than letting it defer. In that case the interest up to the time of your benefactor's death must be included on his or her final return.

When you have the same or a lower tax rate than your benefactor, the best choice is to continue deferring the tax rather than paying it on your benefactor's final return. You can pay the tax at your lower rate when you redeem the bonds. This also avoids any chance that you'll be caught in the double-taxation trap and end up paying the income tax a second time.

Use the tax rates in Table 12-1 to determine who has the lower tax rate.

On the other hand, if you have a higher tax rate than your benefactor, it can make sense to pay the income tax due on the Savings Bond interest earned up to the time of your benefactor's death on his or her final return. However, this opens the door to both the deferred tax time bomb and the double taxation trap.

If your benefactor's Executor does pay the income tax on the interest earned up to the time of your benefactor's death, ask the Executor to provide you with a copy of your benefactor's final tax return as proof that the taxes have been paid. Without this proof, the IRS can force you to pay the tax a second time.

Of course, you also have to remember when you redeem the bonds that part of the tax you owe has already been paid. Typically this detail is forgotten and you get snared in the double-taxation trap.

In addition, in the year that you cash the bonds and report the interest, you can claim a deduction for any federal estate tax that was paid on the interest. So you will also want to obtain documentation on this from the Executor of the estate.

Redemption or reissue?

No matter who will pay the tax, you also have to decide whether to redeem the bonds you've inherited or to keep them.

Keeping them involves having the bonds reissued so that they are registered in your name.

However, reissue isn't an option for stinker bonds (bonds that have reached final maturity and stopped earning interest) or for bonds within a month of final maturity. These bonds must be redeemed.

Otherwise, to determine whether to redeem the bonds or have them reissued, there are two primary issues you have to consider:

★ how will cashing them impact your income taxes?

★ can you get a better return on the money elsewhere at a level of risk you're comfortable with?

In order to determine the impact of cashing the bonds on your income taxes, you need to know:

★ the amount of deferred interest you would have to pay tax on if you cashed the bonds (see the tables in Chapter 17)

★ your current tax rate (see the first section of Chapter 12)

When you cash a bond, you'll receive a 1099-INT tax form for that year reporting all the interest the bond has earned. The IRS will also get a copy. The fact that the interest was earned while the person who bequeathed the bonds to you was alive makes no difference. Unless your benefactor paid the interest each year and left you proof that the taxes have been paid, the IRS will expect you to pay the income tax, at your rates, on the deferred interest.

Consequently, when you inherit a large amount of Savings Bonds, it often makes sense from a tax perspective to cash them over a period of several years. If you cash them all in one year, the total of the deferred interest income could push you into a higher tax bracket and cause you to pay more tax than you need to.

In order to determine whether you can get a better return, you'll have to determine:

★ the Savings Bond interest rates currently being earned

★ the amount of risk you find acceptable

As you can see elsewhere in this book, depending on the series and issue date, Savings Bonds pay a variety of interest rates. Many are above the general level of interest rates being paid by alternative low-risk investments, but some Savings Bonds pay less. If you are willing to take on more risk, you may be able to get a better return than Savings Bonds over long terms, but there are no guarantees.

In any case, make sure you understand the hidden interest rate penalty discussed in Chapter 14 before you redeem any Savings Bonds you inherit.

When there is a living co-owner or beneficiary

When a registrant listed on a Savings Bond dies, the surviving registrant can redeem the bond in the usual way. Take your personal identification and, if you are the beneficiary, the death certificate of the bond's owner.

If you would prefer to keep the bond, you can update the registration by submitting one of the following forms. The forms include complete instructions.

★ For Series I Savings Bonds, use **Public Debt Form 5387**, *Request for Reissue of Series I United States Savings Bonds.*

See Book Note 16-1

★ For all other Savings Bonds, use **Public Debt Form 4000**, *Request to Reissue United States Savings Bonds.*

See Book Note 16-2

If you don't have internet access, you can order copies of these forms by mail. See the Appendix for complete instructions.

When all bond registrants have died

When all bond registrants have died, things get a bit more complicated. The executor of the estate or heirs must take one or more of the following forms to a bank to have his or her signature certified on the form.

In general, if the bonds are to be redeemed, the back of the bonds should also be signed. If the bonds are to be reissued, on the other hand, the back of the bonds should be left blank.

Required documentation

When all bond registrants have died, reissue and redemption requests require:
- ★ proof of death for everyone named on the bond
- ★ proof of the identity of the person making the request, and
- ★ evidence that the person making the request is entitled to make the request
  - ★ if the estate is open and being administered by a court, documentation – no more than a year old – that the court has appointed the person making the request as the estate's representative
  - ★ otherwise, a certified copy of the decree of distribution, the final account, a small estates affidavit, an agreement among entitled parties, or other appropriate documentation as described below

Acceptable proof of death is a copy of a death certificate that is certified to be true and correct and that includes the visible seal of the certifying authority. Newspaper or funeral home notices are not acceptable proof of death.

Stinker bonds

Bonds that are within a month of reaching final maturity cannot be reissued to the heirs of the deceased. They must be redeemed.

If you don't have internet access, you can order copies of these forms by mail. See the Appendix for complete instructions.

Incapacitated owners

If any of those inheriting the Savings Bonds have a legal disability, such as being a minor or incompetent, the representative signing for the person with the legal disability will need to use one of the following forms to furnish proof of authority:

★   If the representative has been appointed by a court use **Public Debt Form 1455**, *Request by Fiduciary for Reissue or Distribution of United States Savings Bonds* (this form is also used by representatives of estates whether the bond owners are incapacitated or not)

See Book Note 16-1.

★   Otherwise, use **Public Debt Form 2513**, *Application by Voluntary Guardian of Incapacitated Owner of Unites States Bonds or Notes*

See Book Note 16-2

Estate handled with Court Administration

Redemption - A court-appointed representative of a deceased person's estate can redeem some or all of the estate's Savings Bonds by taking the bonds to a financial institution, along with all of the required documentation mentioned earlier, and requesting payment.

The representative will have to sign the back of the bonds in the presence of a bank official and show his or her fiduciary capacity - for example, *John Doe, executor of the will of Mary Doe, deceased.*

The financial institution may cash the bonds immediately but is not obligated to do so. At a minimum, the financial institution will certify the representative's signature on the back of the bonds and provide the address of a Savings Bond processing center where the representative can send the bonds and all required documentation to request payment.

If there are a large number of bonds and a list including serial numbers is readily available, the representative can avoid having to sign all the bonds by having his or her signature certified on **Public Debt Form 1522**, *Special Form for Request of Payment of Unites States Savings and Retirement Securities Where Use of a Detached Request is Authorized.*

See Book Note 16-3

Reissue – A court-appointed representative of the deceased person's estate can have some or all of the estate's Savings Bonds reissued by submitting all required documentation mentioned earlier plus – for each person entitled to the estate's Savings Bonds – a copy of **Public Debt Form 1455**, *Request by Fiduciary for Reissue or Distribution of United States Savings Bonds or Notes.*

See Book Note 16-1

The representative must have a bank officer certify his or her signature on each form. When signing the forms (there's no need for the representative to sign the bonds), the representative should show the fiduciary capacity – for example, *John Doe, executor under the will of Mary Doe, deceased.*

For each copy of Form 1455, if the person inheriting the bonds wants to add a co-owner or beneficiary, also submit a copy of **Public Debt Form 5387** for Series I or **Public Debt Form 4000** for other series of Savings Bonds.

See Book Notes 11-1 and 11-2

Form 1455 can be used to request redemption as well as reissue, which the representative will find useful if there are multiple heirs, some of whom want the bonds redeemed and some of whom want the bonds reissued.

Heirs who want bonds redeemed should sign the back of the bonds and have their signatures certified by a bank officer before the court-appointed representative sends them in with Form 1455.

Estate is closed or settled under state small estate law

If the estate is closed or if the estate was settled under special provisions of a state law relating to small estates (for example, Summary Administration, Small Estates Act, Texas Muniment of Title, Louisiana Judgment of Possession) then what you need to do depends on whether the settlement awarded specific bonds to specific people on not.

Specific bonds awarded to specific people – Each heir can request payment by taking the required documentation mentioned earlier and some or all of his or her bonds to a financial institution and requesting payment.

These heirs can request reissue of some or all of their bonds by sending the required documentation mentioned earlier and the bonds to the Treasury with a copy of **Public Debt Form 5387** for Series I or **Public Debt Form 4000** for other series of Savings Bonds.

Bond awards not specified – If the court did not award specific bonds to specific people, submit the required documentation mentioned earlier, the bonds, and one copy of **Public Debt Form 5394**, *Agreement and Request for Disposition of a Decedent's Treasury Securities,* with the certified signature and disposition instructions of each heir. The form allows each heir the choice of redemption, reissue, both, or transfer of electronic bonds to a TreasuryDirect account.

No court involvement

If the current redemption value of the bonds is more than $100,000, the bonds cannot be distributed without court involvement. Contact a lawyer who handles estates.

Otherwise, Federal law provides that Savings Bonds belonging to an estate being settled without administration must be distributed in a specific order of precedence.

For example, if there is a surviving spouse and no surviving child, the bonds go to the spouse.

If you don't have internet access, you can order copies of these forms by mail. See the Appendix for complete instructions.

See Book Note 11-1 and 11-2

See Book Note 16-4

If there is a surviving spouse and surviving children or descendents of children, one half to the spouse and one half to the others.

And so on.

The complete and detailed order of precedence is in the instructions to **Public Debt Form 5336**, *Disposition of Securities Belonging to a Decedent's Estate Being Settled without Administration.*

See Book Note 16-5

The person or persons highest in the order of precedence should submit the required documentation mentioned earlier and the bonds with the form. The form allows each heir the choice of redemption, reissue, both, or transfer of electronic bonds to a TreasuryDirect account.

Bequeathing Savings Bonds

Savings Bonds can work well as a part of your estate. However, there are some important issues you need to be aware of when you want to pass ownership of your Savings Bonds to your heirs in your Will.

Registration issues

If you've listed a co-owner or beneficiary in the registration on your Savings Bonds (you're allowed to list one or the other, but not both), the person named becomes the owner of your bonds at your death and can redeem them or have them reissued with his or her name as owner. A co-owner or beneficiary registration overrides your Will.

On the other hand, if your bonds are registered in your name only, without a co-owner or beneficiary, the bonds become a part of your estate.

In this case, distribution among your heirs is determined by your Will, by state law if your estate is administered by a state court, or by federal law if it's not.

For additional information on this issue, including an example of the problems that declaring a beneficiary can create, see *Registration and estate planning issues* in the first section of Chapter 4.

If your estate plans include a trust, see Chapter 11 for information on how to have your bonds reissued to the trust.

Tax issues

To understand the tax issues your heirs will face, see the *Tax Issues* discussion in the previous section of this chapter. In particular, note the following points:

★ There is no *stepped-up basis* with Savings Bonds, because they earn interest, not capital gains.

- ★ Unless you declare the income your bonds earn annually, your executor has the choice of paying the income tax your bonds have earned on your final return or passing the bonds to your heirs untaxed, in which they will pay the tax when they redeem the bonds. The best strategy is to have the person with the lowest tax rate pay the tax.
- ★ Stinker bonds cannot be reissued to your heirs. The income tax on the interest you have earned will be paid in the year of your death either on your final return or by your heirs.

Make sure your heirs know you own Savings Bonds

It is essential that your heirs and Executor know that you own Savings Bonds and can easily find them. Over 5% of all Savings Bonds have stopped earning interest and have never been cashed. In many cases the owners have died and the heirs didn't know to look for them.

Part IV –
Savings Bond tables

Savings Bond values, rates, and Alert Recommendations

Chapter 17

Savings Bond values, rates, and Alert Recommendations

How to use our tables

Series I tables

Series EE tables

Series E (still paying interest) tables

Series E (no longer paying interest) table

Series H / HH table

Savings Notes (Freedom Shares) table

How to use our tables

There are three types of tables in this section of the book:

★ Tables for bonds that are growing in value:
  ★ Series EE
  ★ Series I
  ★ some Series E issues

★ Tables of bonds not growing in value, but paying interest:
  ★ Series H and HH

★ Tables of bonds no longer paying interest:
  ★ some Series E issues
  ★ Savings Notes (also called Freedom Shares)

There are major differences between the three types of tables. However, one thing they have in common is that they are all two pages wide.

Bonds no longer paying interest

The two-page header for bonds no longer paying interest looks like this:

Series	Year Issued	Redemption value per $ of face value Issued in:					
		Jan	**Feb**	**Mar**	**Apr**	**May**	**Jun**
E	**1941**					3.6236	3.6784
	1942	3.7740	3.7740	3.7740	3.7740	3.8400	3.8980
	1943	3.9980	3.9980	3.9980	3.9980	4.0364	4.0992

The only information this type of table provides is the current redemption value of these Savings Bonds.

To read the table, double-check that you have the correct **series** in the far-left or far-right column and find the row / column intersection that represents the **year** and **month** your bond was issued.

So, for example, you can see in the sample above that for a Series E bond issued in March 1943, the redemption value per dollar of face value is 3.9980.

To determine a bond's actual redemption value, multiply the number the table gives you by the face value of the bond. For

Redemption value per $ of face value Issued in:						Year Issued	Series
Jul	Aug	Sep	Oct	Nov	Dec		
3.6784	3.6784	3.6784	3.6784	3.7144	3.7740	1941	
3.8980	3.8980	3.8980	3.8980	3.9360	3.9980	1942	E
4.0992	4.0992	4.0992	4.0992	4.1392	4.2036	1943	

example, if the face value of a bond is $100 and the number is 3.9980, its redemption value is $399.80.

You can do this calculation in your head by just moving the decimal point for $100, $1,000, and $10,000 bonds. For other face values you can use a calculator or a spreadsheet.

Bonds not growing in value, but paying interest

Here's the header for the Series H and HH bonds that are in this category:

Series	Year Issued	Interest rate as of May 2005 Issued in:						
		Jan	**Feb**	**Mar**	**Apr**	**May**	**Jun**	**Jul**
H	1952 1974	H bonds issued from 1952 to 1974 are no longer earning interest						
	1975	0.0%	0.0%	0.0%	0.0%	0.0%	4.0%	4.0%
	1976	4.0%	4.0%	4.0%	4.0%	4.0%	4.0%	4.0%
	1977	4.0%	4.0%	4.0%	4.0%	4.0%	4.0%	4.0%

The redemption value of Series H and HH bonds is always the face value of the bond, so this table doesn't include that information. Instead, it gives you the current interest rate being paid by these bonds.

To use these tables you begin by checking the **series**, then you find the row / column intersection for the bonds's **year** and **month** of issue. The number at that location is the bond's current interest rate.

And additional feature of this table is the **Alert Recommendation**, which you'll find at the right side of the table. These recommendations are given as letter grades and allow you to compare bonds within and between Savings Bond series.

The letter grades range from A++++ (the more pluses, the better) to D. Just like in school, an A- is better than a B+.

The recommendations also point out, as in the 1975 sample here, if a bond's grade will soon change.

Interest rate as of May 2005 Issued in:					Alert Recommendation	Year Issued	Series
Aug	**Sep**	**Oct**	**Nov**	**Dec**			
H bonds issued from 1952 to 1974 are no longer earning interest					Redeem	1952 1974	**H**
4.0%	4.0%	4.0%	4.0%	4.0%	A until issue month	1975	
4.0%	4.0%	4.0%	4.0%	4.0%	A	1976	
4.0%	4.0%	4.0%	4.0%	4.0%	A	1977	

Bonds still growing in value

This is the type of table that provides the most information. Here's a sample of the header:

Year and Series	Issue month	Current interest rate and redemption value per $ of face value							To avoid rate penalty, redeem:	Fixed-base rate
		May 05	Jun 05	Jul 05	Aug 05	Sep 05	Oct 05	Nov 05		
1998 **I**	Sep	6.11% 1.4612	6.11% 1.4688	6.11% 1.4760	6.11% 1.4836	7.04% 1.4908	7.04% 1.4996	7.04% 1.5080	1st of any month	3.40%
	Oct	6.11% 1.4540	6.11% 1.4612	6.11% 1.4688	6.11% 1.4760	6.11% 1.4836	7.04% 1.4908	7.04% 1.4996	1st of any month	3.40%

First of all, note that in this table, unlike the others, there is a separate row for each issue month. The far-right and -left columns show you the issue **year**, **month** and **series**.

The months shown in the next seven columns are **redemption months**. Since these bonds are still earning interest, their redemption values change regularly. If the months in this table are in the past, you can get an updated copy of this book – with current redemption values – at a special price on our web site.

Look at the cell for the September 1998 I bond in the May 2005 column. The top number is the annual interest rate this bond will earn in May 2005. The lower number is the redemption value of the bond per dollar of face value in May 2005. Just multiply this number by the face value of a bond to get its redemption value.

In the table for Series EE bonds, the redemption value is often less than 1.0 because Series EE bonds are purchased at half of face value. Consequently, until the bond doubles in value, the redemption value per dollar will be between 0.5000 and 1.0000.

The next-to-the last column on this page shows the months in which the bond can be redeemed without an interest rate penalty. The last column shows, for I bonds, the fixed base-rate for that issue and for EE bonds when the current maturity period ends.

On the right page, this table has two columns related to interest paid in 2004; three columns related to lifetime interest as of the end of 2004; whether the bond is eligible for the **education deduction**; the **Alert Recommendation** (see the previous

2004 only		Issue date through Dec 2004			Educa-tion eligible?	Alert Recommendation	Stops paying interest:	Issue month	Year and Series
Annual APY	Interest per $FV	Lifetime APY	Interest per $FV	% interest					
5.50%	0.0744	5.76%	0.4264	30%	Yes	A+++	Sep 2028	Sep	**1998**
5.63%	0.0756	5.76%	0.4196	30%	Yes	A+++	Oct 2028	Oct	I

section for more information); and when the bond stops paying interest.

The **Annual and Lifetime APY** columns show the *Annual Percentage Yield* for the bond in the two time periods.

The **Interest per $FV** columns show how much interest a bond has earned during these two time periods, per dollar of face value. If you have, for example, a $500 bond, you would multiply this number by 500 to determine the amount of interest earned. If it would be advantageous for you to pay tax on your bond's earnings annually, the number in the second column is the one you'd use to calculate the amount of interest to declare on your tax return.

The **% interest** column tells you what percentage of your bond's redemption value is made up of interest. You can multiply your bond's value times this number and your tax rate to calculate how much tax you'd pay if you redeemed the bond.

Alert Recommendations range from A++++ to D. If you are redeeming bonds, it makes sense to redeem the ones with the lowest letter grade. Just like in school, A- is better than B+.

Year and Series	Issue month	Current interest rate and redemption value per $ of face value							To avoid rate penalty, redeem:	Fixed-base rate
		May 05	Jun 05	Jul 05	Aug 05	Sep 05	Oct 05	Nov 05		
1998 **I**	Sep	6.11% 1.4612	6.11% 1.4688	6.11% 1.4760	6.11% 1.4836	7.04% 1.4908	7.04% 1.4996	7.04% 1.5080	1st of any month	3.40%
	Oct	6.11% 1.4540	6.11% 1.4612	6.11% 1.4688	6.11% 1.4760	6.11% 1.4836	7.04% 1.4908	7.04% 1.4996	1st of any month	3.40%
	Nov	6.94% 1.4496	6.94% 1.4580	6.94% 1.4660	6.94% 1.4744	6.94% 1.4828	6.94% 1.4912	??? 1.5000	1st of any month	3.30%
	Dec	6.00% 1.4424	6.94% 1.4496	6.94% 1.4580	6.94% 1.4660	6.94% 1.4744	6.94% 1.4828	6.94% 1.4912	1st of any month	3.30%
1999 **I**	Jan	6.00% 1.4352	6.00% 1.4424	6.94% 1.4496	6.94% 1.4580	6.94% 1.4660	6.94% 1.4744	6.94% 1.4828	1st of any month	3.30%
	Feb	6.00% 1.4280	6.00% 1.4352	6.00% 1.4424	6.94% 1.4496	6.94% 1.4580	6.94% 1.4660	6.94% 1.4744	1st of any month	3.30%
	Mar	6.00% 1.4212	6.00% 1.4280	6.00% 1.4352	6.00% 1.4424	6.94% 1.4496	6.94% 1.4580	6.94% 1.4660	1st of any month	3.30%
	Apr	6.00% 1.4140	6.00% 1.4212	6.00% 1.4280	6.00% 1.4352	6.00% 1.4424	6.94% 1.4496	6.94% 1.4580	1st of any month	3.30%
	May	6.94% 1.4128	6.94% 1.4208	6.94% 1.4288	6.94% 1.4372	6.94% 1.4452	6.94% 1.4536	??? 1.4620	1st of any month	3.30%
	Jun	6.00% 1.4060	6.94% 1.4128	6.94% 1.4208	6.94% 1.4288	6.94% 1.4372	6.94% 1.4452	6.94% 1.4536	1st of any month	3.30%
	Jul	6.00% 1.3988	6.00% 1.4060	6.94% 1.4128	6.94% 1.4208	6.94% 1.4288	6.94% 1.4372	6.94% 1.4452	1st of any month	3.30%
	Aug	6.00% 1.3920	6.00% 1.3988	6.00% 1.4060	6.94% 1.4128	6.94% 1.4208	6.94% 1.4288	6.94% 1.4372	1st of any month	3.30%
	Sep	6.00% 1.3852	6.00% 1.3920	6.00% 1.3988	6.00% 1.4060	6.94% 1.4128	6.94% 1.4208	6.94% 1.4288	1st of any month	3.30%
	Oct	6.00% 1.3784	6.00% 1.3852	6.00% 1.3920	6.00% 1.3988	6.00% 1.4060	6.94% 1.4128	6.94% 1.4208	1st of any month	3.30%
	Nov	7.04% 1.3852	7.04% 1.3932	7.04% 1.4012	7.04% 1.4092	7.04% 1.4176	7.04% 1.4256	??? 1.4340	1st of any month	3.40%
	Dec	6.11% 1.3780	7.04% 1.3852	7.04% 1.3932	7.04% 1.4012	7.04% 1.4092	7.04% 1.4176	7.04% 1.4256	1st of any month	3.40%

2004 only		Issue date through Dec 2004			Educa-tion eligible?	Alert Recommendation	Stops paying interest:	Issue month	Year and Series
Annual APY	Interest per $FV	Lifetime APY	Interest per $FV	% interest					
5.50%	0.0744	5.76%	0.4264	30%	Yes	A+++	Sep 2028	**Sep**	**1998**
5.63%	0.0756	5.76%	0.4196	30%	Yes	A+++	Oct 2028	**Oct**	**I**
5.27%	0.0708	5.78%	0.4140	29%	Yes	A++	Nov 2028	**Nov**	
5.14%	0.0688	5.78%	0.4072	29%	Yes	A++	Dec 2028	**Dec**	
7.03%	0.0920	5.77%	0.4004	29%	Yes	A++	Jan 2029	**Jan**	**1999**
7.16%	0.0932	5.78%	0.3940	28%	Yes	A++	Feb 2029	**Feb**	**I**
7.27%	0.0940	5.78%	0.3876	28%	Yes	A++	Mar 2029	**Mar**	
7.24%	0.0932	5.78%	0.3808	28%	Yes	A++	Apr 2029	**Apr**	
6.85%	0.0884	5.83%	0.3784	27%	Yes	A++	May 2029	**May**	
6.92%	0.0888	5.83%	0.3716	27%	Yes	A++	Jun 2029	**Jun**	
7.02%	0.0896	5.83%	0.3652	27%	Yes	A++	Jul 2029	**Jul**	
7.13%	0.0904	5.83%	0.3588	26%	Yes	A++	Aug 2029	**Aug**	
7.23%	0.0912	5.83%	0.3524	26%	Yes	A++	Sep 2029	**Sep**	
7.23%	0.0908	5.83%	0.3460	26%	Yes	A++	Oct 2029	**Oct**	
6.97%	0.0880	6.00%	0.3508	26%	Yes	A+++	Nov 2029	**Nov**	
7.04%	0.0884	6.00%	0.3440	26%	Yes	A+++	Dec 2029	**Dec**	

Year and Series	Issue month	Current interest rate and redemption value per $ of face value							To avoid rate penalty, redeem:	Fixed-base rate
		May 05	Jun 05	Jul 05	Aug 05	Sep 05	Oct 05	Nov 05		
2000 **I**	Jan	6.11% 1.3712	6.11% 1.3780	7.04% 1.3852	7.04% 1.3932	7.04% 1.4012	7.04% 1.4092	7.04% 1.4176	1st of any month	3.40%
	Feb	6.11% 1.3644	6.11% 1.3712	6.11% 1.3780	7.04% 1.3852	7.04% 1.3932	7.04% 1.4012	7.04% 1.4092	1st of any month	3.40%
	Mar	6.11% 1.3576	6.11% 1.3644	6.11% 1.3712	6.11% 1.3780	7.04% 1.3852	7.04% 1.3932	7.04% 1.4012	1st of any month	3.40%
	Apr	6.11% 1.3508	6.11% 1.3576	6.11% 1.3644	6.11% 1.3712	6.11% 1.3780	7.04% 1.3852	7.04% 1.3932	1st of any month	3.40%
	May	7.24% 1.3520	7.24% 1.3600	7.24% 1.3680	7.24% 1.3764	7.24% 1.3844	7.24% 1.3928	??? 1.4008	After May 2005	3.60%
	Jun	6.31% 1.3244	7.24% 1.3520	7.24% 1.3600	7.24% 1.3680	7.24% 1.3764	7.24% 1.3844	7.24% 1.3928	After Jun 2005	3.60%
	Jul	6.31% 1.3176	6.31% 1.3244	7.24% 1.3520	7.24% 1.3600	7.24% 1.3680	7.24% 1.3764	7.24% 1.3844	After Jul 2005	3.60%
	Aug	6.31% 1.3108	6.31% 1.3176	6.31% 1.3244	7.24% 1.3520	7.24% 1.3600	7.24% 1.3680	7.24% 1.3764	After Aug 2005	3.60%
	Sep	6.31% 1.3044	6.31% 1.3108	6.31% 1.3176	6.31% 1.3244	7.24% 1.3520	7.24% 1.3600	7.24% 1.3680	After Sep 2005	3.60%
	Oct	6.31% 1.2980	6.31% 1.3044	6.31% 1.3108	6.31% 1.3176	6.31% 1.3244	7.24% 1.3520	7.24% 1.3600	After Oct 2005	3.60%
	Nov	7.04% 1.2720	7.04% 1.2784	7.04% 1.2852	7.04% 1.2916	7.04% 1.2992	7.04% 1.3064	??? 1.3372	After Nov 2005	3.40%
	Dec	6.11% 1.2660	7.04% 1.2720	7.04% 1.2784	7.04% 1.2852	7.04% 1.2916	7.04% 1.2992	7.04% 1.3064	After Dec 2005	3.40%
2001 **I**	Jan	6.11% 1.2596	6.11% 1.2660	7.04% 1.2720	7.04% 1.2784	7.04% 1.2852	7.04% 1.2916	7.04% 1.2992	After Jan 2006	3.40%
	Feb	6.11% 1.2532	6.11% 1.2596	6.11% 1.2660	7.04% 1.2720	7.04% 1.2784	7.04% 1.2852	7.04% 1.2916	After Feb 2006	3.40%
	Mar	6.11% 1.2472	6.11% 1.2532	6.11% 1.2596	6.11% 1.2660	7.04% 1.2720	7.04% 1.2784	7.04% 1.2852	After Mar 2006	3.40%
	Apr	6.11% 1.2412	6.11% 1.2472	6.11% 1.2532	6.11% 1.2596	6.11% 1.2660	7.04% 1.2720	7.04% 1.2784	After Apr 2006	3.40%
	May	6.63% 1.2144	6.63% 1.2204	6.63% 1.2260	6.63% 1.2316	6.63% 1.2384	6.63% 1.2452	??? 1.2520	After May 2006	3.00%
	Jun	5.70% 1.2088	6.63% 1.2144	6.63% 1.2204	6.63% 1.2260	6.63% 1.2316	6.63% 1.2384	6.63% 1.2452	After Jun 2006	3.00%
	Jul	5.70% 1.2032	5.70% 1.2088	6.63% 1.2144	6.63% 1.2204	6.63% 1.2260	6.63% 1.2316	6.63% 1.2384	After Jul 2006	3.00%

2004 only		Issue date through Dec 2004			Educa-tion eligible?	Alert Recommendation	Stops paying interest:	Issue month	Year and Series
Annual APY	Interest per $FV	Lifetime APY	Interest per $FV	% interest					
5.61%	0.0700	5.70%	0.3184	24%	Yes	A+++	Jan 2030	**Jan**	**2000**
5.74%	0.0712	5.70%	0.3124	24%	Yes	A+++	Feb 2030	**Feb**	**I**
5.83%	0.0720	5.70%	0.3060	23%	Yes	A+++	Mar 2030	**Mar**	
5.96%	0.0732	5.72%	0.3012	23%	Yes	A+++	Apr 2030	**Apr**	
5.63%	0.0692	5.77%	0.2980	23%	Yes	A++++	May 2030	**May**	
5.73%	0.0700	5.77%	0.2916	23%	Yes	A++++ Hold till Jun 2005	Jun 2030	**Jun**	
5.83%	0.0708	5.76%	0.2852	22%	Yes	A++++ Hold till Jul 2005	Jul 2030	**Jul**	
5.93%	0.0716	5.76%	0.2788	22%	Yes	A++++ Hold till Aug 2005	Aug 2030	**Aug**	
6.03%	0.0724	5.75%	0.2724	21%	Yes	A++++ Hold till Sep 2005	Sep 2030	**Sep**	
6.16%	0.0736	5.77%	0.2676	21%	Yes	A++++ Hold till Oct 2005	Oct 2030	**Oct**	
5.44%	0.0640	5.36%	0.2412	19%	Yes	A+++ Hold till Nov 2005	Nov 2030	**Nov**	
5.54%	0.0648	5.35%	0.2352	19%	Yes	A+++ Hold till Dec 2005	Dec 2030	**Dec**	
5.64%	0.0656	5.34%	0.2292	19%	Yes	A+++ Hold till Jan 2006	Jan 2031	**Jan**	**2001**
5.74%	0.0664	5.33%	0.2236	18%	Yes	A+++ Hold till Feb 2006	Feb 2031	**Feb**	**I**
5.84%	0.0672	5.32%	0.2176	18%	Yes	A+++ Hold till Mar 2006	Mar 2031	**Mar**	
5.94%	0.0680	5.34%	0.2132	18%	Yes	A+++ Hold till Apr 2006	Apr 2031	**Apr**	
5.03%	0.0568	4.84%	0.1868	16%	Yes	A+ Hold till May 2006	May 2031	**May**	
5.12%	0.0576	4.82%	0.1816	15%	Yes	A+ Hold till Jun 2006	Jun 2031	**Jun**	
5.22%	0.0584	4.81%	0.1764	15%	Yes	A+ Hold till Jul 2006	Jul 2031	**Jul**	

Year and Series	Issue month	Current interest rate and redemption value per $ of face value							To avoid rate penalty, redeem:	Fixed-base rate
		May 05	Jun 05	Jul 05	Aug 05	Sep 05	Oct 05	Nov 05		
2001 **I**	Aug	5.70% 1.1976	5.70% 1.2032	5.70% 1.2088	6.63% 1.2144	6.63% 1.2204	6.63% 1.2260	6.63% 1.2316	After Aug 2006	3.00%
	Sep	5.70% 1.1924	5.70% 1.1976	5.70% 1.2032	5.70% 1.2088	6.63% 1.2144	6.63% 1.2204	6.63% 1.2260	After Sep 2006	3.00%
	Oct	5.70% 1.1868	5.70% 1.1924	5.70% 1.1976	5.70% 1.2032	5.70% 1.2088	6.63% 1.2144	6.63% 1.2204	After Oct 2006	3.00%
	Nov	5.62% 1.1424	5.62% 1.1468	5.62% 1.1512	5.62% 1.1556	5.62% 1.1608	5.62% 1.1664	??? 1.1716	After Nov 2006	2.00%
	Dec	4.69% 1.1380	5.62% 1.1424	5.62% 1.1468	5.62% 1.1512	5.62% 1.1556	5.62% 1.1608	5.62% 1.1664	After Dec 2006	2.00%
2002 **I**	Jan	4.69% 1.1336	4.69% 1.1380	5.62% 1.1424	5.62% 1.1468	5.62% 1.1512	5.62% 1.1556	5.62% 1.1608	After Jan 2007	2.00%
	Feb	4.69% 1.1292	4.69% 1.1336	4.69% 1.1380	5.62% 1.1424	5.62% 1.1468	5.62% 1.1512	5.62% 1.1556	After Feb 2007	2.00%
	Mar	4.69% 1.1252	4.69% 1.1292	4.69% 1.1336	4.69% 1.1380	5.62% 1.1424	5.62% 1.1468	5.62% 1.1512	After Mar 2007	2.00%
	Apr	4.69% 1.1208	4.69% 1.1252	4.69% 1.1292	4.69% 1.1336	4.69% 1.1380	5.62% 1.1424	5.62% 1.1468	After Apr 2007	2.00%
	May	5.62% 1.1172	5.62% 1.1216	5.62% 1.1260	5.62% 1.1304	5.62% 1.1356	5.62% 1.1408	??? 1.1460	After May 2007	2.00%
	Jun	4.69% 1.1128	5.62% 1.1172	5.62% 1.1216	5.62% 1.1260	5.62% 1.1304	5.62% 1.1356	5.62% 1.1408	After Jun 2007	2.00%
	Jul	4.69% 1.1088	4.69% 1.1128	5.62% 1.1172	5.62% 1.1216	5.62% 1.1260	5.62% 1.1304	5.62% 1.1356	After Jul 2007	2.00%
	Aug	4.69% 1.1044	4.69% 1.1088	4.69% 1.1128	5.62% 1.1172	5.62% 1.1216	5.62% 1.1260	5.62% 1.1304	After Aug 2007	2.00%
	Sep	4.69% 1.1004	4.69% 1.1044	4.69% 1.1088	4.69% 1.1128	5.62% 1.1172	5.62% 1.1216	5.62% 1.1260	After Sep 2007	2.00%
	Oct	4.69% 1.0964	4.69% 1.1004	4.69% 1.1044	4.69% 1.1088	4.69% 1.1128	5.62% 1.1172	5.62% 1.1216	After Oct 2007	2.00%
	Nov	5.21% 1.0936	5.21% 1.0972	5.21% 1.1012	5.21% 1.1052	5.21% 1.1100	5.21% 1.1148	??? 1.1196	After Nov 2007	1.60%
	Dec	4.28% 1.0896	5.21% 1.0936	5.21% 1.0972	5.21% 1.1012	5.21% 1.1052	5.21% 1.1100	5.21% 1.1148	After Dec 2007	1.60%

2004 only		Issue date through Dec 2004			Educa-tion eligible?	Alert Recommendation	Stops paying interest:	Issue month	Year and Series
Annual APY	Interest per $FV	Lifetime APY	Interest per $FV	% interest					
5.32%	0.0592	4.80%	0.1712	15%	Yes	A+ Hold till Aug 2006	Aug 2031	Aug	2001
5.43%	0.0600	4.78%	0.1660	14%	Yes	A+ Hold till Sep 2006	Sep 2031	Sep	I
5.52%	0.0608	4.80%	0.1620	14%	Yes	A+ Hold till Oct 2006	Oct 2031	Oct	
3.97%	0.0428	3.73%	0.1208	11%	Yes	A Hold till Nov 2006	Nov 2031	Nov	
4.06%	0.0436	3.72%	0.1168	10%	Yes	A	Dec 2031	Dec	
4.19%	0.0448	3.70%	0.1128	10%	Yes	A	Jan 2032	Jan	2002
4.29%	0.0456	3.68%	0.1088	10%	Yes	A	Feb 2032	Feb	I
4.38%	0.0464	3.66%	0.1048	9%	Yes	A	Mar 2032	Mar	
4.51%	0.0476	3.68%	0.1020	9%	Yes	A	Apr 2032	Apr	
3.94%	0.0416	3.59%	0.0964	9%	Yes	A	May 2032	May	
4.08%	0.0428	3.58%	0.0928	8%	Yes	A	Jun 2032	Jun	
4.17%	0.0436	3.55%	0.0888	8%	Yes	A	Jul 2032	Jul	
4.27%	0.0444	3.52%	0.0848	8%	Yes	A	Aug 2032	Aug	
4.36%	0.0452	3.48%	0.0808	7%	Yes	A	Sep 2032	Sep	
4.50%	0.0464	3.50%	0.0780	7%	Yes	A	Oct 2032	Oct	
3.55%	0.0368	3.49%	0.0748	7%	Yes	B+	Nov 2032	Nov	
3.64%	0.0376	3.47%	0.0712	7%	Yes	B+	Dec 2032	Dec	

Year and Series	Issue month	Current interest rate and redemption value per $ of face value							To avoid rate penalty, redeem:	Fixed-base rate
		May 05	Jun 05	Jul 05	Aug 05	Sep 05	Oct 05	Nov 05		
2003 I	Jan	4.28% 1.0860	4.28% 1.0896	5.21% 1.0936	5.21% 1.0972	5.21% 1.1012	5.21% 1.1052	5.21% 1.1100	After Jan 2008	1.60%
	Feb	4.28% 1.0820	4.28% 1.0860	4.28% 1.0896	5.21% 1.0936	5.21% 1.0972	5.21% 1.1012	5.21% 1.1052	After Feb 2008	1.60%
	Mar	4.28% 1.0784	4.28% 1.0820	4.28% 1.0860	4.28% 1.0896	5.21% 1.0936	5.21% 1.0972	5.21% 1.1012	After Mar 2008	1.60%
	Apr	4.28% 1.0748	4.28% 1.0784	4.28% 1.0820	4.28% 1.0860	4.28% 1.0896	5.21% 1.0936	5.21% 1.0972	After Apr 2008	1.60%
	May	4.70% 1.0624	4.70% 1.0656	4.70% 1.0688	4.70% 1.0724	4.70% 1.0764	4.70% 1.0808	??? 1.0848	After May 2008	1.10%
	Jun	3.77% 1.0588	4.70% 1.0624	4.70% 1.0656	4.70% 1.0688	4.70% 1.0724	4.70% 1.0764	4.70% 1.0808	After Jun 2008	1.10%
	Jul	3.77% 1.0556	3.77% 1.0588	4.70% 1.0624	4.70% 1.0656	4.70% 1.0688	4.70% 1.0724	4.70% 1.0764	After Jul 2008	1.10%
	Aug	3.77% 1.0524	3.77% 1.0556	3.77% 1.0588	4.70% 1.0624	4.70% 1.0656	4.70% 1.0688	4.70% 1.0724	After Aug 2008	1.10%
	Sep	3.77% 1.0496	3.77% 1.0524	3.77% 1.0556	3.77% 1.0588	4.70% 1.0624	4.70% 1.0656	4.70% 1.0688	After Sep 2008	1.10%
	Oct	3.77% 1.0464	3.77% 1.0496	3.77% 1.0524	3.77% 1.0556	3.77% 1.0588	4.70% 1.0624	4.70% 1.0656	After Oct 2008	1.10%
	Nov	4.70% 1.0380	4.70% 1.0412	4.70% 1.0444	4.70% 1.0476	4.70% 1.0516	4.70% 1.0556	??? 1.0600	After Nov 2008	1.10%
	Dec	3.77% 1.0348	4.70% 1.0380	4.70% 1.0412	4.70% 1.0444	4.70% 1.0476	4.70% 1.0516	4.70% 1.0556	After Dec 2008	1.10%
2004 I	Jan	3.77% 1.0316	3.77% 1.0348	4.70% 1.0380	4.70% 1.0412	4.70% 1.0444	4.70% 1.0476	4.70% 1.0516	After Jan 2009	1.10%
	Feb	3.77% 1.0284	3.77% 1.0316	3.77% 1.0348	4.70% 1.0380	4.70% 1.0412	4.70% 1.0444	4.70% 1.0476	After Feb 2009	1.10%
	Mar	3.77% 1.0256	3.77% 1.0284	3.77% 1.0316	3.77% 1.0348	4.70% 1.0380	4.70% 1.0412	4.70% 1.0444	After Mar 2009	1.10%
	Apr	3.77% 1.0224	3.77% 1.0256	3.77% 1.0284	3.77% 1.0316	3.77% 1.0348	4.70% 1.0380	4.70% 1.0412	After Apr 2009	1.10%
	May	4.60% 1.0260	4.60% 1.0292	4.60% 1.0324	4.60% 1.0356	4.60% 1.0396	4.60% 1.0436	??? 1.0476	After May 2009	1.00%
	Jun	3.67% 1.0228	4.60% 1.0260	4.60% 1.0292	4.60% 1.0324	4.60% 1.0356	4.60% 1.0396	4.60% 1.0436	After Jun 2009	1.00%

2004 only		Issue date through Dec 2004			Educa-tion eligible?	Alert Recommendation	Stops paying interest:	Issue month	Year and Series
Annual APY	Interest per $FV	Lifetime APY	Interest per $FV	% interest					
3.77%	0.0388	3.46%	0.0680	6%	Yes	B+	Jan 2033	**Jan**	**2003**
3.86%	0.0396	3.43%	0.0644	6%	Yes	B+	Feb 2033	**Feb**	**I**
3.96%	0.0404	3.40%	0.0608	6%	Yes	B+	Mar 2033	**Mar**	
4.09%	0.0416	3.43%	0.0584	6%	Yes	B+	Apr 2033	**Apr**	
3.03%	0.0308	2.89%	0.0464	4%	Yes	B	May 2033	**May**	
3.12%	0.0316	2.84%	0.0432	4%	Yes	B	Jun 2033	**Jun**	
3.26%	0.0328	2.82%	0.0404	4%	Yes	B	Jul 2033	**Jul**	
3.31%	0.0332	2.76%	0.0372	4%	Yes	B	Aug 2033	**Aug**	
3.44%	0.0344	2.72%	0.0344	3%	Yes	B	Sep 2033	**Sep**	
3.24%	0.0324	2.75%	0.0324	3%	Yes	B	Oct 2033	**Oct**	
2.24%	0.0224	2.06%	0.0224	2%	Yes	B	Nov 2033	**Nov**	
1.96%	0.0196	1.95%	0.0196	2%	Yes	B	Dec 2033	**Dec**	
1.83%	0.0168	1.83%	0.0168	2%	Yes	B	Jan 2034	**Jan**	**2004**
1.63%	0.0136	1.63%	0.0136	1%	Yes	B	Feb 2034	**Feb**	**I**
1.44%	0.0108	1.44%	0.0108	1%	Yes	B	Mar 2034	**Mar**	
1.38%	0.0092	1.38%	0.0092	1%	Yes	B	Apr 2034	**Apr**	
1.92%	0.0112	1.92%	0.0112	1%	Yes	B	May 2034	**May**	
1.68%	0.0084	1.68%	0.0084	1%	Yes	B	Jun 2034	**Jun**	

Year and Series	Issue month	Current interest rate and redemption value per $ of face value							To avoid rate penalty, redeem:	Fixed-base rate
		May 05	Jun 05	Jul 05	Aug 05	Sep 05	Oct 05	Nov 05		
2004 I	Jul	3.67% 1.0200	3.67% 1.0228	4.60% 1.0260	4.60% 1.0292	4.60% 1.0324	4.60% 1.0356	4.60% 1.0396	After Jul 2009	1.00%
	Aug	3.67% 1.0168	3.67% 1.0200	3.67% 1.0228	4.60% 1.0260	4.60% 1.0292	4.60% 1.0324	4.60% 1.0356	After Aug 2009	1.00%
	Sep	3.67% 1.0140	3.67% 1.0168	3.67% 1.0200	3.67% 1.0228	4.60% 1.0260	4.60% 1.0292	4.60% 1.0324	After Sep 2009	1.00%
	Oct	3.67% 1.0112	3.67% 1.0140	3.67% 1.0168	3.67% 1.0200	3.67% 1.0228	4.60% 1.0260	4.60% 1.0292	After Oct 2009	1.00%
	Nov	4.60% 1.0092	4.60% 1.0120	4.60% 1.0152	4.60% 1.0184	4.60% 1.0224	4.60% 1.0260	??? 1.0300	After Nov 2009	1.00%
	Dec	3.67% 1.0060	4.60% 1.0092	4.60% 1.0120	4.60% 1.0152	4.60% 1.0184	4.60% 1.0224	4.60% 1.0260	After Dec 2009	1.00%
2005 I	Jan	3.67% 1.0032	3.67% 1.0060	4.60% 1.0092	4.60% 1.0120	4.60% 1.0152	4.60% 1.0184	4.60% 1.0224	After Jan 2010	1.00%
	Feb	3.67% 1.0000	3.67% 1.0032	3.67% 1.0060	4.60% 1.0092	4.60% 1.0120	4.60% 1.0152	4.60% 1.0184	After Feb 2010	1.00%
	Mar	3.67% 1.0000	3.67% 1.0000	3.67% 1.0032	3.67% 1.0060	4.60% 1.0092	4.60% 1.0120	4.60% 1.0152	After Mar 2010	1.00%
	Apr	3.67% 1.0000	3.67% 1.0000	3.67% 1.0000	3.67% 1.0032	3.67% 1.0060	4.60% 1.0092	4.60% 1.0120	After Apr 2010	1.00%
	May	4.80% 1.0000	4.80% 1.0000	4.80% 1.0000	4.80% 1.0000	4.80% 1.0040	4.80% 1.0080	??? 1.0120	After May 2010	1.20%
	Jun	--- ---	4.80% 1.0000	4.80% 1.0000	4.80% 1.0000	4.80% 1.0000	4.80% 1.0040	4.80% 1.0080	After Jun 2010	1.20%
	Jul	--- ---	--- ---	4.80% 1.0000	4.80% 1.0000	4.80% 1.0000	4.80% 1.0000	4.80% 1.0040	After Jul 2010	1.20%
	Aug	--- ---	--- ---	--- ---	4.80% 1.0000	4.80% 1.0000	4.80% 1.0000	4.80% 1.0000	After Aug 2010	1.20%
	Sep	--- ---	--- ---	--- ---	--- ---	4.80% 1.0000	4.80% 1.0000	4.80% 1.0000	After Sep 2010	1.20%
	Oct	--- ---	--- ---	--- ---	--- ---	--- ---	4.80% 1.0000	4.80% 1.0000	After Oct 2010	1.20%
	Nov	--- ---	--- ---	--- ---	--- ---	--- ---	--- ---	??? 1.0000	After Nov 2010	1.20%

2004 only		Issue date through Dec 2004			Educa-tion eligible?	Alert Recommendation	Stops paying interest:	Issue month	Year and Series
Annual APY	Interest per $FV	Lifetime APY	Interest per $FV	% interest					
1.34%	0.0056	1.34%	0.0056	1%	Yes	B	Jul 2034	Jul	**2004**
0.84%	0.0028	0.84%	0.0028	0%	Yes	B	Aug 2034	Aug	I
0.00%	0.0000	0.00%	0.0000	0%	Yes	B	Sep 2034	Sep	
0.00%	0.0000	0.00%	0.0000	0%	Yes	B	Oct 2034	Oct	
0.00%	0.0000	0.00%	0.0000	0%	Yes	B	Nov 2034	Nov	
0.00%	0.0000	0.00%	0.0000	0%	Yes	B	Dec 2034	Dec	
---	---	---	---	---	Yes	B	Jan 2035	Jan	**2005**
---	---	---	---	---	Yes	B	Feb 2035	Feb	I
---	---	---	---	---	Yes	B	Mar 2035	Mar	
---	---	---	---	---	Yes	B	Apr 2035	Apr	
---	---	---	---	---	Yes	B	May 2035	May	
---	---	---	---	---	Yes	B	Jun 2035	Jun	
---	---	---	---	---	Yes	B	Jul 2035	Jul	
---	---	---	---	---	Yes	B	Aug 2035	Aug	
---	---	---	---	---	Yes	B	Sep 2035	Sep	
---	---	---	---	---	Yes	B	Oct 2035	Oct	
---	---	---	---	---	Yes	B	Nov 2035	Nov	

Year and Series	Issue month	Current interest rate and redemption value per $ of face value							To avoid rate penalty, redeem:	Maturity period ends:
		May 05	Jun 05	Jul 05	Aug 05	Sep 05	Oct 05	Nov 05		
1980 **EE**	Jan	4.00% 2.7192	4.00% 2.7192	4.00% 2.7736	4.00% 2.7736	4.00% 2.7736	4.00% 2.7736	4.00% 2.7736	Jan or Jul	Jan 2010
	Feb	4.00% 2.7192	4.00% 2.7192	4.00% 2.7192	4.00% 2.7736	4.00% 2.7736	4.00% 2.7736	4.00% 2.7736	Feb or Aug	Feb 2010
	Mar	4.00% 2.7192	4.00% 2.7192	4.00% 2.7192	4.00% 2.7192	4.00% 2.7736	4.00% 2.7736	4.00% 2.7736	Mar or Sep	Mar 2010
	Apr	4.00% 2.7192	4.00% 2.7192	4.00% 2.7192	4.00% 2.7192	4.00% 2.7192	4.00% 2.7736	4.00% 2.7736	Apr or Oct	Apr 2010
	May	4.00% 2.7464	4.00% 2.7464	4.00% 2.7464	4.00% 2.7464	4.00% 2.7464	4.00% 2.7464	??? 2.8016	May or Nov	May 2010
	Jun	4.00% 2.6928	4.00% 2.7464	4.00% 2.7464	4.00% 2.7464	4.00% 2.7464	4.00% 2.7464	4.00% 2.7464	Jun or Dec	Jun 2010
	Jul	4.00% 2.6928	4.00% 2.6928	4.00% 2.7464	4.00% 2.7464	4.00% 2.7464	4.00% 2.7464	4.00% 2.7464	Jan or Jul	Jul 2010
	Aug	4.00% 2.6928	4.00% 2.6928	4.00% 2.6928	4.00% 2.7464	4.00% 2.7464	4.00% 2.7464	4.00% 2.7464	Feb or Aug	Aug 2010
	Sep	4.00% 2.6928	4.00% 2.6928	4.00% 2.6928	4.00% 2.6928	4.00% 2.7464	4.00% 2.7464	4.00% 2.7464	Mar or Sep	Sep 2010
	Oct	4.00% 2.6928	4.00% 2.6928	4.00% 2.6928	4.00% 2.6928	4.00% 2.6928	4.00% 2.7464	4.00% 2.7464	Apr or Oct	Oct 2010
	Nov	4.00% 2.4680	4.00% 2.4680	4.00% 2.4680	4.00% 2.4680	4.00% 2.4680	4.00% 2.4680	??? 2.5176	May or Nov	Nov 2009
	Dec	4.00% 2.4196	4.00% 2.4680	4.00% 2.4680	4.00% 2.4680	4.00% 2.4680	4.00% 2.4680	4.00% 2.4680	Jun or Dec	Dec 2009
1981 **EE**	Jan	4.00% 2.4196	4.00% 2.4196	4.00% 2.4680	4.00% 2.4680	4.00% 2.4680	4.00% 2.4680	4.00% 2.4680	Jan or Jul	Jan 2010
	Feb	4.00% 2.4196	4.00% 2.4196	4.00% 2.4196	4.00% 2.4680	4.00% 2.4680	4.00% 2.4680	4.00% 2.4680	Feb or Aug	Feb 2010
	Mar	4.00% 2.4196	4.00% 2.4196	4.00% 2.4196	4.00% 2.4196	4.00% 2.4680	4.00% 2.4680	4.00% 2.4680	Mar or Sep	Mar 2010
	Apr	4.00% 2.4196	4.00% 2.4196	4.00% 2.4196	4.00% 2.4196	4.00% 2.4196	4.00% 2.4680	4.00% 2.4680	Apr or Oct	Apr 2010
	May	4.00% 2.3164	4.00% 2.3164	4.00% 2.3164	4.00% 2.3164	4.00% 2.3164	4.00% 2.3164	??? 2.3628	May or Nov	May 2009
	Jun	4.00% 2.2712	4.00% 2.3164	4.00% 2.3164	4.00% 2.3164	4.00% 2.3164	4.00% 2.3164	4.00% 2.3164	Jun or Dec	Jun 2009

2004 only		Issue date through Dec 2004			Educa-tion eligible?	Alert Recommendation	Stops paying interest:	Issue month	Year and Series
Annual APY	Interest per $FV	Lifetime APY	Interest per $FV	% interest					
4.04%	0.1036	6.95%	2.1660	81%	No	A	Jan 2010	**Jan**	**1980**
4.04%	0.1036	6.95%	2.1660	81%	No	A	Feb 2010	**Feb**	**EE**
4.04%	0.1036	6.95%	2.1660	81%	No	A	Mar 2010	**Mar**	
4.04%	0.1036	6.95%	2.1660	81%	No	A	Apr 2010	**Apr**	
4.05%	0.1048	6.99%	2.1928	81%	No	A	May 2010	**May**	
4.05%	0.1048	6.99%	2.1928	81%	No	A	Jun 2010	**Jun**	
4.04%	0.1024	7.05%	2.1400	81%	No	A	Jul 2010	**Jul**	
4.04%	0.1024	7.05%	2.1400	81%	No	A	Aug 2010	**Aug**	
4.04%	0.1024	7.05%	2.1400	81%	No	A	Sep 2010	**Sep**	
4.04%	0.1024	7.05%	2.1400	81%	No	A	Oct 2010	**Oct**	
4.04%	0.0940	6.68%	1.9196	79%	No	A	Nov 2010	**Nov**	
4.04%	0.0940	6.68%	1.9196	79%	No	A	Dec 2010	**Dec**	
4.05%	0.0924	6.74%	1.8724	79%	No	A	Jan 2011	**Jan**	**1981**
4.05%	0.0924	6.74%	1.8724	79%	No	A	Feb 2011	**Feb**	**EE**
4.05%	0.0924	6.74%	1.8724	79%	No	A	Mar 2011	**Mar**	
4.05%	0.0924	6.74%	1.8724	79%	No	A	Apr 2011	**Apr**	
4.05%	0.0884	6.55%	1.7712	78%	No	A	May 2011	**May**	
4.05%	0.0884	6.55%	1.7712	78%	No	A	Jun 2011	**Jun**	

Year and Series	Issue month	Current interest rate and redemption value per $ of face value							To avoid rate penalty, redeem:	Maturity period ends:
		May 05	Jun 05	Jul 05	Aug 05	Sep 05	Oct 05	Nov 05		
1981 **EE**	Jul	4.00% 2.2712	4.00% 2.2712	4.00% 2.3164	4.00% 2.3164	4.00% 2.3164	4.00% 2.3164	4.00% 2.3164	Jan or Jul	Jul 2009
	Aug	4.00% 2.2712	4.00% 2.2712	4.00% 2.2712	4.00% 2.3164	4.00% 2.3164	4.00% 2.3164	4.00% 2.3164	Feb or Aug	Aug 2009
	Sep	4.00% 2.2712	4.00% 2.2712	4.00% 2.2712	4.00% 2.2712	4.00% 2.3164	4.00% 2.3164	4.00% 2.3164	Mar or Sep	Sep 2009
	Oct	4.00% 2.2712	4.00% 2.2712	4.00% 2.2712	4.00% 2.2712	4.00% 2.2712	4.00% 2.3164	4.00% 2.3164	Apr or Oct	Oct 2009
	Nov	4.00% 2.2712	4.00% 2.2712	4.00% 2.2712	4.00% 2.2712	4.00% 2.2712	4.00% 2.2712	??? 2.3164	May or Nov	Nov 2009
	Dec	4.00% 2.2264	4.00% 2.2712	4.00% 2.2712	4.00% 2.2712	4.00% 2.2712	4.00% 2.2712	4.00% 2.2712	Jun or Dec	Dec 2009
1982 **EE**	Jan	4.00% 2.2264	4.00% 2.2264	4.00% 2.2712	4.00% 2.2712	4.00% 2.2712	4.00% 2.2712	4.00% 2.2712	Jan or Jul	Jan 2010
	Feb	4.00% 2.2264	4.00% 2.2264	4.00% 2.2264	4.00% 2.2712	4.00% 2.2712	4.00% 2.2712	4.00% 2.2712	Feb or Aug	Feb 2010
	Mar	4.00% 2.2264	4.00% 2.2264	4.00% 2.2264	4.00% 2.2264	4.00% 2.2712	4.00% 2.2712	4.00% 2.2712	Mar or Sep	Mar 2010
	Apr	4.00% 2.2264	4.00% 2.2264	4.00% 2.2264	4.00% 2.2264	4.00% 2.2264	4.00% 2.2712	4.00% 2.2712	Apr or Oct	Apr 2010
	May	4.00% 2.2264	4.00% 2.2264	4.00% 2.2264	4.00% 2.2264	4.00% 2.2264	4.00% 2.2264	??? 2.2712	May or Nov	May 2010
	Jun	4.00% 2.1828	4.00% 2.2264	4.00% 2.2264	4.00% 2.2264	4.00% 2.2264	4.00% 2.2264	4.00% 2.2264	Jun or Dec	Jun 2010
	Jul	4.00% 2.1828	4.00% 2.1828	4.00% 2.2264	4.00% 2.2264	4.00% 2.2264	4.00% 2.2264	4.00% 2.2264	Jan or Jul	Jul 2010
	Aug	4.00% 2.1828	4.00% 2.1828	4.00% 2.1828	4.00% 2.2264	4.00% 2.2264	4.00% 2.2264	4.00% 2.2264	Feb or Aug	Aug 2010
	Sep	4.00% 2.1828	4.00% 2.1828	4.00% 2.1828	4.00% 2.1828	4.00% 2.2264	4.00% 2.2264	4.00% 2.2264	Mar or Sep	Sep 2010
	Oct	4.00% 2.1828	4.00% 2.1828	4.00% 2.1828	4.00% 2.1828	4.00% 2.1828	4.00% 2.2264	4.00% 2.2264	Apr or Oct	Oct 2010
	Nov	4.00% 2.0828	4.00% 2.0828	4.00% 2.0828	4.00% 2.0828	4.00% 2.0828	4.00% 2.0828	??? 2.1244	May or Nov	Nov 2012
	Dec	4.00% 2.0420	4.00% 2.0828	4.00% 2.0828	4.00% 2.0828	4.00% 2.0828	4.00% 2.0828	4.00% 2.0828	Jun or Dec	Dec 2012

2004 only		Issue date through Dec 2004			Educa-tion eligible?	Alert Recommendation	Stops paying interest:	Issue month	Year and Series
Annual APY	Interest per $FV	Lifetime APY	Interest per $FV	% interest					
4.04%	0.0864	6.60%	1.7264	78%	No	A	Jul 2011	Jul	**1981**
4.04%	0.0864	6.60%	1.7264	78%	No	A	Aug 2011	Aug	**EE**
4.04%	0.0864	6.60%	1.7264	78%	No	A	Sep 2011	Sep	
4.04%	0.0864	6.60%	1.7264	78%	No	A	Oct 2011	Oct	
4.04%	0.0864	6.60%	1.7264	78%	No	A	Nov 2011	Nov	
4.04%	0.0864	6.60%	1.7264	78%	No	A	Dec 2011	Dec	
4.04%	0.0848	6.66%	1.6828	77%	No	A	Jan 2012	Jan	**1982**
4.04%	0.0848	6.66%	1.6828	77%	No	A	Feb 2012	Feb	**EE**
4.04%	0.0848	6.66%	1.6828	77%	No	A	Mar 2012	Mar	
4.04%	0.0848	6.66%	1.6828	77%	No	A	Apr 2012	Apr	
4.04%	0.0848	6.66%	1.6828	77%	No	A	May 2012	May	
4.04%	0.0848	6.66%	1.6828	77%	No	A	Jun 2012	Jun	
4.02%	0.0828	6.72%	1.6400	77%	No	A	Jul 2012	Jul	
4.02%	0.0828	6.72%	1.6400	77%	No	A	Aug 2012	Aug	
4.02%	0.0828	6.72%	1.6400	77%	No	A	Sep 2012	Sep	
4.02%	0.0828	6.72%	1.6400	77%	No	A	Oct 2012	Oct	
4.04%	0.0792	6.50%	1.5420	76%	No	A	Nov 2012	Nov	
4.04%	0.0792	6.50%	1.5420	76%	No	A	Dec 2012	Dec	

Year and Series	Issue month	Current interest rate and redemption value per $ of face value							To avoid rate penalty, redeem:	Maturity period ends:
		May 05	Jun 05	Jul 05	Aug 05	Sep 05	Oct 05	Nov 05		
1983 EE	Jan	4.00% 2.0420	4.00% 2.0420	4.00% 2.0828	4.00% 2.0828	4.00% 2.0828	4.00% 2.0828	4.00% 2.0828	Jan or Jul	Jan 2013
	Feb	4.00% 2.0420	4.00% 2.0420	4.00% 2.0420	4.00% 2.0828	4.00% 2.0828	4.00% 2.0828	4.00% 2.0828	Feb or Aug	Feb 2013
	Mar	3.32% 1.8360	3.32% 1.8360	3.32% 1.8360	3.32% 1.8360	3.20% 1.8664	3.20% 1.8664	3.20% 1.8664	Mar or Sep	Mar 2013
	Apr	3.32% 1.8360	3.32% 1.8360	3.32% 1.8360	3.32% 1.8360	3.32% 1.8360	3.20% 1.8664	3.20% 1.8664	Apr or Oct	Apr 2013
	May	3.14% 1.7668	3.14% 1.7668	3.14% 1.7668	3.14% 1.7668	3.14% 1.7668	3.14% 1.7668	??? 1.7944	May or Nov	May 2013
	Jun	2.83% 1.7420	3.14% 1.7668	3.14% 1.7668	3.14% 1.7668	3.14% 1.7668	3.14% 1.7668	3.14% 1.7668	Jun or Dec	Jun 2013
	Jul	2.83% 1.7420	2.83% 1.7420	3.14% 1.7668	3.14% 1.7668	3.14% 1.7668	3.14% 1.7668	3.14% 1.7668	Jan or Jul	Jul 2013
	Aug	2.83% 1.7420	2.83% 1.7420	2.83% 1.7420	3.14% 1.7668	3.14% 1.7668	3.14% 1.7668	3.14% 1.7668	Feb or Aug	Aug 2013
	Sep	2.83% 1.7420	2.83% 1.7420	2.83% 1.7420	2.83% 1.7420	3.14% 1.7668	3.14% 1.7668	3.14% 1.7668	Mar or Sep	Sep 2013
	Oct	2.83% 1.7420	2.83% 1.7420	2.83% 1.7420	2.83% 1.7420	2.83% 1.7420	3.14% 1.7668	3.14% 1.7668	Apr or Oct	Oct 2013
	Nov	3.14% 1.6952	3.14% 1.6952	3.14% 1.6952	3.14% 1.6952	3.14% 1.6952	3.14% 1.6952	??? 1.7220	May or Nov	Nov 2013
	Dec	3.26% 1.6680	3.14% 1.6952	3.14% 1.6952	3.14% 1.6952	3.14% 1.6952	3.14% 1.6952	3.14% 1.6952	Jun or Dec	Dec 2013
1984 EE	Jan	3.26% 1.6680	3.26% 1.6680	3.14% 1.6952	3.14% 1.6952	3.14% 1.6952	3.14% 1.6952	3.14% 1.6952	Jan or Jul	Jan 2014
	Feb	3.26% 1.6680	3.26% 1.6680	3.26% 1.6680	3.14% 1.6952	3.14% 1.6952	3.14% 1.6952	3.14% 1.6952	Feb or Aug	Feb 2014
	Mar	3.26% 1.6680	3.26% 1.6680	3.26% 1.6680	3.26% 1.6680	3.14% 1.6952	3.14% 1.6952	3.14% 1.6952	Mar or Sep	Mar 2014
	Apr	3.26% 1.6680	3.26% 1.6680	3.26% 1.6680	3.26% 1.6680	3.26% 1.6680	3.14% 1.6952	3.14% 1.6952	Apr or Oct	Apr 2014
	May	4.00% 1.6180	4.00% 1.6180	4.00% 1.6180	4.00% 1.6180	4.00% 1.6180	4.00% 1.6180	??? 1.6472	May or Nov	May 2014
	Jun	3.23% 1.5920	4.00% 1.6180	4.00% 1.6180	4.00% 1.6180	4.00% 1.6180	4.00% 1.6180	4.00% 1.6180	Jun or Dec	Jun 2014

2004 only		Issue date through Dec 2004			Educa-tion eligible?	Alert Recommendation	Stops paying interest:	Issue month	Year and Series
Annual APY	Interest per $FV	Lifetime APY	Interest per $FV	% interest					
4.03%	0.0776	6.56%	1.5020	75%	No	A	Jan 2013	Jan	1983
4.03%	0.0776	6.56%	1.5020	75%	No	A	Feb 2013	Feb	EE
2.44%	0.0432	6.08%	1.3124	72%	No	B	Mar 2013	Mar	
2.44%	0.0432	6.08%	1.3124	72%	No	B	Apr 2013	Apr	
2.66%	0.0452	5.89%	1.2420	71%	No	B-	May 2013	May	
2.66%	0.0452	5.89%	1.2420	71%	No	B-	Jun 2013	Jun	
2.41%	0.0404	5.96%	1.2164	71%	No	B-	Jul 2013	Jul	
2.41%	0.0404	5.96%	1.2164	71%	No	B-	Aug 2013	Aug	
2.41%	0.0404	5.96%	1.2164	71%	No	B-	Sep 2013	Sep	
2.41%	0.0404	5.96%	1.2164	71%	No	B-	Oct 2013	Oct	
2.66%	0.0432	5.82%	1.1680	70%	No	B	Nov 2013	Nov	
2.66%	0.0432	5.82%	1.1680	70%	No	B	Dec 2013	Dec	
2.64%	0.0424	5.90%	1.1472	70%	No	B	Jan 2014	Jan	1984
2.64%	0.0424	5.90%	1.1472	70%	No	B	Feb 2014	Feb	EE
2.64%	0.0424	5.90%	1.1472	70%	No	B	Mar 2014	Mar	
2.64%	0.0424	5.90%	1.1472	70%	No	B	Apr 2014	Apr	
2.45%	0.0380	5.73%	1.0920	69%	No	A	May 2014	May	
2.45%	0.0380	5.73%	1.0920	69%	No	A	Jun 2014	Jun	

Year and Series	Issue month	Current interest rate and redemption value per $ of face value							To avoid rate penalty, redeem:	Maturity period ends:
		May 05	Jun 05	Jul 05	Aug 05	Sep 05	Oct 05	Nov 05		
1984 EE	Jul	3.23% 1.5920	3.23% 1.5920	4.00% 1.6180	4.00% 1.6180	4.00% 1.6180	4.00% 1.6180	4.00% 1.6180	Jan or Jul	Jul 2014
	Aug	3.23% 1.5920	3.23% 1.5920	3.23% 1.5920	4.00% 1.6180	4.00% 1.6180	4.00% 1.6180	4.00% 1.6180	Feb or Aug	Aug 2014
	Sep	3.23% 1.5920	3.23% 1.5920	3.23% 1.5920	3.23% 1.5920	4.00% 1.6180	4.00% 1.6180	4.00% 1.6180	Mar or Sep	Sep 2014
	Oct	3.23% 1.5920	3.23% 1.5920	3.23% 1.5920	3.23% 1.5920	3.23% 1.5920	4.00% 1.6180	4.00% 1.6180	Apr or Oct	Oct 2014
	Nov	4.00% 1.5832	4.00% 1.5832	4.00% 1.5832	4.00% 1.5832	4.00% 1.5832	4.00% 1.5832	??? 1.6148	May or Nov	Nov 2014
	Dec	4.00% 1.5520	4.00% 1.5832	4.00% 1.5832	4.00% 1.5832	4.00% 1.5832	4.00% 1.5832	4.00% 1.5832	Jun or Dec	Dec 2014
1985 EE	Jan	4.00% 1.5520	4.00% 1.5520	4.00% 1.5832	4.00% 1.5832	4.00% 1.5832	4.00% 1.5832	4.00% 1.5832	Jan or Jul	Jan 2015
	Feb	4.00% 1.5520	4.00% 1.5520	4.00% 1.5520	4.00% 1.5832	4.00% 1.5832	4.00% 1.5832	4.00% 1.5832	Feb or Aug	Feb 2015
	Mar	4.00% 1.5520	4.00% 1.5520	4.00% 1.5520	4.00% 1.5520	4.00% 1.5832	4.00% 1.5832	4.00% 1.5832	Mar or Sep	Mar 2015
	Apr	4.00% 1.5520	4.00% 1.5520	4.00% 1.5520	4.00% 1.5520	4.00% 1.5520	4.00% 1.5832	4.00% 1.5832	Apr or Oct	Apr 2015
	May	4.00% 1.5520	4.00% 1.5520	4.00% 1.5520	4.00% 1.5520	4.00% 1.5520	4.00% 1.5520	??? 1.5832	May or Nov	May 2015
	Jun	4.00% 1.5216	4.00% 1.5520	4.00% 1.5520	4.00% 1.5520	4.00% 1.5520	4.00% 1.5520	4.00% 1.5520	Jun or Dec	Jun 2005
	Jul	4.00% 1.5216	4.00% 1.5216	4.00% 1.5520	4.00% 1.5520	4.00% 1.5520	4.00% 1.5520	4.00% 1.5520	Jan or Jul	Jul 2005
	Aug	4.00% 1.5216	4.00% 1.5216	4.00% 1.5216	4.00% 1.5520	4.00% 1.5520	4.00% 1.5520	4.00% 1.5520	Feb or Aug	Aug 2005
	Sep	4.00% 1.5216	4.00% 1.5216	4.00% 1.5216	4.00% 1.5216	4.00% 1.5520	4.00% 1.5520	4.00% 1.5520	Mar or Sep	Sep 2005
	Oct	4.00% 1.5216	4.00% 1.5216	4.00% 1.5216	4.00% 1.5216	4.00% 1.5216	4.00% 1.5520	4.00% 1.5520	Apr or Oct	Oct 2005
	Nov	4.00% 1.5216	4.00% 1.5216	4.00% 1.5216	4.00% 1.5216	4.00% 1.5216	4.00% 1.5216	??? 1.5520	May or Nov	Nov 2005
	Dec	4.00% 1.4920	4.00% 1.5216	4.00% 1.5216	4.00% 1.5216	4.00% 1.5216	4.00% 1.5216	4.00% 1.5216	Jun or Dec	Dec 2005

2004 only		Issue date through Dec 2004			Educa-tion eligible?	Alert Recommendation	Stops paying interest:	Issue month	Year and Series
Annual APY	Interest per $FV	Lifetime APY	Interest per $FV	% interest					
2.61%	0.0400	5.81%	1.0720	68%	No	A	Jul 2014	Jul	1984
2.61%	0.0400	5.81%	1.0720	68%	No	A	Aug 2014	Aug	EE
2.61%	0.0400	5.81%	1.0720	68%	No	A	Sep 2014	Sep	
2.61%	0.0400	5.81%	1.0720	68%	No	A	Oct 2014	Oct	
4.02%	0.0600	5.74%	1.0520	68%	No	A	Nov 2014	Nov	
4.02%	0.0600	5.74%	1.0520	68%	No	A	Dec 2014	Dec	
4.02%	0.0588	5.79%	1.0216	67%	No	A	Jan 2015	Jan	1985
4.02%	0.0588	5.79%	1.0216	67%	No	A	Feb 2015	Feb	EE
4.02%	0.0588	5.79%	1.0216	67%	No	A	Mar 2015	Mar	
4.02%	0.0588	5.79%	1.0216	67%	No	A	Apr 2015	Apr	
4.02%	0.0588	5.79%	1.0216	67%	No	A	May 2015	May	
4.02%	0.0588	5.79%	1.0216	67%	No	A	Jun 2015	Jun	
4.04%	0.0580	5.84%	0.9920	66%	No	A	Jul 2015	Jul	
4.04%	0.0580	5.84%	0.9920	66%	No	A	Aug 2015	Aug	
4.04%	0.0580	5.84%	0.9920	66%	No	A	Sep 2015	Sep	
4.04%	0.0580	5.84%	0.9920	66%	No	A	Oct 2015	Oct	
4.04%	0.0580	5.84%	0.9920	66%	No	A	Nov 2015	Nov	
4.04%	0.0580	5.84%	0.9920	66%	No	A	Dec 2015	Dec	

Year and Series	Issue month	Current interest rate and redemption value per $ of face value							To avoid rate penalty, redeem:	Maturity period ends:
		May 05	Jun 05	Jul 05	Aug 05	Sep 05	Oct 05	Nov 05		
1986 EE	Jan	4.00% 1.4920	4.00% 1.4920	4.00% 1.5216	4.00% 1.5216	4.00% 1.5216	4.00% 1.5216	4.00% 1.5216	Jan or Jul	Jan 2006
	Feb	4.00% 1.4920	4.00% 1.4920	4.00% 1.4920	4.00% 1.5216	4.00% 1.5216	4.00% 1.5216	4.00% 1.5216	Feb or Aug	Feb 2006
	Mar	4.00% 1.4920	4.00% 1.4920	4.00% 1.4920	4.00% 1.4920	4.00% 1.5216	4.00% 1.5216	4.00% 1.5216	Mar or Sep	Mar 2006
	Apr	4.00% 1.4920	4.00% 1.4920	4.00% 1.4920	4.00% 1.4920	4.00% 1.4920	4.00% 1.5216	4.00% 1.5216	Apr or Oct	Apr 2006
	May	4.00% 1.4920	4.00% 1.4920	4.00% 1.4920	4.00% 1.4920	4.00% 1.4920	4.00% 1.4920	??? 1.5216	May or Nov	May 2006
	Jun	4.00% 1.4628	4.00% 1.4920	4.00% 1.4920	4.00% 1.4920	4.00% 1.4920	4.00% 1.4920	4.00% 1.4920	Jun or Dec	Jun 2006
	Jul	4.00% 1.4628	4.00% 1.4628	4.00% 1.4920	4.00% 1.4920	4.00% 1.4920	4.00% 1.4920	4.00% 1.4920	Jan or Jul	Jul 2006
	Aug	4.00% 1.4628	4.00% 1.4628	4.00% 1.4628	4.00% 1.4920	4.00% 1.4920	4.00% 1.4920	4.00% 1.4920	Feb or Aug	Aug 2006
	Sep	4.00% 1.4628	4.00% 1.4628	4.00% 1.4628	4.00% 1.4628	4.00% 1.4920	4.00% 1.4920	4.00% 1.4920	Mar or Sep	Sep 2006
	Oct	4.00% 1.4628	4.00% 1.4628	4.00% 1.4628	4.00% 1.4628	4.00% 1.4628	4.00% 1.4920	4.00% 1.4920	Apr or Oct	Oct 2006
	Nov	4.00% 1.3152	4.00% 1.3152	4.00% 1.3152	4.00% 1.3152	4.00% 1.3152	4.00% 1.3152	??? 1.3412	May or Nov	Nov 2008
	Dec	4.00% 1.2892	4.00% 1.3152	4.00% 1.3152	4.00% 1.3152	4.00% 1.3152	4.00% 1.3152	4.00% 1.3152	Jun or Dec	Dec 2008
1987 EE	Jan	4.00% 1.2892	4.00% 1.2892	4.00% 1.3152	4.00% 1.3152	4.00% 1.3152	4.00% 1.3152	4.00% 1.3152	Jan or Jul	Jan 2009
	Feb	4.00% 1.2892	4.00% 1.2892	4.00% 1.2892	4.00% 1.3152	4.00% 1.3152	4.00% 1.3152	4.00% 1.3152	Feb or Aug	Feb 2009
	Mar	4.00% 1.2892	4.00% 1.2892	4.00% 1.2892	4.00% 1.2892	4.00% 1.3152	4.00% 1.3152	4.00% 1.3152	Mar or Sep	Mar 2009
	Apr	4.00% 1.2892	4.00% 1.2892	4.00% 1.2892	4.00% 1.2892	4.00% 1.2892	4.00% 1.3152	4.00% 1.3152	Apr or Oct	Apr 2009
	May	4.00% 1.2892	4.00% 1.2892	4.00% 1.2892	4.00% 1.2892	4.00% 1.2892	4.00% 1.2892	??? 1.3152	May or Nov	May 2009
	Jun	4.00% 1.2640	4.00% 1.2892	4.00% 1.2892	4.00% 1.2892	4.00% 1.2892	4.00% 1.2892	4.00% 1.2892	Jun or Dec	Jun 2009

2004 only		Issue date through Dec 2004			Educa-tion eligible?	Alert Recommendation	Stops paying interest:	Issue month	Year and Series
Annual APY	Interest per $FV	Lifetime APY	Interest per $FV	% interest					
4.04%	0.0568	5.89%	0.9628	66%	No	A	Jan 2016	Jan	**1986**
4.04%	0.0568	5.89%	0.9628	66%	No	A	Feb 2016	Feb	**EE**
4.04%	0.0568	5.89%	0.9628	66%	No	A	Mar 2016	Mar	
4.04%	0.0568	5.89%	0.9628	66%	No	A	Apr 2016	Apr	
4.04%	0.0568	5.89%	0.9628	66%	No	A	May 2016	May	
4.04%	0.0568	5.89%	0.9628	66%	No	A	Jun 2016	Jun	
4.03%	0.0556	5.94%	0.9340	65%	No	A	Jul 2016	Jul	
4.03%	0.0556	5.94%	0.9340	65%	No	A	Aug 2016	Aug	
4.03%	0.0556	5.94%	0.9340	65%	No	A	Sep 2016	Sep	
4.03%	0.0556	5.94%	0.9340	65%	No	A	Oct 2016	Oct	
3.87%	0.0480	5.33%	0.7892	61%	No	A	Nov 2016	Nov	
3.87%	0.0480	5.33%	0.7892	61%	No	A	Dec 2016	Dec	
3.27%	0.0400	5.37%	0.7640	60%	No	A	Jan 2017	Jan	**1987**
3.27%	0.0400	5.37%	0.7640	60%	No	A	Feb 2017	Feb	**EE**
3.27%	0.0400	5.37%	0.7640	60%	No	A	Mar 2017	Mar	
3.27%	0.0400	5.37%	0.7640	60%	No	A	Apr 2017	Apr	
4.05%	0.0492	5.37%	0.7640	60%	No	A	May 2017	May	
4.05%	0.0492	5.37%	0.7640	60%	No	A	Jun 2017	Jun	

Year and Series	Issue month	Current interest rate and redemption value per $ of face value							To avoid rate penalty, redeem:	Maturity period ends:
		May 05	Jun 05	Jul 05	Aug 05	Sep 05	Oct 05	Nov 05		
1987 **EE**	Jul	4.00% 1.2640	4.00% 1.2640	4.00% 1.2892	4.00% 1.2892	4.00% 1.2892	4.00% 1.2892	4.00% 1.2892	Jan or Jul	Jul 2009
	Aug	4.00% 1.2640	4.00% 1.2640	4.00% 1.2640	4.00% 1.2892	4.00% 1.2892	4.00% 1.2892	4.00% 1.2892	Feb or Aug	Aug 2009
	Sep	4.00% 1.2640	4.00% 1.2640	4.00% 1.2640	4.00% 1.2640	4.00% 1.2892	4.00% 1.2892	4.00% 1.2892	Mar or Sep	Sep 2009
	Oct	4.00% 1.2640	4.00% 1.2640	4.00% 1.2640	4.00% 1.2640	4.00% 1.2640	4.00% 1.2892	4.00% 1.2892	Apr or Oct	Oct 2009
	Nov	4.00% 1.2640	4.00% 1.2640	4.00% 1.2640	4.00% 1.2640	4.00% 1.2640	4.00% 1.2640	??? 1.2892	May or Nov	Nov 2009
	Dec	4.00% 1.2392	4.00% 1.2640	4.00% 1.2640	4.00% 1.2640	4.00% 1.2640	4.00% 1.2640	4.00% 1.2640	Jun or Dec	Dec 2009
1988 **EE**	Jan	4.00% 1.2392	4.00% 1.2392	4.00% 1.2640	4.00% 1.2640	4.00% 1.2640	4.00% 1.2640	4.00% 1.2640	Jan or Jul	Jan 2010
	Feb	4.00% 1.2392	4.00% 1.2392	4.00% 1.2392	4.00% 1.2640	4.00% 1.2640	4.00% 1.2640	4.00% 1.2640	Feb or Aug	Feb 2010
	Mar	4.00% 1.2392	4.00% 1.2392	4.00% 1.2392	4.00% 1.2392	4.00% 1.2640	4.00% 1.2640	4.00% 1.2640	Mar or Sep	Mar 2010
	Apr	4.00% 1.2392	4.00% 1.2392	4.00% 1.2392	4.00% 1.2392	4.00% 1.2392	4.00% 1.2640	4.00% 1.2640	Apr or Oct	Apr 2010
	May	4.00% 1.2392	4.00% 1.2392	4.00% 1.2392	4.00% 1.2392	4.00% 1.2392	4.00% 1.2392	??? 1.2640	May or Nov	May 2010
	Jun	4.00% 1.2148	4.00% 1.2392	4.00% 1.2392	4.00% 1.2392	4.00% 1.2392	4.00% 1.2392	4.00% 1.2392	Jun or Dec	Jun 2010
	Jul	4.00% 1.2148	4.00% 1.2148	4.00% 1.2392	4.00% 1.2392	4.00% 1.2392	4.00% 1.2392	4.00% 1.2392	Jan or Jul	Jul 2010
	Aug	4.00% 1.2148	4.00% 1.2148	4.00% 1.2148	4.00% 1.2392	4.00% 1.2392	4.00% 1.2392	4.00% 1.2392	Feb or Aug	Aug 2010
	Sep	4.00% 1.2148	4.00% 1.2148	4.00% 1.2148	4.00% 1.2148	4.00% 1.2392	4.00% 1.2392	4.00% 1.2392	Mar or Sep	Sep 2010
	Oct	4.00% 1.2148	4.00% 1.2148	4.00% 1.2148	4.00% 1.2148	4.00% 1.2148	4.00% 1.2392	4.00% 1.2392	Apr or Oct	Oct 2010
	Nov	4.00% 1.2148	4.00% 1.2148	4.00% 1.2148	4.00% 1.2148	4.00% 1.2148	4.00% 1.2148	??? 1.2392	May or Nov	Nov 2010
	Dec	4.00% 1.1912	4.00% 1.2148	4.00% 1.2148	4.00% 1.2148	4.00% 1.2148	4.00% 1.2148	4.00% 1.2148	Jun or Dec	Dec 2010

2004 only		Issue date through Dec 2004			Educa-tion eligible?	Alert Recommendation	Stops paying interest:	Issue month	Year and Series
Annual APY	Interest per $FV	Lifetime APY	Interest per $FV	% interest					
4.03%	0.0480	5.41%	0.7392	60%	No	A	Jul 2017	Jul	1987
4.03%	0.0480	5.41%	0.7392	60%	No	A	Aug 2017	Aug	EE
4.03%	0.0480	5.41%	0.7392	60%	No	A	Sep 2017	Sep	
4.03%	0.0480	5.41%	0.7392	60%	No	A	Oct 2017	Oct	
4.03%	0.0480	5.41%	0.7392	60%	No	A	Nov 2017	Nov	
4.03%	0.0480	5.41%	0.7392	60%	No	A	Dec 2017	Dec	
4.04%	0.0472	5.45%	0.7148	59%	No	A	Jan 2018	Jan	1988
4.04%	0.0472	5.45%	0.7148	59%	No	A	Feb 2018	Feb	EE
4.04%	0.0472	5.45%	0.7148	59%	No	A	Mar 2018	Mar	
4.04%	0.0472	5.45%	0.7148	59%	No	A	Apr 2018	Apr	
4.04%	0.0472	5.45%	0.7148	59%	No	A	May 2018	May	
4.04%	0.0472	5.45%	0.7148	59%	No	A	Jun 2018	Jun	
4.05%	0.0464	5.50%	0.6912	58%	No	A	Jul 2018	Jul	
4.05%	0.0464	5.50%	0.6912	58%	No	A	Aug 2018	Aug	
4.05%	0.0464	5.50%	0.6912	58%	No	A	Sep 2018	Sep	
4.05%	0.0464	5.50%	0.6912	58%	No	A	Oct 2018	Oct	
4.05%	0.0464	5.50%	0.6912	58%	No	A	Nov 2018	Nov	
4.05%	0.0464	5.50%	0.6912	58%	No	A	Dec 2018	Dec	

Year and Series	Issue month	Current interest rate and redemption value per $ of face value							To avoid rate penalty, redeem:	Maturity period ends:
		May 05	Jun 05	Jul 05	Aug 05	Sep 05	Oct 05	Nov 05		
1989 EE	Jan	4.00% 1.1912	4.00% 1.1912	4.00% 1.2148	4.00% 1.2148	4.00% 1.2148	4.00% 1.2148	4.00% 1.2148	Jan or Jul	Jan 2011
	Feb	4.00% 1.1912	4.00% 1.1912	4.00% 1.1912	4.00% 1.2148	4.00% 1.2148	4.00% 1.2148	4.00% 1.2148	Feb or Aug	Feb 2011
	Mar	4.00% 1.1912	4.00% 1.1912	4.00% 1.1912	4.00% 1.1912	4.00% 1.2148	4.00% 1.2148	4.00% 1.2148	Mar or Sep	Mar 2011
	Apr	4.00% 1.1912	4.00% 1.1912	4.00% 1.1912	4.00% 1.1912	4.00% 1.1912	4.00% 1.2148	4.00% 1.2148	Apr or Oct	Apr 2011
	May	4.00% 1.1912	4.00% 1.1912	4.00% 1.1912	4.00% 1.1912	4.00% 1.1912	4.00% 1.1912	??? 1.2148	May or Nov	May 2011
	Jun	4.00% 1.1676	4.00% 1.1912	4.00% 1.1912	4.00% 1.1912	4.00% 1.1912	4.00% 1.1912	4.00% 1.1912	Jun or Dec	Jun 2011
	Jul	4.00% 1.1676	4.00% 1.1676	4.00% 1.1912	4.00% 1.1912	4.00% 1.1912	4.00% 1.1912	4.00% 1.1912	Jan or Jul	Jul 2011
	Aug	4.00% 1.1676	4.00% 1.1676	4.00% 1.1676	4.00% 1.1912	4.00% 1.1912	4.00% 1.1912	4.00% 1.1912	Feb or Aug	Aug 2011
	Sep	4.00% 1.1676	4.00% 1.1676	4.00% 1.1676	4.00% 1.1676	4.00% 1.1912	4.00% 1.1912	4.00% 1.1912	Mar or Sep	Sep 2011
	Oct	4.00% 1.1676	4.00% 1.1676	4.00% 1.1676	4.00% 1.1676	4.00% 1.1676	4.00% 1.1912	4.00% 1.1912	Apr or Oct	Oct 2011
	Nov	4.00% 1.1676	4.00% 1.1676	4.00% 1.1676	4.00% 1.1676	4.00% 1.1676	4.00% 1.1676	??? 1.1912	May or Nov	Nov 2011
	Dec	4.00% 1.1448	4.00% 1.1676	4.00% 1.1676	4.00% 1.1676	4.00% 1.1676	4.00% 1.1676	4.00% 1.1676	Jun or Dec	Dec 2011
1990 EE	Jan	4.00% 1.1448	4.00% 1.1448	4.00% 1.1676	4.00% 1.1676	4.00% 1.1676	4.00% 1.1676	4.00% 1.1676	Jan or Jul	Jan 2012
	Feb	4.00% 1.1448	4.00% 1.1448	4.00% 1.1448	4.00% 1.1676	4.00% 1.1676	4.00% 1.1676	4.00% 1.1676	Feb or Aug	Feb 2012
	Mar	4.00% 1.1448	4.00% 1.1448	4.00% 1.1448	4.00% 1.1448	4.00% 1.1676	4.00% 1.1676	4.00% 1.1676	Mar or Sep	Mar 2012
	Apr	4.00% 1.1448	4.00% 1.1448	4.00% 1.1448	4.00% 1.1448	4.00% 1.1448	4.00% 1.1676	4.00% 1.1676	Apr or Oct	Apr 2012
	May	4.00% 1.1448	4.00% 1.1448	4.00% 1.1448	4.00% 1.1448	4.00% 1.1448	4.00% 1.1448	??? 1.1676	May or Nov	May 2012
	Jun	4.00% 1.1224	4.00% 1.1448	4.00% 1.1448	4.00% 1.1448	4.00% 1.1448	4.00% 1.1448	4.00% 1.1448	Jun or Dec	Jun 2012

2004 only		Issue date through Dec 2004			Educa-tion eligible?	Alert Recommendation	Stops paying interest:	Issue month	Year and Series
Annual APY	Interest per $FV	Lifetime APY	Interest per $FV	% interest					
4.03%	0.0452	5.55%	0.6676	57%	No	A	Jan 2019	Jan	**1989**
4.03%	0.0452	5.55%	0.6676	57%	No	A	Feb 2019	Feb	EE
4.03%	0.0452	5.55%	0.6676	57%	No	A	Mar 2019	Mar	
4.03%	0.0452	5.55%	0.6676	57%	No	A	Apr 2019	Apr	
4.03%	0.0452	5.55%	0.6676	57%	No	A	May 2019	May	
4.03%	0.0452	5.55%	0.6676	57%	No	A	Jun 2019	Jun	
4.03%	0.0444	5.60%	0.6448	56%	No	A	Jul 2019	Jul	
4.03%	0.0444	5.60%	0.6448	56%	No	A	Aug 2019	Aug	
4.03%	0.0444	5.60%	0.6448	56%	No	A	Sep 2019	Sep	
4.03%	0.0444	5.60%	0.6448	56%	No	A	Oct 2019	Oct	
4.03%	0.0444	5.60%	0.6448	56%	No	A	Nov 2019	Nov	
4.03%	0.0444	5.60%	0.6448	56%	No	A	Dec 2019	Dec	
4.04%	0.0436	5.66%	0.6224	55%	Yes	A	Jan 2020	Jan	**1990**
4.04%	0.0436	5.66%	0.6224	55%	Yes	A	Feb 2020	Feb	EE
4.04%	0.0436	5.66%	0.6224	55%	Yes	A	Mar 2020	Mar	
4.04%	0.0436	5.66%	0.6224	55%	Yes	A	Apr 2020	Apr	
4.04%	0.0436	5.66%	0.6224	55%	Yes	A	May 2020	May	
4.04%	0.0436	5.66%	0.6224	55%	Yes	A	Jun 2020	Jun	

Year and Series	Issue month	Current interest rate and redemption value per $ of face value							To avoid rate penalty, redeem:	Maturity period ends:
		May 05	Jun 05	Jul 05	Aug 05	Sep 05	Oct 05	Nov 05		
1990 EE	Jul	4.00% 1.1224	4.00% 1.1224	4.00% 1.1448	4.00% 1.1448	4.00% 1.1448	4.00% 1.1448	4.00% 1.1448	Jan or Jul	Jul 2012
	Aug	4.00% 1.1224	4.00% 1.1224	4.00% 1.1224	4.00% 1.1448	4.00% 1.1448	4.00% 1.1448	4.00% 1.1448	Feb or Aug	Aug 2012
	Sep	4.00% 1.1224	4.00% 1.1224	4.00% 1.1224	4.00% 1.1224	4.00% 1.1448	4.00% 1.1448	4.00% 1.1448	Mar or Sep	Sep 2012
	Oct	4.00% 1.1224	4.00% 1.1224	4.00% 1.1224	4.00% 1.1224	4.00% 1.1224	4.00% 1.1448	4.00% 1.1448	Apr or Oct	Oct 2012
	Nov	4.00% 1.1224	4.00% 1.1224	4.00% 1.1224	4.00% 1.1224	4.00% 1.1224	4.00% 1.1224	??? 1.1448	May or Nov	Nov 2012
	Dec	4.00% 1.1004	4.00% 1.1224	4.00% 1.1224	4.00% 1.1224	4.00% 1.1224	4.00% 1.1224	4.00% 1.1224	Jun or Dec	Dec 2012
1991 EE	Jan	4.00% 1.1004	4.00% 1.1004	4.00% 1.1224	4.00% 1.1224	4.00% 1.1224	4.00% 1.1224	4.00% 1.1224	Jan or Jul	Jan 2013
	Feb	4.00% 1.1004	4.00% 1.1004	4.00% 1.1004	4.00% 1.1224	4.00% 1.1224	4.00% 1.1224	4.00% 1.1224	Feb or Aug	Feb 2013
	Mar	4.00% 1.1004	4.00% 1.1004	4.00% 1.1004	4.00% 1.1004	4.00% 1.1224	4.00% 1.1224	4.00% 1.1224	Mar or Sep	Mar 2013
	Apr	4.00% 1.1004	4.00% 1.1004	4.00% 1.1004	4.00% 1.1004	4.00% 1.1004	4.00% 1.1224	4.00% 1.1224	Apr or Oct	Apr 2013
	May	4.00% 1.1004	4.00% 1.1004	4.00% 1.1004	4.00% 1.1004	4.00% 1.1004	4.00% 1.1004	??? 1.1224	May or Nov	May 2013
	Jun	4.00% 1.0788	4.00% 1.1004	4.00% 1.1004	4.00% 1.1004	4.00% 1.1004	4.00% 1.1004	4.00% 1.1004	Jun or Dec	Jun 2013
	Jul	4.00% 1.0788	4.00% 1.0788	4.00% 1.1004	4.00% 1.1004	4.00% 1.1004	4.00% 1.1004	4.00% 1.1004	Jan or Jul	Jul 2013
	Aug	4.00% 1.0788	4.00% 1.0788	4.00% 1.0788	4.00% 1.1004	4.00% 1.1004	4.00% 1.1004	4.00% 1.1004	Feb or Aug	Aug 2013
	Sep	4.00% 1.0788	4.00% 1.0788	4.00% 1.0788	4.00% 1.0788	4.00% 1.1004	4.00% 1.1004	4.00% 1.1004	Mar or Sep	Sep 2013
	Oct	4.00% 1.0788	4.00% 1.0788	4.00% 1.0788	4.00% 1.0788	4.00% 1.0788	4.00% 1.1004	4.00% 1.1004	Apr or Oct	Oct 2013
	Nov	4.00% 1.0788	4.00% 1.0788	4.00% 1.0788	4.00% 1.0788	4.00% 1.0788	4.00% 1.0788	??? 1.1004	May or Nov	Nov 2013
	Dec	4.00% 1.0576	4.00% 1.0788	4.00% 1.0788	4.00% 1.0788	4.00% 1.0788	4.00% 1.0788	4.00% 1.0788	Jun or Dec	Dec 2013

2004 only		Issue date through Dec 2004			Educa-tion eligible?	Alert Recommendation	Stops paying interest:	Issue month	Year and Series
Annual APY	Interest per $FV	Lifetime APY	Interest per $FV	% interest					
4.05%	0.0428	5.71%	0.6004	55%	Yes	A	Jul 2020	Jul	1990
4.05%	0.0428	5.71%	0.6004	55%	Yes	A	Aug 2020	Aug	EE
4.05%	0.0428	5.71%	0.6004	55%	Yes	A	Sep 2020	Sep	
4.05%	0.0428	5.71%	0.6004	55%	Yes	A	Oct 2020	Oct	
4.05%	0.0428	5.71%	0.6004	55%	Yes	A	Nov 2020	Nov	
4.05%	0.0428	5.71%	0.6004	55%	Yes	A	Dec 2020	Dec	
4.05%	0.0420	5.78%	0.5788	54%	Yes	A	Jan 2021	Jan	1991
4.05%	0.0420	5.78%	0.5788	54%	Yes	A	Feb 2021	Feb	EE
4.05%	0.0420	5.78%	0.5788	54%	Yes	A	Mar 2021	Mar	
4.05%	0.0420	5.78%	0.5788	54%	Yes	A	Apr 2021	Apr	
4.05%	0.0420	5.78%	0.5788	54%	Yes	A	May 2021	May	
4.05%	0.0420	5.78%	0.5788	54%	Yes	A	Jun 2021	Jun	
4.05%	0.0412	5.85%	0.5576	53%	Yes	A	Jul 2021	Jul	
4.05%	0.0412	5.85%	0.5576	53%	Yes	A	Aug 2021	Aug	
4.05%	0.0412	5.85%	0.5576	53%	Yes	A	Sep 2021	Sep	
4.05%	0.0412	5.85%	0.5576	53%	Yes	A	Oct 2021	Oct	
4.05%	0.0412	5.85%	0.5576	53%	Yes	A	Nov 2021	Nov	
4.05%	0.0412	5.85%	0.5576	53%	Yes	A	Dec 2021	Dec	

Year and Series	Issue month	Current interest rate and redemption value per $ of face value							To avoid rate penalty, redeem:	Maturity period ends:
		May 05	Jun 05	Jul 05	Aug 05	Sep 05	Oct 05	Nov 05		
1992 **EE**	Jan	4.00% 1.0576	4.00% 1.0576	4.00% 1.0788	4.00% 1.0788	4.00% 1.0788	4.00% 1.0788	4.00% 1.0788	Jan or Jul	Jan 2014
	Feb	4.00% 1.0576	4.00% 1.0576	4.00% 1.0576	4.00% 1.0788	4.00% 1.0788	4.00% 1.0788	4.00% 1.0788	Feb or Aug	Feb 2014
	Mar	4.00% 1.0576	4.00% 1.0576	4.00% 1.0576	4.00% 1.0576	4.00% 1.0788	4.00% 1.0788	4.00% 1.0788	Mar or Sep	Mar 2014
	Apr	4.00% 1.0576	4.00% 1.0576	4.00% 1.0576	4.00% 1.0576	4.00% 1.0576	4.00% 1.0788	4.00% 1.0788	Apr or Oct	Apr 2014
	May	4.00% 1.0576	4.00% 1.0576	4.00% 1.0576	4.00% 1.0576	4.00% 1.0576	4.00% 1.0576	??? 1.0788	May or Nov	May 2014
	Jun	4.00% 1.0368	4.00% 1.0576	4.00% 1.0576	4.00% 1.0576	4.00% 1.0576	4.00% 1.0576	4.00% 1.0576	Jun or Dec	Jun 2014
	Jul	4.00% 1.0368	4.00% 1.0368	4.00% 1.0576	4.00% 1.0576	4.00% 1.0576	4.00% 1.0576	4.00% 1.0576	Jan or Jul	Jul 2014
	Aug	4.00% 1.0368	4.00% 1.0368	4.00% 1.0368	4.00% 1.0576	4.00% 1.0576	4.00% 1.0576	4.00% 1.0576	Feb or Aug	Aug 2014
	Sep	4.00% 1.0368	4.00% 1.0368	4.00% 1.0368	4.00% 1.0368	4.00% 1.0576	4.00% 1.0576	4.00% 1.0576	Mar or Sep	Sep 2014
	Oct	4.00% 1.0368	4.00% 1.0368	4.00% 1.0368	4.00% 1.0368	4.00% 1.0368	4.00% 1.0576	4.00% 1.0576	Apr or Oct	Oct 2014
	Nov	4.00% 1.0368	4.00% 1.0368	4.00% 1.0368	4.00% 1.0368	4.00% 1.0368	4.00% 1.0368	??? 1.0576	May or Nov	Nov 2014
	Dec	4.00% 1.0164	4.00% 1.0368	4.00% 1.0368	4.00% 1.0368	4.00% 1.0368	4.00% 1.0368	4.00% 1.0368	Jun or Dec	Dec 2014
1993 **EE**	Jan	4.00% 1.0164	4.00% 1.0164	4.00% 1.0368	4.00% 1.0368	4.00% 1.0368	4.00% 1.0368	4.00% 1.0368	Jan or Jul	Jan 2015
	Feb	4.00% 1.0164	4.00% 1.0164	4.00% 1.0164	4.00% 1.0368	4.00% 1.0368	4.00% 1.0368	4.00% 1.0368	Feb or Aug	Feb 2015
	Mar	3.03% 0.8552	3.03% 0.8552	3.03% 0.8552	3.03% 0.8552	3.16% 0.8680	3.16% 0.8680	3.16% 0.8680	Mar or Sep	Mar 2011
	Apr	3.03% 0.8552	3.03% 0.8552	3.03% 0.8552	3.03% 0.8552	3.03% 0.8552	3.16% 0.8680	3.16% 0.8680	Apr or Oct	Apr 2011
	May	3.19% 0.8472	3.19% 0.8472	3.19% 0.8472	3.19% 0.8472	3.19% 0.8472	3.19% 0.8472	??? 0.8608	May or Nov	May 2011
	Jun	3.06% 0.8344	3.19% 0.8472	3.19% 0.8472	3.19% 0.8472	3.19% 0.8472	3.19% 0.8472	3.19% 0.8472	Jun or Dec	Jun 2011

2004 only		Issue date through Dec 2004			Educa-tion eligible?	Alert Recommendation	Stops paying interest:	Issue month	Year and Series
Annual APY	Interest per $FV	Lifetime APY	Interest per $FV	% interest					
5.07%	0.0500	5.92%	0.5368	52%	Yes	A	Jan 2022	Jan	**1992**
5.07%	0.0500	5.92%	0.5368	52%	Yes	A	Feb 2022	Feb	**EE**
5.07%	0.0500	5.92%	0.5368	52%	Yes	A	Mar 2022	Mar	
5.07%	0.0500	5.92%	0.5368	52%	Yes	A	Apr 2022	Apr	
5.07%	0.0500	5.92%	0.5368	52%	Yes	A	May 2022	May	
5.07%	0.0500	5.92%	0.5368	52%	Yes	A	Jun 2022	Jun	
6.05%	0.0580	6.00%	0.5164	51%	Yes	A	Jul 2022	Jul	
6.05%	0.0580	6.00%	0.5164	51%	Yes	A	Aug 2022	Aug	
6.05%	0.0580	6.00%	0.5164	51%	Yes	A	Sep 2022	Sep	
6.05%	0.0580	6.00%	0.5164	51%	Yes	A	Oct 2022	Oct	
6.05%	0.0580	6.00%	0.5164	51%	Yes	A	Nov 2022	Nov	
6.05%	0.0580	6.00%	0.5164	51%	Yes	A	Dec 2022	Dec	
6.06%	0.0564	6.00%	0.4868	49%	Yes	A	Jan 2023	Jan	**1993**
6.06%	0.0564	6.00%	0.4868	49%	Yes	A	Feb 2023	Feb	**EE**
2.53%	0.0208	4.60%	0.3436	41%	Yes	B-	Mar 2023	Mar	
2.53%	0.0208	4.60%	0.3436	41%	Yes	B-	Apr 2023	Apr	
2.66%	0.0216	4.50%	0.3344	40%	Yes	B-	May 2023	May	
2.66%	0.0216	4.50%	0.3344	40%	Yes	B-	Jun 2023	Jun	

Year and Series	Issue month	Current interest rate and redemption value per $ of face value							To avoid rate penalty, redeem:	Maturity period ends:
		May 05	Jun 05	Jul 05	Aug 05	Sep 05	Oct 05	Nov 05		
1993 **EE**	Jul	3.06% 0.8344	3.06% 0.8344	3.19% 0.8472	3.19% 0.8472	3.19% 0.8472	3.19% 0.8472	3.19% 0.8472	Jan or Jul	Jul 2011
	Aug	3.06% 0.8344	3.06% 0.8344	3.06% 0.8344	3.19% 0.8472	3.19% 0.8472	3.19% 0.8472	3.19% 0.8472	Feb or Aug	Aug 2011
	Sep	3.06% 0.8344	3.06% 0.8344	3.06% 0.8344	3.06% 0.8344	3.19% 0.8472	3.19% 0.8472	3.19% 0.8472	Mar or Sep	Sep 2011
	Oct	3.06% 0.8344	3.06% 0.8344	3.06% 0.8344	3.06% 0.8344	3.06% 0.8344	3.19% 0.8472	3.19% 0.8472	Apr or Oct	Oct 2011
	Nov	3.22% 0.8268	3.22% 0.8268	3.22% 0.8268	3.22% 0.8268	3.22% 0.8268	3.22% 0.8268	??? 0.8400	May or Nov	Nov 2011
	Dec	3.10% 0.8144	3.22% 0.8268	3.22% 0.8268	3.22% 0.8268	3.22% 0.8268	3.22% 0.8268	3.22% 0.8268	Jun or Dec	Dec 2011
1994 **EE**	Jan	3.10% 0.8144	3.10% 0.8144	3.22% 0.8268	3.22% 0.8268	3.22% 0.8268	3.22% 0.8268	3.22% 0.8268	Jan or Jul	Jan 2012
	Feb	3.10% 0.8144	3.10% 0.8144	3.10% 0.8144	3.22% 0.8268	3.22% 0.8268	3.22% 0.8268	3.22% 0.8268	Feb or Aug	Feb 2012
	Mar	3.10% 0.8144	3.10% 0.8144	3.10% 0.8144	3.10% 0.8144	3.22% 0.8268	3.22% 0.8268	3.22% 0.8268	Mar or Sep	Mar 2012
	Apr	3.10% 0.8144	3.10% 0.8144	3.10% 0.8144	3.10% 0.8144	3.10% 0.8144	3.22% 0.8268	3.22% 0.8268	Apr or Oct	Apr 2012
	May	3.28% 0.8100	3.28% 0.8100	3.28% 0.8100	3.28% 0.8100	3.28% 0.8100	3.28% 0.8100	??? 0.8232	May or Nov	May 2012
	Jun	2.97% 0.7980	3.28% 0.8100	3.28% 0.8100	3.28% 0.8100	3.28% 0.8100	3.28% 0.8100	3.28% 0.8100	Jun or Dec	Jun 2012
	Jul	2.97% 0.7980	2.97% 0.7980	3.28% 0.8100	3.28% 0.8100	3.28% 0.8100	3.28% 0.8100	3.28% 0.8100	Jan or Jul	Jul 2012
	Aug	2.97% 0.7980	2.97% 0.7980	2.97% 0.7980	3.28% 0.8100	3.28% 0.8100	3.28% 0.8100	3.28% 0.8100	Feb or Aug	Aug 2012
	Sep	2.97% 0.7980	2.97% 0.7980	2.97% 0.7980	2.97% 0.7980	3.28% 0.8100	3.28% 0.8100	3.28% 0.8100	Mar or Sep	Sep 2012
	Oct	2.97% 0.7980	2.97% 0.7980	2.97% 0.7980	2.97% 0.7980	2.97% 0.7980	3.28% 0.8100	3.28% 0.8100	Apr or Oct	Oct 2012
	Nov	3.10% 0.7916	3.10% 0.7916	3.10% 0.7916	3.10% 0.7916	3.10% 0.7916	3.10% 0.7916	??? 0.8036	May or Nov	Nov 2012
	Dec	3.03% 0.7796	3.10% 0.7916	3.10% 0.7916	3.10% 0.7916	3.10% 0.7916	3.10% 0.7916	3.10% 0.7916	Jun or Dec	Dec 2012

2004 only		Issue date through Dec 2004			Educa-tion eligible?	Alert Recommendation	Stops paying interest:	Issue month	Year and Series
Annual APY	Interest per $FV	Lifetime APY	Interest per $FV	% interest					
2.54%	0.0204	4.58%	0.3232	39%	Yes	B-	Jul 2023	Jul	1993
2.54%	0.0204	4.58%	0.3232	39%	Yes	B-	Aug 2023	Aug	EE
2.54%	0.0204	4.58%	0.3232	39%	Yes	B-	Sep 2023	Sep	
2.54%	0.0204	4.58%	0.3232	39%	Yes	B-	Oct 2023	Oct	
2.52%	0.0200	4.48%	0.3144	39%	Yes	B-	Nov 2023	Nov	
2.52%	0.0200	4.48%	0.3144	39%	Yes	B-	Dec 2023	Dec	
2.50%	0.0196	4.57%	0.3036	38%	Yes	B-	Jan 2024	Jan	1994
2.50%	0.0196	4.57%	0.3036	38%	Yes	B-	Feb 2024	Feb	EE
2.50%	0.0196	4.57%	0.3036	38%	Yes	B-	Mar 2024	Mar	
2.50%	0.0196	4.57%	0.3036	38%	Yes	B-	Apr 2024	Apr	
2.62%	0.0204	4.50%	0.2980	37%	Yes	B-	May 2024	May	
2.62%	0.0204	4.50%	0.2980	37%	Yes	B-	Jun 2024	Jun	
2.55%	0.0196	4.59%	0.2872	36%	Yes	B-	Jul 2024	Jul	
2.55%	0.0196	4.59%	0.2872	36%	Yes	B-	Aug 2024	Aug	
2.55%	0.0196	4.59%	0.2872	36%	Yes	B-	Sep 2024	Sep	
2.55%	0.0196	4.59%	0.2872	36%	Yes	B-	Oct 2024	Oct	
2.63%	0.0200	4.49%	0.2796	36%	Yes	B--	Nov 2024	Nov	
2.63%	0.0200	4.49%	0.2796	36%	Yes	B--	Dec 2024	Dec	

Year and Series	Issue month	Current interest rate and redemption value per $ of face value							To avoid rate penalty, redeem:	Maturity period ends:
		May 05	**Jun 05**	**Jul 05**	**Aug 05**	**Sep 05**	**Oct 05**	**Nov 05**		
1995 EE	Jan	3.03% 0.7796	3.03% 0.7796	3.10% 0.7916	3.10% 0.7916	3.10% 0.7916	3.10% 0.7916	3.10% 0.7916	Jan or Jul	Jan 2013
	Feb	3.03% 0.7796	3.03% 0.7796	3.03% 0.7796	3.10% 0.7916	3.10% 0.7916	3.10% 0.7916	3.10% 0.7916	Feb or Aug	Feb 2013
	Mar	3.03% 0.7796	3.03% 0.7796	3.03% 0.7796	3.03% 0.7796	3.10% 0.7916	3.10% 0.7916	3.10% 0.7916	Mar or Sep	Mar 2013
	Apr	3.03% 0.7796	3.03% 0.7796	3.03% 0.7796	3.03% 0.7796	3.03% 0.7796	3.10% 0.7916	3.10% 0.7916	Apr or Oct	Apr 2013
	May	3.23% 0.7464	3.23% 0.7464	3.23% 0.7464	3.23% 0.7464	3.23% 0.7464	3.23% 0.7464	??? 0.7584	May or Nov	May 2012
	Jun	3.07% 0.7352	3.23% 0.7464	3.23% 0.7464	3.23% 0.7464	3.23% 0.7464	3.23% 0.7464	3.23% 0.7464	Jun or Dec	Jun 2012
	Jul	3.07% 0.7352	3.07% 0.7352	3.23% 0.7464	3.23% 0.7464	3.23% 0.7464	3.23% 0.7464	3.23% 0.7464	Jan or Jul	Jul 2012
	Aug	3.07% 0.7352	3.07% 0.7352	3.07% 0.7352	3.23% 0.7464	3.23% 0.7464	3.23% 0.7464	3.23% 0.7464	Feb or Aug	Aug 2012
	Sep	3.07% 0.7352	3.07% 0.7352	3.07% 0.7352	3.07% 0.7352	3.23% 0.7464	3.23% 0.7464	3.23% 0.7464	Mar or Sep	Sep 2012
	Oct	3.07% 0.7352	3.07% 0.7352	3.07% 0.7352	3.07% 0.7352	3.07% 0.7352	3.23% 0.7464	3.23% 0.7464	Apr or Oct	Oct 2012
	Nov	3.23% 0.7272	3.23% 0.7272	3.23% 0.7272	3.23% 0.7272	3.23% 0.7272	3.23% 0.7272	??? 0.7388	May or Nov	Nov 2012
	Dec	3.07% 0.7164	3.23% 0.7272	3.23% 0.7272	3.23% 0.7272	3.23% 0.7272	3.23% 0.7272	3.23% 0.7272	Jun or Dec	Dec 2012
1996 EE	Jan	3.07% 0.7164	3.07% 0.7164	3.23% 0.7272	3.23% 0.7272	3.23% 0.7272	3.23% 0.7272	3.23% 0.7272	Jan or Jul	Jan 2013
	Feb	3.07% 0.7164	3.07% 0.7164	3.07% 0.7164	3.23% 0.7272	3.23% 0.7272	3.23% 0.7272	3.23% 0.7272	Feb or Aug	Feb 2013
	Mar	3.07% 0.7164	3.07% 0.7164	3.07% 0.7164	3.07% 0.7164	3.23% 0.7272	3.23% 0.7272	3.23% 0.7272	Mar or Sep	Mar 2013
	Apr	3.07% 0.7164	3.07% 0.7164	3.07% 0.7164	3.07% 0.7164	3.07% 0.7164	3.23% 0.7272	3.23% 0.7272	Apr or Oct	Apr 2013
	May	3.23% 0.7100	3.23% 0.7100	3.23% 0.7100	3.23% 0.7100	3.23% 0.7100	3.23% 0.7100	??? 0.7216	May or Nov	May 2013
	Jun	3.07% 0.6992	3.23% 0.7100	3.23% 0.7100	3.23% 0.7100	3.23% 0.7100	3.23% 0.7100	3.23% 0.7100	Jun or Dec	Jun 2013

2004 only		Issue date through Dec 2004			Educa-tion eligible?	Alert Recommendation	Stops paying interest:	Issue month	Year and Series
Annual APY	Interest per $FV	Lifetime APY	Interest per $FV	% interest					
2.45%	0.0184	4.58%	0.2688	35%	Yes	B--	Jan 2025	Jan	**1995**
2.45%	0.0184	4.58%	0.2688	35%	Yes	B--	Feb 2025	Feb	**EE**
2.45%	0.0184	4.58%	0.2688	35%	Yes	B--	Mar 2025	Mar	
2.45%	0.0184	4.58%	0.2688	35%	Yes	B--	Apr 2025	Apr	
2.57%	0.0184	4.10%	0.2352	32%	Yes	B-	May 2025	May	
2.57%	0.0184	4.10%	0.2352	32%	Yes	B-	Jun 2025	Jun	
2.49%	0.0176	4.18%	0.2256	31%	Yes	B-	Jul 2025	Jul	
2.49%	0.0176	4.18%	0.2256	31%	Yes	B-	Aug 2025	Aug	
2.49%	0.0176	4.18%	0.2256	31%	Yes	B-	Sep 2025	Sep	
2.49%	0.0176	4.18%	0.2256	31%	Yes	B-	Oct 2025	Oct	
2.64%	0.0184	4.04%	0.2164	30%	Yes	B-	Nov 2025	Nov	
2.64%	0.0184	4.04%	0.2164	30%	Yes	B-	Dec 2025	Dec	
2.55%	0.0176	4.11%	0.2068	29%	Yes	B-	Jan 2026	Jan	**1996**
2.55%	0.0176	4.11%	0.2068	29%	Yes	B-	Feb 2026	Feb	**EE**
2.55%	0.0176	4.11%	0.2068	29%	Yes	B-	Mar 2026	Mar	
2.55%	0.0176	4.11%	0.2068	29%	Yes	B-	Apr 2026	Apr	
2.58%	0.0176	3.98%	0.1992	28%	Yes	B-	May 2026	May	
2.58%	0.0176	3.98%	0.1992	28%	Yes	D-	Jun 2026	Jun	

Year and Series	Issue month	Current interest rate and redemption value per $ of face value							To avoid rate penalty, redeem:	Maturity period ends:
		May 05	Jun 05	Jul 05	Aug 05	Sep 05	Oct 05	Nov 05		
1996 **EE**	Jul	3.07% 0.6992	3.07% 0.6992	3.23% 0.7100	3.23% 0.7100	3.23% 0.7100	3.23% 0.7100	3.23% 0.7100	Jan or Jul	Jul 2013
	Aug	3.07% 0.6992	3.07% 0.6992	3.07% 0.6992	3.23% 0.7100	3.23% 0.7100	3.23% 0.7100	3.23% 0.7100	Feb or Aug	Aug 2013
	Sep	3.07% 0.6992	3.07% 0.6992	3.07% 0.6992	3.07% 0.6992	3.23% 0.7100	3.23% 0.7100	3.23% 0.7100	Mar or Sep	Sep 2013
	Oct	3.07% 0.6992	3.07% 0.6992	3.07% 0.6992	3.07% 0.6992	3.07% 0.6992	3.23% 0.7100	3.23% 0.7100	Apr or Oct	Oct 2013
	Nov	3.23% 0.6944	3.23% 0.6944	3.23% 0.6944	3.23% 0.6944	3.23% 0.6944	3.23% 0.6944	??? 0.7056	May or Nov	Nov 2013
	Dec	3.07% 0.6840	3.23% 0.6944	3.23% 0.6944	3.23% 0.6944	3.23% 0.6944	3.23% 0.6944	3.23% 0.6944	Jun or Dec	Dec 2013
1997 **EE**	Jan	3.07% 0.6840	3.07% 0.6840	3.23% 0.6944	3.23% 0.6944	3.23% 0.6944	3.23% 0.6944	3.23% 0.6944	Jan or Jul	Jan 2014
	Feb	3.07% 0.6840	3.07% 0.6840	3.07% 0.6840	3.23% 0.6944	3.23% 0.6944	3.23% 0.6944	3.23% 0.6944	Feb or Aug	Feb 2014
	Mar	3.07% 0.6840	3.07% 0.6840	3.07% 0.6840	3.07% 0.6840	3.23% 0.6944	3.23% 0.6944	3.23% 0.6944	Mar or Sep	Mar 2014
	Apr	3.07% 0.6840	3.07% 0.6840	3.07% 0.6840	3.07% 0.6840	3.07% 0.6840	3.23% 0.6944	3.23% 0.6944	Apr or Oct	Apr 2014
	May	3.42% 0.7032	3.42% 0.7052	3.42% 0.7072	3.42% 0.7092	3.42% 0.7112	3.42% 0.7132	??? 0.7152	1st of any month	May 2014
	Jun	3.25% 0.7012	3.42% 0.7032	3.42% 0.7052	3.42% 0.7072	3.42% 0.7092	3.42% 0.7112	3.42% 0.7132	1st of any month	Jun 2014
	Jul	3.25% 0.6996	3.25% 0.7012	3.42% 0.7032	3.42% 0.7052	3.42% 0.7072	3.42% 0.7092	3.42% 0.7112	1st of any month	Jul 2014
	Aug	3.25% 0.6976	3.25% 0.6996	3.25% 0.7012	3.42% 0.7032	3.42% 0.7052	3.42% 0.7072	3.42% 0.7092	1st of any month	Aug 2014
	Sep	3.25% 0.6956	3.25% 0.6976	3.25% 0.6996	3.25% 0.7012	3.42% 0.7032	3.42% 0.7052	3.42% 0.7072	1st of any month	Sep 2014
	Oct	3.25% 0.6940	3.25% 0.6956	3.25% 0.6976	3.25% 0.6996	3.25% 0.7012	3.42% 0.7032	3.42% 0.7052	1st of any month	Oct 2014
	Nov	3.42% 0.6832	3.42% 0.6852	3.42% 0.6872	3.42% 0.6892	3.42% 0.6908	3.42% 0.6928	??? 0.6948	1st of any month	Nov 2014
	Dec	3.25% 0.6816	3.42% 0.6832	3.42% 0.6852	3.42% 0.6872	3.42% 0.6892	3.42% 0.6908	3.42% 0.6928	1st of any month	Dec 2014

2004 only		Issue date through Dec 2004			Educa-tion eligible?	Alert Recommendation	Stops paying interest:	Issue month	Year and Series
Annual APY	Interest per $FV	Lifetime APY	Interest per $FV	% interest					
2.50%	0.0168	4.07%	0.1900	28%	Yes	B-	Jul 2026	**Jul**	**1996**
2.50%	0.0168	4.07%	0.1900	28%	Yes	B-	Aug 2026	**Aug**	**EE**
2.50%	0.0168	4.07%	0.1900	28%	Yes	B-	Sep 2026	**Sep**	
2.50%	0.0168	4.07%	0.1900	28%	Yes	B-	Oct 2026	**Oct**	
2.64%	0.0176	3.96%	0.1840	27%	Yes	B-	Nov 2026	**Nov**	
2.64%	0.0176	3.96%	0.1840	27%	Yes	B-	Dec 2026	**Dec**	
2.55%	0.0168	4.04%	0.1748	26%	Yes	B-	Jan 2027	**Jan**	**1997**
2.55%	0.0168	4.04%	0.1748	26%	Yes	B-	Feb 2027	**Feb**	**EE**
2.55%	0.0168	4.04%	0.1748	26%	Yes	B-	Mar 2027	**Mar**	
2.55%	0.0168	4.04%	0.1748	26%	Yes	B-	Apr 2027	**Apr**	
2.78%	0.0188	4.37%	0.1940	28%	Yes	B	May 2027	**May**	
2.73%	0.0184	4.38%	0.1920	28%	Yes	B	Jun 2027	**Jun**	
2.74%	0.0184	4.40%	0.1904	28%	Yes	B	Jul 2027	**Jul**	
2.68%	0.0180	4.42%	0.1888	27%	Yes	B	Aug 2027	**Aug**	
2.69%	0.0180	4.43%	0.1872	27%	Yes	B	Sep 2027	**Sep**	
2.70%	0.0180	4.45%	0.1856	27%	Yes	B	Oct 2027	**Oct**	
2.80%	0.0184	4.27%	0.1744	26%	Yes	B	Nov 2027	**Nov**	
2.75%	0.0180	4.28%	0.1724	26%	Yes	B	Dec 2027	**Dec**	

Year and Series	Issue month	Current interest rate and redemption value per $ of face value							To avoid rate penalty, redeem:	Maturity period ends:
		May 05	Jun 05	Jul 05	Aug 05	Sep 05	Oct 05	Nov 05		
1998 **EE**	Jan	3.25% 0.6796	3.25% 0.6816	3.42% 0.6832	3.42% 0.6852	3.42% 0.6872	3.42% 0.6892	3.42% 0.6908	1st of any month	Jan 2015
	Feb	3.25% 0.6780	3.25% 0.6796	3.25% 0.6816	3.42% 0.6832	3.42% 0.6852	3.42% 0.6872	3.42% 0.6892	1st of any month	Feb 2015
	Mar	3.25% 0.6760	3.25% 0.6780	3.25% 0.6796	3.25% 0.6816	3.42% 0.6832	3.42% 0.6852	3.42% 0.6872	1st of any month	Mar 2015
	Apr	3.25% 0.6744	3.25% 0.6760	3.25% 0.6780	3.25% 0.6796	3.25% 0.6816	3.42% 0.6832	3.42% 0.6852	1st of any month	Apr 2015
	May	3.42% 0.6648	3.42% 0.6668	3.42% 0.6684	3.42% 0.6704	3.42% 0.6724	3.42% 0.6744	??? 0.6760	1st of any month	May 2015
	Jun	3.25% 0.6628	3.42% 0.6648	3.42% 0.6668	3.42% 0.6684	3.42% 0.6704	3.42% 0.6724	3.42% 0.6744	1st of any month	Jun 2015
	Jul	3.25% 0.6612	3.25% 0.6628	3.42% 0.6648	3.42% 0.6668	3.42% 0.6684	3.42% 0.6704	3.42% 0.6724	1st of any month	Jul 2015
	Aug	3.25% 0.6592	3.25% 0.6612	3.25% 0.6628	3.42% 0.6648	3.42% 0.6668	3.42% 0.6684	3.42% 0.6704	1st of any month	Aug 2015
	Sep	3.25% 0.6576	3.25% 0.6592	3.25% 0.6612	3.25% 0.6628	3.42% 0.6648	3.42% 0.6668	3.42% 0.6684	1st of any month	Sep 2015
	Oct	3.25% 0.6556	3.25% 0.6576	3.25% 0.6592	3.25% 0.6612	3.25% 0.6628	3.42% 0.6648	3.42% 0.6668	1st of any month	Oct 2015
	Nov	3.42% 0.6476	3.42% 0.6496	3.42% 0.6512	3.42% 0.6532	3.42% 0.6548	3.42% 0.6568	??? 0.6588	1st of any month	Nov 2015
	Dec	3.25% 0.6460	3.42% 0.6476	3.42% 0.6496	3.42% 0.6512	3.42% 0.6532	3.42% 0.6548	3.42% 0.6568	1st of any month	Dec 2015
1999 **EE**	Jan	3.25% 0.6440	3.25% 0.6460	3.42% 0.6476	3.42% 0.6496	3.42% 0.6512	3.42% 0.6532	3.42% 0.6548	1st of any month	Jan 2016
	Feb	3.25% 0.6424	3.25% 0.6440	3.25% 0.6460	3.42% 0.6476	3.42% 0.6496	3.42% 0.6512	3.42% 0.6532	1st of any month	Feb 2016
	Mar	3.25% 0.6408	3.25% 0.6424	3.25% 0.6440	3.25% 0.6460	3.42% 0.6476	3.42% 0.6496	3.42% 0.6512	1st of any month	Mar 2016
	Apr	3.25% 0.6388	3.25% 0.6408	3.25% 0.6424	3.25% 0.6440	3.25% 0.6460	3.42% 0.6476	3.42% 0.6496	1st of any month	Apr 2016
	May	3.42% 0.6340	3.42% 0.6356	3.42% 0.6376	3.42% 0.6392	3.42% 0.6412	3.42% 0.6432	??? 0.6448	1st of any month	May 2016
	Jun	3.25% 0.6324	3.42% 0.6340	3.42% 0.6356	3.42% 0.6376	3.42% 0.6392	3.42% 0.6412	3.42% 0.6432	1st of any month	Jun 2016

2004 only		Issue date through Dec 2004			Educa-tion eligible?	Alert Recommendation	Stops paying interest:	Issue month	Year and Series
Annual APY	Interest per $FV	Lifetime APY	Interest per $FV	% interest					
2.69%	0.0176	4.29%	0.1708	25%	Yes	B	Jan 2028	Jan	**1998**
2.70%	0.0176	4.31%	0.1692	25%	Yes	B	Feb 2028	Feb	**EE**
2.64%	0.0172	4.33%	0.1676	25%	Yes	B	Mar 2028	Mar	
2.65%	0.0172	4.35%	0.1660	25%	Yes	B	Apr 2028	Apr	
2.82%	0.0180	4.16%	0.1556	24%	Yes	B	May 2028	May	
2.77%	0.0176	4.17%	0.1540	24%	Yes	B	Jun 2028	Jun	
2.77%	0.0176	4.19%	0.1524	23%	Yes	B	Jul 2028	Jul	
2.71%	0.0172	4.21%	0.1508	23%	Yes	B	Aug 2028	Aug	
2.72%	0.0172	4.22%	0.1492	23%	Yes	B	Sep 2028	Sep	
2.73%	0.0172	4.25%	0.1480	23%	Yes	B	Oct 2028	Oct	
2.77%	0.0172	4.07%	0.1388	22%	Yes	B	Nov 2028	Nov	
2.71%	0.0168	4.08%	0.1372	22%	Yes	B	Dec 2028	Dec	
3.38%	0.0208	4.11%	0.1360	21%	Yes	B	Jan 2029	Jan	**1999**
3.39%	0.0208	4.12%	0.1344	21%	Yes	B	Feb 2029	Feb	**EE**
3.33%	0.0204	4.14%	0.1328	21%	Yes	B	Mar 2029	Mar	
3.34%	0.0204	4.15%	0.1312	21%	Yes	B	Apr 2029	Apr	
3.51%	0.0212	4.05%	0.1256	20%	Yes	B	May 2029	May	
3.45%	0.0208	4.07%	0.1240	20%	Yes	B	Jun 2029	Jun	

Year and Series	Issue month	Current interest rate and redemption value per $ of face value							To avoid rate penalty, redeem:	Maturity period ends:
		May 05	Jun 05	Jul 05	Aug 05	Sep 05	Oct 05	Nov 05		
1999 **EE**	Jul	3.25% 0.6308	3.25% 0.6324	3.42% 0.6340	3.42% 0.6356	3.42% 0.6376	3.42% 0.6392	3.42% 0.6412	1st of any month	Jul 2016
	Aug	3.25% 0.6292	3.25% 0.6308	3.25% 0.6324	3.42% 0.6340	3.42% 0.6356	3.42% 0.6376	3.42% 0.6392	1st of any month	Aug 2016
	Sep	3.25% 0.6272	3.25% 0.6292	3.25% 0.6308	3.25% 0.6324	3.42% 0.6340	3.42% 0.6356	3.42% 0.6376	1st of any month	Sep 2016
	Oct	3.25% 0.6256	3.25% 0.6272	3.25% 0.6292	3.25% 0.6308	3.25% 0.6324	3.42% 0.6340	3.42% 0.6356	1st of any month	Oct 2016
	Nov	3.42% 0.6200	3.42% 0.6216	3.42% 0.6236	3.42% 0.6252	3.42% 0.6272	3.42% 0.6288	??? 0.6308	1st of any month	Nov 2016
	Dec	3.25% 0.6184	3.42% 0.6200	3.42% 0.6216	3.42% 0.6236	3.42% 0.6252	3.42% 0.6272	3.42% 0.6288	1st of any month	Dec 2016
2000 **EE**	Jan	3.25% 0.6164	3.25% 0.6184	3.42% 0.6200	3.42% 0.6216	3.42% 0.6236	3.42% 0.6252	3.42% 0.6272	1st of any month	Jan 2017
	Feb	3.25% 0.6148	3.25% 0.6164	3.25% 0.6184	3.42% 0.6200	3.42% 0.6216	3.42% 0.6236	3.42% 0.6252	1st of any month	Feb 2017
	Mar	3.25% 0.6132	3.25% 0.6148	3.25% 0.6164	3.25% 0.6184	3.42% 0.6200	3.42% 0.6216	3.42% 0.6236	1st of any month	Mar 2017
	Apr	3.25% 0.6116	3.25% 0.6132	3.25% 0.6148	3.25% 0.6164	3.25% 0.6184	3.42% 0.6200	3.42% 0.6216	1st of any month	Apr 2017
	May	3.42% 0.6052	3.42% 0.6068	3.42% 0.6088	3.42% 0.6104	3.42% 0.6120	3.42% 0.6140	??? 0.6156	After May 2005	May 2017
	Jun	3.25% 0.5988	3.42% 0.6052	3.42% 0.6068	3.42% 0.6088	3.42% 0.6104	3.42% 0.6120	3.42% 0.6140	After Jun 2005	Jun 2017
	Jul	3.25% 0.5972	3.25% 0.5988	3.42% 0.6052	3.42% 0.6068	3.42% 0.6088	3.42% 0.6104	3.42% 0.6120	After Jul 2005	Jul 2017
	Aug	3.25% 0.5956	3.25% 0.5972	3.25% 0.5988	3.42% 0.6052	3.42% 0.6068	3.42% 0.6088	3.42% 0.6104	After Aug 2005	Aug 2017
	Sep	3.25% 0.5940	3.25% 0.5956	3.25% 0.5972	3.25% 0.5988	3.42% 0.6052	3.42% 0.6068	3.42% 0.6088	After Sep 2005	Sep 2017
	Oct	3.25% 0.5928	3.25% 0.5940	3.25% 0.5956	3.25% 0.5972	3.25% 0.5988	3.42% 0.6052	3.42% 0.6068	After Oct 2005	Oct 2017
	Nov	3.42% 0.5832	3.42% 0.5848	3.42% 0.5864	3.42% 0.5876	3.42% 0.5892	3.42% 0.5908	??? 0.5976	After Nov 2005	Nov 2017
	Dec	3.25% 0.5816	3.42% 0.5832	3.42% 0.5848	3.42% 0.5864	3.42% 0.5876	3.42% 0.5892	3.42% 0.5908	After Dec 2005	Dec 2017

2004 only		Issue date through Dec 2004			Educa-tion eligible?	Alert Recommendation	Stops paying interest:	Issue month	Year and Series
Annual APY	Interest per $FV	Lifetime APY	Interest per $FV	% interest					
3.39%	0.0204	4.08%	0.1224	20%	Yes	B	Jul 2029	Jul	**1999**
3.46%	0.0208	4.11%	0.1212	20%	Yes	B	Aug 2029	Aug	**EE**
3.40%	0.0204	4.13%	0.1196	19%	Yes	B	Sep 2029	Sep	
3.41%	0.0204	4.14%	0.1180	19%	Yes	B	Oct 2029	Oct	
3.38%	0.0200	4.00%	0.1116	18%	Yes	B	Nov 2029	Nov	
3.32%	0.0196	4.02%	0.1100	18%	Yes	B	Dec 2029	Dec	
2.65%	0.0156	3.89%	0.1044	17%	Yes	B	Jan 2030	Jan	**2000**
2.65%	0.0156	3.92%	0.1032	17%	Yes	B	Feb 2030	Feb	**EE**
2.59%	0.0152	3.93%	0.1016	17%	Yes	B	Mar 2030	Mar	
2.60%	0.0152	3.96%	0.1004	17%	Yes	B	Apr 2030	Apr	
2.70%	0.0156	3.75%	0.0928	16%	Yes	B	May 2030	May	
2.71%	0.0156	3.76%	0.0912	15%	Yes	B Hold till Jun 2005	Jun 2030	Jun	
2.72%	0.0156	3.78%	0.0900	15%	Yes	B Hold till Jul 2005	Jul 2030	Jul	
2.65%	0.0152	3.79%	0.0884	15%	Yes	B Hold till Aug 2005	Aug 2030	Aug	
2.66%	0.0152	3.82%	0.0872	15%	Yes	B Hold till Sep 2005	Sep 2030	Sep	
2.74%	0.0156	3.85%	0.0860	15%	Yes	B Hold till Oct 2005	Oct 2030	Oct	
2.64%	0.0148	3.48%	0.0756	13%	Yes	B Hold till Nov 2005	Nov 2030	Nov	
2.64%	0.0148	3.50%	0.0744	13%	Yes	B Hold till Dec 2005	Dec 2030	Dec	

Year and Series	Issue month	Current interest rate and redemption value per $ of face value							To avoid rate penalty, redeem:	Maturity period ends:
		May 05	Jun 05	Jul 05	Aug 05	Sep 05	Oct 05	Nov 05		
2001 EE	Jan	3.25% 0.5800	3.25% 0.5816	3.42% 0.5832	3.42% 0.5848	3.42% 0.5864	3.42% 0.5876	3.42% 0.5892	After Jan 2006	Jan 2018
	Feb	3.25% 0.5784	3.25% 0.5800	3.25% 0.5816	3.42% 0.5832	3.42% 0.5848	3.42% 0.5864	3.42% 0.5876	After Feb 2006	Feb 2018
	Mar	3.25% 0.5772	3.25% 0.5784	3.25% 0.5800	3.25% 0.5816	3.42% 0.5832	3.42% 0.5848	3.42% 0.5864	After Mar 2006	Mar 2018
	Apr	3.25% 0.5756	3.25% 0.5772	3.25% 0.5784	3.25% 0.5800	3.25% 0.5816	3.42% 0.5832	3.42% 0.5848	After Apr 2006	Apr 2018
	May	3.42% 0.5676	3.42% 0.5692	3.42% 0.5708	3.42% 0.5724	3.42% 0.5740	3.42% 0.5756	??? 0.5772	After May 2006	May 2018
	Jun	3.25% 0.5664	3.42% 0.5676	3.42% 0.5692	3.42% 0.5708	3.42% 0.5724	3.42% 0.5740	3.42% 0.5756	After Jun 2006	Jun 2018
	Jul	3.25% 0.5648	3.25% 0.5664	3.42% 0.5676	3.42% 0.5692	3.42% 0.5708	3.42% 0.5724	3.42% 0.5740	After Jul 2006	Jul 2018
	Aug	3.25% 0.5632	3.25% 0.5648	3.25% 0.5664	3.42% 0.5676	3.42% 0.5692	3.42% 0.5708	3.42% 0.5724	After Aug 2006	Aug 2018
	Sep	3.25% 0.5616	3.25% 0.5632	3.25% 0.5648	3.25% 0.5664	3.42% 0.5676	3.42% 0.5692	3.42% 0.5708	After Sep 2006	Sep 2018
	Oct	3.25% 0.5604	3.25% 0.5616	3.25% 0.5632	3.25% 0.5648	3.25% 0.5664	3.42% 0.5676	3.42% 0.5692	After Oct 2006	Oct 2018
	Nov	3.42% 0.5544	3.42% 0.5560	3.42% 0.5576	3.42% 0.5588	3.42% 0.5604	3.42% 0.5620	??? 0.5636	After Nov 2006	Nov 2018
	Dec	3.25% 0.5528	3.42% 0.5544	3.42% 0.5560	3.42% 0.5576	3.42% 0.5588	3.42% 0.5604	3.42% 0.5620	After Dec 2006	Dec 2018
2002 EE	Jan	3.25% 0.5516	3.25% 0.5528	3.42% 0.5544	3.42% 0.5560	3.42% 0.5576	3.42% 0.5588	3.42% 0.5604	After Jan 2007	Jan 2019
	Feb	3.25% 0.5500	3.25% 0.5516	3.25% 0.5528	3.42% 0.5544	3.42% 0.5560	3.42% 0.5576	3.42% 0.5588	After Feb 2007	Feb 2019
	Mar	3.25% 0.5488	3.25% 0.5500	3.25% 0.5516	3.25% 0.5528	3.42% 0.5544	3.42% 0.5560	3.42% 0.5576	After Mar 2007	Mar 2019
	Apr	3.25% 0.5476	3.25% 0.5488	3.25% 0.5500	3.25% 0.5516	3.25% 0.5528	3.42% 0.5544	3.42% 0.5560	After Apr 2007	Apr 2019
	May	3.42% 0.5440	3.42% 0.5456	3.42% 0.5468	3.42% 0.5484	3.42% 0.5500	3.42% 0.5516	??? 0.5532	After May 2007	May 2019
	Jun	3.25% 0.5424	3.42% 0.5440	3.42% 0.5456	3.42% 0.5468	3.42% 0.5484	3.42% 0.5500	3.42% 0.5516	After Jun 2007	Jun 2019

2004 only		Issue date through Dec 2004			Educa-tion eligible?	Alert Recommendation	Stops paying interest:	Issue month	Year and Series
Annual APY	Interest per $FV	Lifetime APY	Interest per $FV	% interest					
2.65%	0.0148	3.52%	0.0732	13%	Yes	B Hold till Jan 2006	Jan 2031	Jan	**2001**
2.58%	0.0144	3.52%	0.0716	13%	Yes	B Hold till Feb 2006	Feb 2031	Feb	**EE**
2.59%	0.0144	3.54%	0.0704	12%	Yes	B Hold till Mar 2006	Mar 2031	Mar	
2.60%	0.0144	3.57%	0.0692	12%	Yes	B Hold till Apr 2006	Apr 2031	Apr	
2.71%	0.0148	3.21%	0.0604	11%	Yes	B Hold till May 2006	May 2031	May	
2.72%	0.0148	3.22%	0.0592	11%	Yes	B Hold till Jun 2006	Jun 2031	Jun	
2.72%	0.0148	3.24%	0.0580	10%	Yes	B Hold till Jul 2006	Jul 2031	Jul	
2.66%	0.0144	3.23%	0.0564	10%	Yes	B Hold till Aug 2006	Aug 2031	Aug	
2.66%	0.0144	3.25%	0.0552	10%	Yes	B Hold till Sep 2006	Sep 2031	Sep	
2.74%	0.0148	3.26%	0.0540	10%	Yes	B Hold till Oct 2006	Oct 2031	Oct	
2.70%	0.0144	2.97%	0.0476	9%	Yes	B Hold till Nov 2006	Nov 2031	Nov	
2.71%	0.0144	2.98%	0.0464	8%	Yes	B	Dec 2031	Dec	
2.64%	0.0140	2.96%	0.0448	8%	Yes	B	Jan 2032	Jan	**2002**
2.64%	0.0140	2.97%	0.0436	8%	Yes	B	Feb 2032	Feb	**EE**
2.65%	0.0140	2.98%	0.0424	8%	Yes	B	Mar 2032	Mar	
2.73%	0.0144	3.02%	0.0416	8%	Yes	B	Apr 2032	Apr	
2.75%	0.0144	2.80%	0.0372	7%	Yes	B	May 2032	May	
2.61%	0.0136	2.77%	0.0356	7%	Yes	B	Jun 2032	Jun	

Year and Series	Issue month	Current interest rate and redemption value per $ of face value							To avoid rate penalty, redeem:	Maturity period ends:
		May 05	Jun 05	Jul 05	Aug 05	Sep 05	Oct 05	Nov 05		
2002 **EE**	Jul	3.25% 0.5412	3.25% 0.5424	3.42% 0.5440	3.42% 0.5456	3.42% 0.5468	3.42% 0.5484	3.42% 0.5500	After Jul 2007	Jul 2019
	Aug	3.25% 0.5396	3.25% 0.5412	3.25% 0.5424	3.42% 0.5440	3.42% 0.5456	3.42% 0.5468	3.42% 0.5484	After Aug 2007	Aug 2019
	Sep	3.25% 0.5384	3.25% 0.5396	3.25% 0.5412	3.25% 0.5424	3.42% 0.5440	3.42% 0.5456	3.42% 0.5468	After Sep 2007	Sep 2019
	Oct	3.25% 0.5372	3.25% 0.5384	3.25% 0.5396	3.25% 0.5412	3.25% 0.5424	3.42% 0.5440	3.42% 0.5456	After Oct 2007	Oct 2019
	Nov	3.42% 0.5336	3.42% 0.5348	3.42% 0.5364	3.42% 0.5376	3.42% 0.5392	3.42% 0.5408	??? 0.5420	After Nov 2007	Nov 2019
	Dec	3.25% 0.5320	3.42% 0.5336	3.42% 0.5348	3.42% 0.5364	3.42% 0.5376	3.42% 0.5392	3.42% 0.5408	After Dec 2007	Dec 2019
2003 **EE**	Jan	3.25% 0.5308	3.25% 0.5320	3.42% 0.5336	3.42% 0.5348	3.42% 0.5364	3.42% 0.5376	3.42% 0.5392	After Jan 2008	Jan 2020
	Feb	3.25% 0.5292	3.25% 0.5308	3.25% 0.5320	3.42% 0.5336	3.42% 0.5348	3.42% 0.5364	3.42% 0.5376	After Feb 2008	Feb 2020
	Mar	3.25% 0.5276	3.25% 0.5292	3.25% 0.5308	3.25% 0.5320	3.42% 0.5336	3.42% 0.5348	3.42% 0.5364	After Mar 2008	Mar 2020
	Apr	3.25% 0.5264	3.25% 0.5276	3.25% 0.5292	3.25% 0.5308	3.25% 0.5320	3.42% 0.5336	3.42% 0.5348	After Apr 2008	Apr 2020
	May	3.42% 0.5252	3.42% 0.5264	3.42% 0.5280	3.42% 0.5292	3.42% 0.5308	3.42% 0.5320	??? 0.5336	After May 2008	May 2020
	Jun	3.25% 0.5236	3.42% 0.5252	3.42% 0.5264	3.42% 0.5280	3.42% 0.5292	3.42% 0.5308	3.42% 0.5320	After Jun 2008	Jun 2023
	Jul	3.25% 0.5224	3.25% 0.5236	3.42% 0.5252	3.42% 0.5264	3.42% 0.5280	3.42% 0.5292	3.42% 0.5308	After Jul 2008	Jul 2023
	Aug	3.25% 0.5208	3.25% 0.5224	3.25% 0.5236	3.42% 0.5252	3.42% 0.5264	3.42% 0.5280	3.42% 0.5292	After Aug 2008	Aug 2023
	Sep	3.25% 0.5196	3.25% 0.5208	3.25% 0.5224	3.25% 0.5236	3.42% 0.5252	3.42% 0.5264	3.42% 0.5280	After Sep 2008	Sep 2023
	Oct	3.25% 0.5184	3.25% 0.5196	3.25% 0.5208	3.25% 0.5224	3.25% 0.5236	3.42% 0.5252	3.42% 0.5264	After Oct 2008	Oct 2023
	Nov	3.42% 0.5176	3.42% 0.5192	3.42% 0.5204	3.42% 0.5220	3.42% 0.5236	3.42% 0.5248	??? 0.5264	After Nov 2008	Nov 2023
	Dec	3.25% 0.5164	3.42% 0.5176	3.42% 0.5192	3.42% 0.5204	3.42% 0.5220	3.42% 0.5236	3.42% 0.5248	After Dec 2008	Dec 2023

2004 only		Issue date through Dec 2004			Educa-tion eligible?	Alert Recommendation	Stops paying interest:	Issue month	Year and Series
Annual APY	Interest per $FV	Lifetime APY	Interest per $FV	% interest					
2.61%	0.0136	2.77%	0.0344	6%	Yes	B	Jul 2032	Jul	2002
2.62%	0.0136	2.77%	0.0332	6%	Yes	B	Aug 2032	Aug	EE
2.62%	0.0136	2.78%	0.0320	6%	Yes	B	Sep 2032	Sep	
2.71%	0.0140	2.78%	0.0308	6%	Yes	B	Oct 2032	Oct	
2.73%	0.0140	2.49%	0.0264	5%	Yes	B	Nov 2032	Nov	
2.74%	0.0140	2.47%	0.0252	5%	Yes	B	Dec 2032	Dec	
2.66%	0.0136	2.46%	0.0240	5%	Yes	B	Jan 2033	Jan	2003
2.67%	0.0136	2.45%	0.0228	4%	Yes	B	Feb 2033	Feb	EE
2.68%	0.0136	2.43%	0.0216	4%	Yes	B	Mar 2033	Mar	
2.68%	0.0136	2.41%	0.0204	4%	Yes	B	Apr 2033	Apr	
2.78%	0.0140	2.30%	0.0184	4%	Yes	B	May 2033	May	
2.78%	0.0140	2.27%	0.0172	3%	Yes	B	Jun 2033	Jun	
2.71%	0.0136	2.24%	0.0160	3%	Yes	B	Jul 2033	Jul	
2.71%	0.0136	2.20%	0.0148	3%	Yes	B	Aug 2033	Aug	
2.72%	0.0136	2.16%	0.0136	3%	Yes	B	Sep 2033	Sep	
2.48%	0.0124	2.11%	0.0124	2%	Yes	B	Oct 2033	Oct	
2.24%	0.0112	2.06%	0.0112	2%	Yes	B	Nov 2033	Nov	
2.00%	0.0100	1.99%	0.0100	2%	Yes	B	Dec 2033	Dec	

Year and Series	Issue month	Current interest rate and redemption value per $ of face value							To avoid rate penalty, redeem:	Maturity period ends:
		May 05	Jun 05	Jul 05	Aug 05	Sep 05	Oct 05	Nov 05		
2004 EE	Jan	3.25% 0.5148	3.25% 0.5164	3.42% 0.5176	3.42% 0.5192	3.42% 0.5204	3.42% 0.5220	3.42% 0.5236	After Jan 2009	Jan 2024
	Feb	3.25% 0.5136	3.25% 0.5148	3.25% 0.5164	3.42% 0.5176	3.42% 0.5192	3.42% 0.5204	3.42% 0.5220	After Feb 2009	Feb 2024
	Mar	3.25% 0.5124	3.25% 0.5136	3.25% 0.5148	3.25% 0.5164	3.42% 0.5176	3.42% 0.5192	3.42% 0.5204	After Mar 2009	Mar 2024
	Apr	3.25% 0.5112	3.25% 0.5124	3.25% 0.5136	3.25% 0.5148	3.25% 0.5164	3.42% 0.5176	3.42% 0.5192	After Apr 2009	Apr 2024
	May	3.42% 0.5112	3.42% 0.5128	3.42% 0.5140	3.42% 0.5156	3.42% 0.5172	3.42% 0.5184	??? 0.5200	After May 2009	May 2024
	Jun	3.25% 0.5100	3.42% 0.5112	3.42% 0.5128	3.42% 0.5140	3.42% 0.5156	3.42% 0.5172	3.42% 0.5184	After Jun 2009	Jun 2024
	Jul	3.25% 0.5084	3.25% 0.5100	3.42% 0.5112	3.42% 0.5128	3.42% 0.5140	3.42% 0.5156	3.42% 0.5172	After Jul 2009	Jul 2024
	Aug	3.25% 0.5072	3.25% 0.5084	3.25% 0.5100	3.42% 0.5112	3.42% 0.5128	3.42% 0.5140	3.42% 0.5156	After Aug 2009	Aug 2024
	Sep	3.25% 0.5060	3.25% 0.5072	3.25% 0.5084	3.25% 0.5100	3.42% 0.5112	3.42% 0.5128	3.42% 0.5140	After Sep 2009	Sep 2024
	Oct	3.25% 0.5048	3.25% 0.5060	3.25% 0.5072	3.25% 0.5084	3.25% 0.5100	3.42% 0.5112	3.42% 0.5128	After Oct 2009	Oct 2024
	Nov	3.42% 0.5040	3.42% 0.5056	3.42% 0.5068	3.42% 0.5080	3.42% 0.5096	3.42% 0.5108	??? 0.5124	After Nov 2009	Nov 2024
	Dec	3.25% 0.5028	3.42% 0.5040	3.42% 0.5056	3.42% 0.5068	3.42% 0.5080	3.42% 0.5096	3.42% 0.5108	After Dec 2009	Dec 2024
2005 EE	Jan	3.25% 0.5012	3.25% 0.5028	3.42% 0.5040	3.42% 0.5056	3.42% 0.5068	3.42% 0.5080	3.42% 0.5096	After Jan 2010	Jan 2025
	Feb	3.25% 0.5000	3.25% 0.5012	3.25% 0.5028	3.42% 0.5040	3.42% 0.5056	3.42% 0.5068	3.42% 0.5080	After Feb 2010	Feb 2025
	Mar	3.25% 0.5000	3.25% 0.5000	3.25% 0.5012	3.25% 0.5028	3.42% 0.5040	3.42% 0.5056	3.42% 0.5068	After Mar 2010	Mar 2025
	Apr	3.25% 0.5000	3.25% 0.5000	3.25% 0.5000	3.25% 0.5012	3.25% 0.5028	3.42% 0.5040	3.42% 0.5056	After Apr 2010	Apr 2025
	May	3.50% fixed rate							After May 2010	May 2025
		0.5000	0.5000	0.5000	0.5000	0.5016	0.5028	0.5044		
	Jun	--- ---	3.50% fixed rate						After Jun 2010	Jun 2025
			0.5000	0.5000	0.5000	0.5000	0.5016	0.5028		

| 2004 only | | Issue date through Dec 2004 | | | Educa-tion eligible? | Alert Recommendation | Stops paying interest: | Issue month | Year and Series |
Annual APY	Interest per $FV	Lifetime APY	Interest per $FV	% interest					
1.92%	0.0088	1.91%	0.0088	2%	Yes	B	Jan 2034	Jan	**2004**
1.82%	0.0076	1.82%	0.0076	1%	Yes	B	Feb 2034	Feb	**EE**
1.71%	0.0064	1.70%	0.0064	1%	Yes	B	Mar 2034	Mar	
1.68%	0.0056	1.68%	0.0056	1%	Yes	B	Apr 2034	Apr	
1.65%	0.0048	1.64%	0.0048	1%	Yes	B	May 2034	May	
1.44%	0.0036	1.44%	0.0036	1%	Yes	B	Jun 2034	Jun	
1.15%	0.0024	1.15%	0.0024	0%	Yes	B	Jul 2034	Jul	
0.72%	0.0012	0.72%	0.0012	0%	Yes	B	Aug 2034	Aug	
0.00%	0.0000	0.00%	0.0000	0%	Yes	B	Sep 2034	Sep	
0.00%	0.0000	0.00%	0.0000	0%	Yes	B	Oct 2034	Oct	
0.00%	0.0000	0.00%	0.0000	0%	Yes	B	Nov 2034	Nov	
---	---	---	---	---	Yes	B	Dec 2034	Dec	
---	---	---	---	---	Yes	B	Jan 2035	Jan	**2005**
---	---	---	---	---	Yes	B	Feb 2035	Feb	**EE**
---	---	---	---	---	Yes	B	Mar 2035	Mar	
---	---	---	---	---	Yes	B	Apr 2035	Apr	
---	---	---	---	---	Yes	B-	May 2035	May	
---	---	---	---	---	Yes	B-	Jun 2035	Jun	

Year and Series	Issue month	Current interest rate and redemption value per $ of face value							To avoid rate penalty, redeem:	Maturity period ends:
		May 05	Jun 05	Jul 05	Aug 05	Sep 05	Oct 05	Nov 05		
2005	Jul	---	---	3.50% fixed rate					After Jul 2010	Jul 2025
		---	---	0.5000	0.5000	0.5000	0.5000	0.5016		
EE	Aug	---	---	---	3.50% fixed rate				After Aug 2010	Aug 2025
		---	---	---	0.5000	0.5000	0.5000	0.5000		
	Sep	---	---	---	---	3.50% fixed rate			After Sep 2010	Sep 2025
		---	---	---	---	0.5000	0.5000	0.5000		
	Oct	---	---	---	---	---	3.50% fixed rate		After Oct 2010	Oct 2025
		---	---	---	---	---	0.5000	0.5000		
	Nov	---	---	---	---	---	---	???	After Nov 2010	Nov 2025
		---	---	---	---	---	---	0.5000		

2004 only		Issue date through Dec 2004			Educa-tion eligible?	Alert Recommendation	Stops paying interest:	Issue month	Year and Series
Annual APY	Interest per $FV	Lifetime APY	Interest per $FV	% interest					
---	---	---	---	---	Yes	B-	Jul 2035	Jul	2005
---	---	---	---	---	Yes	B-	Aug 2035	Aug	EE
---	---	---	---	---	Yes	B-	Sep 2035	Sep	
---	---	---	---	---	Yes	B-	Oct 2035	Oct	
---	---	---	---	---	Yes	B-	Nov 2035	Nov	

Year and Series	Issue month	Current interest rate and redemption value per $ of face value							To avoid rate penalty, redeem:	Maturity period ends:
		May 05	Jun 05	Jul 05	Aug 05	Sep 05	Oct 05	Nov 05		
1965 **E**		Series E Savings Bonds issued before December 1965 earn interest for 40 years. Those issued before May 1965 have stopped earning interest. See the other Series E table for their redemption values.								
	May	0% 8.6308	0% 8.6308	0% 8.6308	0% 8.6308	0% 8.6308	0% 8.6308	0% 8.6308	Feb or Aug	May 2005
	Jun	6% 7.3296	0% 7.4388	0% 7.4388	0% 7.4388	0% 7.4388	0% 7.4388	0% 7.4388	Mar or Sep	Jun 2005
	Jul	6% 7.3296	6% 7.3296	0% 7.4388	0% 7.4388	0% 7.4388	0% 7.4388	0% 7.4388	Apr or Oct	Jul 2005
	Aug	5.94% 7.2168	5.94% 7.2168	5.94% 7.2168	0% 7.3232	0% 7.3232	0% 7.3232	0% 7.3232	May or Nov	Aug 2005
	Sep	3.32% 7.1360	5.94% 7.2540	5.94% 7.2540	5.94% 7.2540	0% 7.3612	0% 7.3612	0% 7.3612	Jun or Dec	Sep 2005
	Oct	3.32% 7.1360	3.32% 7.1360	5.94% 7.2540	5.94% 7.2540	5.94% 7.2540	0% 7.3612	0% 7.3612	Jan or Jul	Oct 2005
	Nov	3.32% 7.1360	3.32% 7.1360	3.32% 7.1360	5.94% 7.2540	5.94% 7.2540	5.94% 7.2540	0% 7.3612	Feb or Aug	Nov 2005
1975 **E**		Series E Savings Bonds issued in December 1965 and later earn interest for 30 years. Those issued before May 1975 have stopped earning interest. See the other Series E table for their redemption values.								
	May	0% 5.3132	0% 5.3132	0% 5.3132	0% 5.3132	0% 5.3132	0% 5.3132	0% 5.3132	May or Nov	May 2005
	Jun	4% 5.2216	0% 5.3260	0% 5.3260	0% 5.3260	0% 5.3260	0% 5.3260	0% 5.3260	Jun or Dec	Jun 2005
	Jul	4% 5.2216	4% 5.2216	0% 5.3260	0% 5.3260	0% 5.3260	0% 5.3260	0% 5.3260	Jan or Jul	Jul 2005
	Aug	4% 5.2216	4% 5.2216	4% 5.2216	0% 5.3260	0% 5.3260	0% 5.3260	0% 5.3260	Feb or Aug	Aug 2005
	Sep	4% 5.2216	4% 5.2216	4% 5.2216	4% 5.2216	0% 5.3260	0% 5.3260	0% 5.3260	Mar or Sep	Sep 2005
	Oct	4% 5.2216	4% 5.2216	4% 5.2216	4% 5.2216	4% 5.2216	0% 5.3260	0% 5.3260	Apr or Oct	Oct 2005
	Nov	4% 5.2728	4% 5.2728	4% 5.2728	4% 5.2728	4% 5.2728	4% 5.2728	0% 5.3784	May or Nov	Nov 2005
	Dec	4% 5.1808	4% 5.2844	4% 5.2844	4% 5.2844	4% 5.2844	4% 5.2844	4% 5.2844	Jun or Dec	Dec 2005

2004 only		Issue date through Dec 2004			Educa-tion eligible?	Alert Recommendation	Stops paying interest:	Issue month	Year and Series
Annual APY	Interest per $FV	Lifetime APY	Interest per $FV	% interest					
Series E Savings Bonds issued before December 1965 earn interest for 40 years. Those issued before May 1965 have stopped earning interest. See the other Series E table for their redemption values.									**1965** E
4.04%	0.3252	6.30%	7.6280	91%	No	Redeem Now	May 2005	**May**	
2.44%	0.1724	5.95%	6.4860	90%	No	A to Jun, then redeem	Jun 2005	**Jun**	
2.44%	0.1724	5.95%	6.4860	90%	No	A to Jul, then redeem	Jul 2005	**Jul**	
2.48%	0.1716	5.90%	6.3492	89%	No	A to Aug, then redeem	Aug 2005	**Aug**	
2.48%	0.1728	5.91%	6.3860	89%	No	A to Sep, then redeem	Sep 2005	**Sep**	
2.44%	0.1680	5.96%	6.2948	89%	No	A to Oct, then redeem	Oct 2005	**Oct**	
2.44%	0.1680	5.96%	6.2948	89%	No	A to Nov, then redeem	Nov 2005	**Nov**	
Series E Savings Bonds issued in December 1965 and later earn interest for 30 years. Those issued before May 1975 have stopped earning interest. See the other Series E table for their redemption values.									**1975** E
4.04%	0.2024	6.77%	4.4592	86%	No	Redeem Now	May 2005	**May**	
4.04%	0.2028	6.78%	4.4716	86%	No	A to Jun, then redeem	Jun 2005	**Jun**	
4.04%	0.1988	6.83%	4.3692	85%	No	A to Jul, then redeem	Jul 2005	**Jul**	
4.04%	0.1988	6.83%	4.3692	85%	No	A to Aug, then redeem	Aug 2005	**Aug**	
4.04%	0.1988	6.83%	4.3692	85%	No	A to Sep, then redeem	Sep 2005	**Sep**	
4.04%	0.1988	6.83%	4.3692	85%	No	A to Oct, then redeem	Oct 2005	**Oct**	
4.03%	0.2004	6.87%	4.4192	85%	No	A to Nov, then redeem	Nov 2005	**Nov**	
4.04%	0.2012	6.88%	4.4308	86%	No	A	Dec 2005	**Dec**	

Year and Series	Issue month	Current interest rate and redemption value per $ of face value							To avoid rate penalty, redeem:	Maturity period ends:
		May 05	Jun 05	Jul 05	Aug 05	Sep 05	Oct 05	Nov 05		
1976	Jan	4% 5.1812	4% 5.1812	4% 5.2848	4% 5.2848	4% 5.2848	4% 5.2848	4% 5.2848	Jan or Jul	Jan 2006
E	Feb	4% 5.1812	4% 5.1812	4% 5.1812	4% 5.2848	4% 5.2848	4% 5.2848	4% 5.2848	Feb or Aug	Feb 2006
	Mar	4% 5.1812	4% 5.1812	4% 5.1812	4% 5.1812	4% 5.2848	4% 5.2848	4% 5.2848	Mar or Sep	Mar 2006
	Apr	4% 5.1812	4% 5.1812	4% 5.1812	4% 5.1812	4% 5.1812	4% 5.2848	4% 5.2848	Apr or Oct	Apr 2006
	May	4% 5.2304	4% 5.2304	4% 5.2304	4% 5.2304	4% 5.2304	4% 5.2304	??? 5.3348	May or Nov	May 2006
	Jun	4% 5.1392	4% 5.2420	4% 5.2420	4% 5.2420	4% 5.2420	4% 5.2420	4% 5.2420	Jun or Dec	Jun 2006
	Jul	4% 5.1384	4% 5.1384	4% 5.2412	4% 5.2412	4% 5.2412	4% 5.2412	4% 5.2412	Jan or Jul	Jul 2006
	Aug	4% 5.1384	4% 5.1384	4% 5.1384	4% 5.2412	4% 5.2412	4% 5.2412	4% 5.2412	Feb or Aug	Aug 2006
	Sep	4% 5.1384	4% 5.1384	4% 5.1384	4% 5.1384	4% 5.2412	4% 5.2412	4% 5.2412	Mar or Sep	Sep 2006
	Oct	4% 5.1384	4% 5.1384	4% 5.1384	4% 5.1384	4% 5.1384	4% 5.2412	4% 5.2412	Apr or Oct	Oct 2006
	Nov	4% 5.1884	4% 5.1884	4% 5.1884	4% 5.1884	4% 5.1884	4% 5.1884	??? 5.2920	May or Nov	Nov 2006
	Dec	4% 5.1012	4% 5.2032	4% 5.2032	4% 5.2032	4% 5.2032	4% 5.2032	4% 5.2032	Jun or Dec	Dec 2006
1977	Jan	4% 5.1012	4% 5.1012	4% 5.2032	4% 5.2032	4% 5.2032	4% 5.2032	4% 5.2032	Jan or Jul	Jan 2007
E	Feb	4% 5.1012	4% 5.1012	4% 5.1012	4% 5.2032	4% 5.2032	4% 5.2032	4% 5.2032	Feb or Aug	Feb 2007
	Mar	4% 5.1012	4% 5.1012	4% 5.1012	4% 5.1012	4% 5.2032	4% 5.2032	4% 5.2032	Mar or Sep	Mar 2007
	Apr	4% 5.1012	4% 5.1012	4% 5.1012	4% 5.1012	4% 5.1012	4% 5.2032	4% 5.2032	Apr or Oct	Apr 2007
	May	4% 5.1516	4% 5.1516	4% 5.1516	4% 5.1516	4% 5.1516	4% 5.1516	??? 5.2544	May or Nov	May 2007
	Jun	4% 5.0612	4% 5.1624	4% 5.1624	4% 5.1624	4% 5.1624	4% 5.1624	4% 5.1624	Jun or Dec	Jun 2007

2004 only		Issue date through Dec 2004			Educa-tion eligible?	Alert Recommendation	Stops paying interest:	Issue month	Year and Series
Annual APY	Interest per $FV	Lifetime APY	Interest per $FV	% interest					
4.04%	0.1972	6.93%	4.3296	85%	No	A	Jan 2006	Jan	**1976**
4.04%	0.1972	6.93%	4.3296	85%	No	A	Feb 2006	Feb	E
4.04%	0.1972	6.93%	4.3296	85%	No	A	Mar 2006	Mar	
4.04%	0.1972	6.93%	4.3296	85%	No	A	Apr 2006	Apr	
4.03%	0.1988	6.96%	4.3776	85%	No	A	May 2006	May	
4.04%	0.1996	6.97%	4.3892	85%	No	A	Jun 2006	Jun	
4.04%	0.1956	7.03%	4.2876	85%	No	A	Jul 2006	Jul	
4.04%	0.1956	7.03%	4.2876	85%	No	A	Aug 2006	Aug	
4.04%	0.1956	7.03%	4.2876	85%	No	A	Sep 2006	Sep	
4.04%	0.1956	7.03%	4.2876	85%	No	A	Oct 2006	Oct	
4.04%	0.1976	7.07%	4.3368	85%	No	A	Nov 2006	Nov	
4.05%	0.1984	7.08%	4.3512	85%	No	A	Dec 2006	Dec	
4.04%	0.1944	7.13%	4.2512	85%	No	A	Jan 2007	Jan	**1977**
4.04%	0.1944	7.13%	4.2512	85%	No	A	Feb 2007	Feb	E
4.04%	0.1944	7.13%	4.2512	85%	No	A	Mar 2007	Mar	
4.04%	0.1944	7.13%	4.2512	85%	No	A	Apr 2007	Apr	
4.04%	0.1960	7.17%	4.3004	85%	No	A	May 2007	May	
4.05%	0.1968	7.18%	4.3112	85%	No	A	Jun 2007	Jun	

Year and Series	Issue month	Current interest rate and redemption value per $ of face value							To avoid rate penalty, redeem:	Maturity period ends:
		May 05	Jun 05	Jul 05	Aug 05	Sep 05	Oct 05	Nov 05		
1977 **E**	Jul	4% 5.0604	4% 5.0604	4% 5.1616	4% 5.1616	4% 5.1616	4% 5.1616	4% 5.1616	Jan or Jul	Jul 2007
	Aug	4% 5.0604	4% 5.0604	4% 5.0604	4% 5.1616	4% 5.1616	4% 5.1616	4% 5.1616	Feb or Aug	Aug 2007
	Sep	4% 5.0604	4% 5.0604	4% 5.0604	4% 5.0604	4% 5.1616	4% 5.1616	4% 5.1616	Mar or Sep	Sep 2007
	Oct	4% 5.0604	4% 5.0604	4% 5.0604	4% 5.0604	4% 5.0604	4% 5.1616	4% 5.1616	Apr or Oct	Oct 2007
	Nov	4% 4.6408	4% 4.6408	4% 4.6408	4% 4.6408	4% 4.6408	4% 4.6408	??? 4.7336	May or Nov	Nov 2007
	Dec	4% 4.5624	4% 4.6536	4% 4.6536	4% 4.6536	4% 4.6536	4% 4.6536	4% 4.6536	Jun or Dec	Dec 2007
1978 **E**	Jan	4% 4.5624	4% 4.5624	4% 4.6536	4% 4.6536	4% 4.6536	4% 4.6536	4% 4.6536	Jan or Jul	Jan 2008
	Feb	4% 4.5624	4% 4.5624	4% 4.5624	4% 4.6536	4% 4.6536	4% 4.6536	4% 4.6536	Feb or Aug	Feb 2008
	Mar	3.32% 3.8916	3.32% 3.8916	3.32% 3.8916	3.32% 3.8916	3.2% 3.9564	3.2% 3.9564	3.2% 3.9564	Mar or Sep	Mar 2008
	Apr	3.32% 3.8916	3.32% 3.8916	3.32% 3.8916	3.32% 3.8916	3.32% 3.8916	3.2% 3.9564	3.2% 3.9564	Apr or Oct	Apr 2008
	May	4% 3.7888	4% 3.7888	4% 3.7888	4% 3.7888	4% 3.7888	4% 3.7888	??? 3.8648	May or Nov	May 2008
	Jun	4% 3.7240	4% 3.7984	4% 3.7984	4% 3.7984	4% 3.7984	4% 3.7984	4% 3.7984	Jun or Dec	Jun 2008
	Jul	4% 3.7248	4% 3.7248	4% 3.7992	4% 3.7992	4% 3.7992	4% 3.7992	4% 3.7992	Jan or Jul	Jul 2008
	Aug	4% 3.7248	4% 3.7248	4% 3.7248	4% 3.7992	4% 3.7992	4% 3.7992	4% 3.7992	Feb or Aug	Aug 2008
	Sep	4% 3.7248	4% 3.7248	4% 3.7248	4% 3.7248	4% 3.7992	4% 3.7992	4% 3.7992	Mar or Sep	Sep 2008
	Oct	4% 3.7248	4% 3.7248	4% 3.7248	4% 3.7248	4% 3.7248	4% 3.7992	4% 3.7992	Apr or Oct	Oct 2008
	Nov	4% 3.7600	4% 3.7600	4% 3.7600	4% 3.7600	4% 3.7600	4% 3.7600	??? 3.8352	May or Nov	Nov 2008
	Dec	4% 3.6964	4% 3.7704	4% 3.7704	4% 3.7704	4% 3.7704	4% 3.7704	4% 3.7704	Jun or Dec	Dec 2008

2004 only		Issue date through Dec 2004			Educa-tion eligible?	Alert Recommendation	Stops paying interest:	Issue month	Year and Series
Annual APY	Interest per $FV	Lifetime APY	Interest per $FV	% interest					
4.04%	0.1928	7.24%	4.2112	85%	No	A	Jul 2007	Jul	**1977**
4.04%	0.1928	7.24%	4.2112	85%	No	A	Aug 2007	Aug	E
4.04%	0.1928	7.24%	4.2112	85%	No	A	Sep 2007	Sep	
4.04%	0.1928	7.24%	4.2112	85%	No	A	Oct 2007	Oct	
4.03%	0.1764	6.90%	3.7996	84%	No	A	Nov 2007	Nov	
4.04%	0.1772	6.91%	3.8124	84%	No	A	Dec 2007	Dec	
4.04%	0.1736	6.97%	3.7228	83%	No	A	Jan 2008	Jan	**1978**
4.04%	0.1736	6.97%	3.7228	83%	No	A	Feb 2008	Feb	E
2.44%	0.0916	6.41%	3.0920	80%	No	B	Mar 2008	Mar	
2.44%	0.0916	6.41%	3.0920	80%	No	B	Apr 2008	Apr	
4.04%	0.1444	6.21%	2.9648	80%	No	A	May 2008	May	
4.05%	0.1448	6.22%	2.9740	80%	No	A	Jun 2008	Jun	
4.05%	0.1420	6.27%	2.9020	79%	No	A	Jul 2008	Jul	
4.05%	0.1420	6.27%	2.9020	79%	No	A	Aug 2008	Aug	
4.05%	0.1420	6.27%	2.9020	79%	No	A	Sep 2008	Sep	
4.05%	0.1420	6.27%	2.9020	79%	No	A	Oct 2008	Oct	
4.04%	0.1432	6.31%	2.9364	80%	No	A	Nov 2008	Nov	
4.04%	0.1436	6.32%	2.9464	80%	No	A	Dec 2008	Dec	

Year and Series	Issue month	Current interest rate and redemption value per $ of face value							To avoid rate penalty, redeem:	Maturity period ends:
		May 05	Jun 05	Jul 05	Aug 05	Sep 05	Oct 05	Nov 05		
1979 **E**	Jan	4% 3.6968	4% 3.6968	4% 3.7708	4% 3.7708	4% 3.7708	4% 3.7708	4% 3.7708	Jan or Jul	Jan 2009
	Feb	4% 3.6968	4% 3.6968	4% 3.6968	4% 3.7708	4% 3.7708	4% 3.7708	4% 3.7708	Feb or Aug	Feb 2009
	Mar	4% 3.6968	4% 3.6968	4% 3.6968	4% 3.6968	4% 3.7708	4% 3.7708	4% 3.7708	Mar or Sep	Mar 2009
	Apr	4% 3.6968	4% 3.6968	4% 3.6968	4% 3.6968	4% 3.6968	4% 3.7708	4% 3.7708	Apr or Oct	Apr 2009
	May	4% 3.7324	4% 3.7324	4% 3.7324	4% 3.7324	4% 3.7324	4% 3.7324	??? 3.8072	May or Nov	May 2009
	Jun	4% 3.6680	4% 3.7412	4% 3.7412	4% 3.7412	4% 3.7412	4% 3.7412	4% 3.7412	Jun or Dec	Jun 2009
	Jul	4% 3.6680	4% 3.6680	4% 3.7412	4% 3.7412	4% 3.7412	4% 3.7412	4% 3.7412	Jan or Jul	Jul 2009
	Aug	4% 3.6680	4% 3.6680	4% 3.6680	4% 3.7412	4% 3.7412	4% 3.7412	4% 3.7412	Feb or Aug	Aug 2009
	Sep	4% 3.6680	4% 3.6680	4% 3.6680	4% 3.6680	4% 3.7412	4% 3.7412	4% 3.7412	Mar or Sep	Sep 2009
	Oct	4% 3.6680	4% 3.6680	4% 3.6680	4% 3.6680	4% 3.6680	4% 3.7412	4% 3.7412	Apr or Oct	Oct 2009
	Nov	4% 3.7028	4% 3.7028	4% 3.7028	4% 3.7028	4% 3.7028	4% 3.7028	??? 3.7768	May or Nov	Nov 2009
	Dec	4% 3.6300	4% 3.7028	4% 3.7028	4% 3.7028	4% 3.7028	4% 3.7028	4% 3.7028	Jun or Dec	Dec 2009
1980 **E**	Jan	4% 3.6300	4% 3.6300	4% 3.7028	4% 3.7028	4% 3.7028	4% 3.7028	4% 3.7028	Jan or Jul	Jan 2010
	Feb	4% 3.6300	4% 3.6300	4% 3.6300	4% 3.7028	4% 3.7028	4% 3.7028	4% 3.7028	Feb or Aug	Feb 2010
	Mar	4% 3.6300	4% 3.6300	4% 3.6300	4% 3.6300	4% 3.7028	4% 3.7028	4% 3.7028	Mar or Sep	Mar 2010
	Apr	4% 3.6300	4% 3.6300	4% 3.6300	4% 3.6300	4% 3.6300	4% 3.7028	4% 3.7028	Apr or Oct	Apr 2010
	May	4% 3.6668	4% 3.6668	4% 3.6668	4% 3.6668	4% 3.6668	4% 3.6668	??? 3.7400	May or Nov	May 2010
	Jun	4% 3.5948	4% 3.6668	4% 3.6668	4% 3.6668	4% 3.6668	4% 3.6668	4% 3.6668	Jun or Dec	Jun 2010

2004 only		Issue date through Dec 2004			Educa-tion eligible?	Alert Recommendation	Stops paying interest:	Issue month	Year and Series
Annual APY	Interest per $FV	Lifetime APY	Interest per $FV	% interest					
4.04%	0.1408	6.37%	2.8744	79%	No	A	Jan 2009	Jan	**1979**
4.04%	0.1408	6.37%	2.8744	79%	No	A	Feb 2009	Feb	E
4.04%	0.1408	6.37%	2.8744	79%	No	A	Mar 2009	Mar	
4.04%	0.1408	6.37%	2.8744	79%	No	A	Apr 2009	Apr	
4.04%	0.1420	6.41%	2.9092	80%	No	A	May 2009	May	
4.04%	0.1424	6.42%	2.9180	80%	No	A	Jun 2009	Jun	
4.04%	0.1396	6.47%	2.8460	79%	No	A	Jul 2009	Jul	
4.04%	0.1396	6.47%	2.8460	79%	No	A	Aug 2009	Aug	
4.04%	0.1396	6.47%	2.8460	79%	No	A	Sep 2009	Sep	
4.04%	0.1396	6.47%	2.8460	79%	No	A	Oct 2009	Oct	
4.05%	0.1412	6.51%	2.8800	79%	No	A	Nov 2009	Nov	
4.05%	0.1412	6.51%	2.8800	79%	No	A	Dec 2009	Dec	
4.05%	0.1384	6.56%	2.8088	79%	No	A	Jan 2010	Jan	**1980**
4.05%	0.1384	6.56%	2.8088	79%	No	A	Feb 2010	Feb	E
4.05%	0.1384	6.56%	2.8088	79%	No	A	Mar 2010	Mar	
4.05%	0.1384	6.56%	2.8088	79%	No	A	Apr 2010	Apr	
4.04%	0.1396	6.61%	2.8448	79%	No	A	May 2010	May	
4.04%	0.1396	6.61%	2.8448	79%	No	A	Jun 2010	Jun	

Series	Year Issued	Redemption value per $ of face value Issued in:					
		Jan	Feb	Mar	Apr	May	Jun
E	1941					3.6236	3.6784
	1942	3.7740	3.7740	3.7740	3.7740	3.8400	3.8980
	1943	3.9980	3.9980	3.9980	3.9980	4.0364	4.0992
	1944	4.2036	4.2036	4.2036	4.2036	4.2444	4.3080
	1945	4.4188	4.4188	4.4188	4.4188	4.4616	4.5332
	1946	4.6912	4.6912	4.6912	4.6912	4.7364	4.8100
	1947	4.9352	4.9352	4.9352	4.9352	4.9828	5.0628
	1948	5.2564	5.2564	5.2564	5.2564	5.2436	5.3292
	1949	5.4676	5.4676	5.4676	5.4676	5.5208	5.7532
	1950	5.8824	5.8824	5.8824	5.8824	5.9392	6.0212
	1951	6.5040	6.5040	6.5040	6.5040	6.5664	6.6644
	1952	6.8264	6.8264	6.8264	6.8264	6.9352	6.9512
	1953	7.1256	7.1256	6.5352	6.6164	6.6164	6.6324
	1954	6.7544	6.7544	6.8204	6.9076	6.9076	6.9248
	1955	7.1012	7.1012	7.1704	7.2628	7.2628	7.2820
	1956	7.4716	7.4716	7.5436	7.7532	7.7532	7.7716
	1957	7.9824	7.9960	7.9960	7.9960	7.9960	8.1088
	1958	7.3248	7.3248	7.3248	7.3248	7.3248	7.3812
	1959	7.6612	7.6612	7.6612	7.6612	7.6612	7.5152
	1960	7.5400	7.6068	7.6944	7.6944	7.6944	7.7076
	1961	7.8872	7.9628	8.0548	8.0544	8.0544	8.0780
	1962	8.2700	8.3500	8.4108	8.4096	8.4096	8.4316
	1963	8.6088	8.6924	8.7328	8.7316	8.7316	8.7980
	1964	8.9820	9.0684	9.1116	9.1108	9.1108	9.1716
	1965	9.3644	8.5896	8.6316	8.6308	8.6308	
	1966	5.1252	5.1252	4.8776	4.8776	4.8808	4.9312
	1967	5.0344	5.0344	5.0344	5.0344	5.0824	5.1384
	1968	5.2512	5.2512	5.2512	5.2512	5.3028	5.3664
	1969	5.4908	5.4908	5.4908	5.4908	5.5440	5.3368
	1970	5.4800	5.4936	5.4944	5.4944	5.4944	5.5200
	1971	5.0520	5.0640	5.0640	5.0640	5.0640	5.0780
	1972	5.0352	5.0468	5.0476	5.0476	5.0476	5.0616
	1973	5.1824	5.1956	5.1956	5.1956	5.1956	5.2080
	1974	5.1392	5.1392	5.1392	5.1392	5.1884	5.2008
	1975	5.2628	5.2628	5.2628	5.2628	5.3132	
	1976-1980	Still earning interest - see other Series E table					

Redemption value per $ of face value Issued in:						Year Issued	Series
Jul	Aug	Sep	Oct	Nov	Dec		
3.6784	3.6784	3.6784	3.6784	3.7144	3.7740	1941	E
3.8980	3.8980	3.8980	3.8980	3.9360	3.9980	1942	
4.0992	4.0992	4.0992	4.0992	4.1392	4.2036	1943	
4.3080	4.3080	4.3080	4.3080	4.3500	4.4188	1944	
4.5332	4.5332	4.5332	4.5332	4.5772	4.6912	1945	
4.8100	4.8100	4.8100	4.8100	4.8568	4.9352	1946	
5.0628	5.0628	5.0628	5.0628	5.1736	5.2564	1947	
5.3292	5.3292	5.3292	5.3292	5.3804	5.4676	1948	
5.7532	5.7532	5.7532	5.7532	5.8092	5.8824	1949	
6.0212	6.0212	6.0212	6.0212	6.0796	6.1704	1950	
6.6640	6.6640	6.6640	6.6640	6.7292	6.8260	1951	
6.9512	6.9512	7.0184	7.1076	7.1064	7.1256	1952	
6.6324	6.6324	6.6532	6.7372	6.7376	6.7544	1953	
6.9248	6.9248	6.9924	7.0864	7.0868	7.1012	1954	
7.2820	7.2820	7.3528	7.4516	7.4516	7.4716	1955	
7.7716	7.7716	7.8476	7.9392	7.9388	7.9824	1956	
8.2032	8.2028	8.2028	8.2028	8.2028	7.2388	1957	
7.4688	7.4684	7.4684	7.4684	7.4684	7.5736	1958	
7.5152	7.4404	7.5240	7.5240	7.5240	7.5400	1959	
7.7076	7.7808	7.8712	7.8716	7.8716	7.8872	1960	
8.0780	8.1552	8.2468	8.2460	8.2460	8.2700	1961	
8.4316	8.5124	8.5728	8.5732	8.5732	8.6088	1962	
8.7980	8.8844	8.9268	8.9268	8.9268	8.9820	1963	
9.1716	9.2608	9.3044	9.3044	9.3044	9.3644	1964	
Still earning interest - see other Series E table					5.1248	1965	
4.9308	4.9308	4.9308	4.9308	4.9784	5.0340	1966	
5.1380	5.1380	5.1380	5.1380	5.1880	5.2512	1967	
5.3656	5.3656	5.3656	5.3656	5.4176	5.4912	1968	
5.3884	5.4004	5.4008	5.4008	5.4008	5.4288	1969	
5.5744	5.5876	5.5876	5.5876	5.5876	5.6004	1970	
5.0424	5.0544	5.0544	5.0544	5.0544	5.0664	1971	
5.1108	5.1220	5.1220	5.1220	5.1220	5.1332	1972	
5.2584	5.2696	5.2704	5.2704	5.2704	5.1392	1973	
5.2008	5.2008	5.2008	5.2008	5.2504	5.2636	1974	
Still earning interest - see other Series E table						1975	
Still earning interest - see other Series E table						1976-1980	

Series	Year Issued	Interest rate as of May 2005 Issued in:						
		Jan	Feb	Mar	Apr	May	Jun	Jul
H	1952 1974	H bonds issued from 1952 to 1974 are no longer earning interest						
	1975	0.0%	0.0%	0.0%	0.0%	0.0%	4.0%	4.0%
	1976	4.0%	4.0%	4.0%	4.0%	4.0%	4.0%	4.0%
	1977	4.0%	4.0%	4.0%	4.0%	4.0%	4.0%	4.0%
	1978	4.0%	4.0%	4.0%	4.0%	4.0%	4.0%	4.0%
	1979	4.0%	4.0%	4.0%	4.0%	4.0%	4.0%	4.0%
HH	1980 1984	HH bonds issued from 1980 to 1984 are no longer earning interest						
	1985	0.0%	0.0%	0.0%	0.0%	0.0%	4.0%	4.0%
	1986	4.0%	4.0%	4.0%	4.0%	4.0%	4.0%	4.0%
	1987	4.0%	4.0%	4.0%	4.0%	4.0%	4.0%	4.0%
	1988	4.0%	4.0%	4.0%	4.0%	4.0%	4.0%	4.0%
	1989	4.0%	4.0%	4.0%	4.0%	4.0%	4.0%	4.0%
	1990	4.0%	4.0%	4.0%	4.0%	4.0%	4.0%	4.0%
	1991	4.0%	4.0%	4.0%	4.0%	4.0%	4.0%	4.0%
	1992	4.0%	4.0%	4.0%	4.0%	4.0%	4.0%	4.0%
	1993	1.5%	1.5%	1.5%	1.5%	1.5%	1.5%	1.5%
	1994	1.5%	1.5%	1.5%	1.5%	1.5%	1.5%	1.5%
	1995	1.5%	1.5%	1.5%	1.5%	1.5%	4.0%	4.0%
	1996	4.0%	4.0%	4.0%	4.0%	4.0%	4.0%	4.0%
	1997	4.0%	4.0%	4.0%	4.0%	4.0%	4.0%	4.0%
	1998	4.0%	4.0%	4.0%	4.0%	4.0%	4.0%	4.0%
	1999	4.0%	4.0%	4.0%	4.0%	4.0%	4.0%	4.0%
	2000	4.0%	4.0%	4.0%	4.0%	4.0%	4.0%	4.0%
	2001	4.0%	4.0%	4.0%	4.0%	4.0%	4.0%	4.0%
	2002	4.0%	4.0%	4.0%	4.0%	4.0%	4.0%	4.0%
	2003	1.5%	1.5%	1.5%	1.5%	1.5%	1.5%	1.5%
	2004	1.5%	1.5%	1.5%	1.5%	1.5%	1.5%	1.5%

Interest rate as of May 2005 Issued in:					Alert Recommendation	Year Issued	Series
Aug	Sep	Oct	Nov	Dec			
H bonds issued from 1952 to 1974 are no longer earning interest					Redeem	1952 1974	H
4.0%	4.0%	4.0%	4.0%	4.0%	A until issue month	1975	
4.0%	4.0%	4.0%	4.0%	4.0%	A	1976	
4.0%	4.0%	4.0%	4.0%	4.0%	A	1977	
4.0%	4.0%	4.0%	4.0%	4.0%	A	1978	
4.0%	4.0%	4.0%	4.0%	4.0%	A	1979	
HH bonds issued from 1980 to 1984 are no longer earning interest					Redeem	1980 1984	HH
4.0%	4.0%	4.0%	4.0%	4.0%	A until issue month	1985	
4.0%	4.0%	4.0%	4.0%	4.0%	A	1986	
4.0%	4.0%	4.0%	4.0%	4.0%	A	1987	
4.0%	4.0%	4.0%	4.0%	4.0%	A	1988	
4.0%	4.0%	4.0%	4.0%	4.0%	A	1989	
4.0%	4.0%	4.0%	4.0%	4.0%	A	1990	
4.0%	4.0%	4.0%	4.0%	4.0%	A	1991	
4.0%	4.0%	4.0%	4.0%	4.0%	A	1992	
1.5%	1.5%	1.5%	1.5%	1.5%	D	1993	
1.5%	1.5%	1.5%	1.5%	1.5%	D	1994	
4.0%	4.0%	4.0%	4.0%	4.0%	A until issue month	1995	
4.0%	4.0%	4.0%	4.0%	4.0%	A	1996	
4.0%	4.0%	4.0%	4.0%	4.0%	A	1997	
4.0%	4.0%	4.0%	4.0%	4.0%	A	1998	
4.0%	4.0%	4.0%	4.0%	4.0%	A	1999	
4.0%	4.0%	4.0%	4.0%	4.0%	A	2000	
4.0%	4.0%	4.0%	4.0%	4.0%	A	2001	
4.0%	4.0%	4.0%	4.0%	4.0%	A	2002	
1.5%	1.5%	1.5%	1.5%	1.5%	D	2003	
1.5%	No longer issued				D	2004	

Series	Year Issued	Redemption value per $ of face value Issued in:					
		Jan	**Feb**	**Mar**	**Apr**	**May**	**Jun**
SN	**1967**					6.1332	6.1616
	1968	6.2516	6.2516	6.2516	6.2516	5.7348	5.8272
	1969	5.4280	5.4280	5.4280	5.4280	5.3748	5.4000
	1970	5.4684	5.4684	5.4684	5.4684	5.5216	5.5480

Redemption value per $ of face value Issued in:						Year Issued	Series
Jul	Aug	Sep	Oct	Nov	Dec		
6.1620	6.1620	6.1620	6.1620	6.2208	6.2512	**1967**	**SN**
5.8272	5.8272	5.4472	5.4472	5.3988	5.4280	**1968**	
5.4000	5.4000	5.4000	5.4000	5.4428	5.4680	**1969**	
5.5480	5.5480	5.5480	5.5480			**1970**	

Appendix

Appendix

All about rate periods

How to obtain the forms you need

Index

All about rate periods

Savings Bonds interest rates are announced by the Treasury every six months on the first business days of May and November. The announced rates apply to a bond's next six-month rate period.

Every Savings Bond has **two six-month rate periods a year**. One period starts at the beginning of the bond's issue month and the other starts exactly six months later.

For example, a bond issued in January has a January-June rate period and a July-December rate period. A bond issued in April has April-September and October-March rate periods.

The announced rates are expressed as an annual rate, but the rate periods only last half a year. You'll earn one-half of the announced rate for your bond's first six-month rate period, then you'll earn one-half of the next announced rate for your bond's second six-month rate period.

Confused? Maybe it would help if you looked at Figure 1-1 on the next page.

Note that for a Savings Bond purchased in April or October, the rate announced in May applies to its October-March rate period, which begins five months after – and ends 11 months after – the rate announcement.

Moreover, the **EE bond announcement** is based on market rates for the six-month period that ends *the day* before the announcement. The **I bond announcement** is based on the average inflation rate for the six-month period that ends *the month* before the announcement.

These features create a rate lag that makes Series I Savings Bonds look very attractive when the long-term interest rate cycle is starts heading down, which may in fact be the time you should be locking in the high fixed rates of Series EE bonds.

On the other hand, when the long term cycle is moving rates up, the adjustable-rate feature of Series I Savings Bonds gives them an advantage over the locked-in rates of Series EE, but the rate lag can make them seem less competitive.

Rate periods are a little complicated, but essential for a Savings Bond investor to understand.

If you're having trouble with this page, start with Figure 1-1 on the next page and come back here when it starts to make sense.

Figure 1-1

Savings Bond rate-setting and interest-earning rate periods

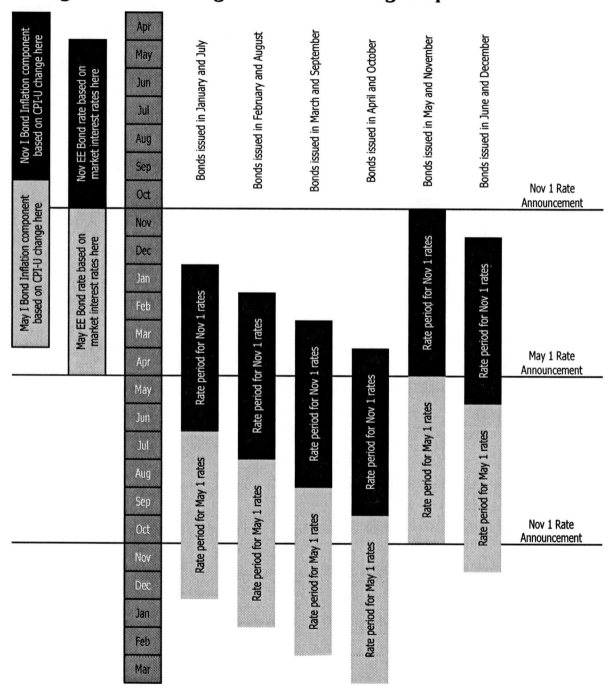

How to obtain the forms you need

In the text of this book we mention a number of forms the Bureau of Public Debt uses for Savings Bonds transactions. Next to each reference, we give a link to our web site where you get an electronic (Adobe Acrobat .pdf file) copy of the form.

If you would prefer to use a pre-printed form, go to our web site, click on Book Notes, and select note 18-1. This will link you to an online form on the Treasury's Savings Bond web site that allows you to order paper forms and have them mailed to you.

If you would prefer to order by mail, send you name and address and a list of the forms you need, including both the Bureau of Public Debt form number (PDF #) and the name of the form. Send your request to:

Savings Bond Form Request
Bureau of the Public Debt
P. O. Box 1328
Parkersburg, WV 26106-1328

Index

Printed in the United States
37922LVS00004B/41